EARTH A.D.

EARTH A.D.

THE POISONING OF THE AMERICAN LANDSCAPE AND THE COMMUNITIES THAT FOUGHT BACK

MICHAEL LEE NIRENBERG

PROCESS

1: HEAVY METAL

2: SLUDGE METAL

"The real problem of humanity is the following: we have Paleolithic emotions; medieval institutions; and god-like technology. And it is terrifically danger- ous, and it is now approaching a point of crisis overall."

— E.O. Wilson

INTRODUCTION

THOSE OF US ALIVE in 21st-century America have inherited a lifestyle beyond anything our forefathers could have possibly imagined: instant global video com- munication, streaming mobile entertainment, cheap travel, robot assistants, artificial intelligence, abundant, high-density calories, and countless conve- niences that have narcotized us and removed most of us from the instability of hunting, gathering, and the drudgery of factory life.

The political mindset of people living during the European migration to what is now the United States from the 1600s to the early 1970s was a philosophy of Manifest Destiny. The phrase was first used in 1845; it made clear the Christian idea that people had "dominion" over the earth. Though what the concept meant in a practical sense was politically contested by lawmakers, nothing would stop this young country from expanding across the continent and developing and exploiting its resources as much as possible. During our first two hundred or so years, it was acceptable to pollute the earth, because the land appeared limit- less. If you worked hard and had innovative ideas, economic growth was for the taking. There were more than enough natural resources for everyone (except for indigenous populations who stood in the way of the American expansion).

In recent decades it's become clear that the destruction of natural resources is the hidden cost we pay for the lifestyle we take for granted. For many, the first indication that the environment was in trouble was in 1969 when NBC News broadcast dramatic footage of the Cuyahoga River in Cleveland, Ohio aflame due to the chemicals in the water. It was a turning point for the environmental move- ment, which had begun organizing around local issues during the 1960s as they gained widespread support and national attention. Politicians responded to ecological problems with robust bipartisan legislation, chiefly among them the Clean Air Act of 1970, the Clean Water Act of 1972, the Endangered Species Act of 1973, and the Safe Drinking Water Act of 1974. There were other landmark legis- lations throughout the decades that followed. After years of education and action, it seemed as if citizens and their elected officials were in lockstep toward a society that valued an ecosystem that didn't make people sick. The consensus was that allegiance to political parties was irrelevant when protecting the earth from destruction. It's hard to believe we used to (mostly) agree that the earth is for everyone.

Hundreds of contaminated sites dot the countryside. Many of them were abandoned, shuttered ghost towns by the 1960s. These sites were the legacy of America's imperialist tendencies colliding with the reality of industrial pollution. And what remained was the epic damage to the landscape, wildlife, communities, and cultures that had been done by the time the laws and politics caught up in the 1970s.

On December 11, 1980, Congress enacted the Comprehensive Environmental Response, Compensation, and Liability Act (CERCLA), more commonly known as the Superfund law. The legislation assured the citizens of the contaminated communities that the taxpayers were going to help them out and be made whole by Superfund. The new law set up a trust fund independent of Congressional budget cycles and paid for with an earmarked excise tax on petroleum and chemical feedstock products and a separate environmental income tax. Additional monies are generated by interest income, fines, and citizen-paid income taxes. In 1980 we believed that we needed to rectify the damage to the citizens who suffered at the hands of the same industries that put people to work, built America, won the World Wars, and made this country the economic and military superpower it is today. Superfund ensures that there will be money to remediate these places as long as people live there—and if the polluters are still around, they're going to pay for it.

Earth A.D.: The Poisoning of the American Landscape and the Communities That Fought Back documents two environmental disasters born of the American Industrial Revolution. When I first started thinking about this book I began by soliciting suggestions from a few longtime environmental activists—"What are some of the worst environmental disasters in this country that perhaps more people should know about?" The name "Tar Creek" was cited over and over.

The Tar Creek Superfund Site is located in the Tri-State Mining District that straddles the corners of three states: Oklahoma, Missouri, and Kansas. This region was rich in natural resources, particularly lead and zinc. So rich, in fact, that the area supplied a substantial amount of the lead for the Allies' bullets in both World Wars. I focus mainly on Picher, Oklahoma—home to the densest lead mines in the region. Picher and the surrounding towns became boomtowns for the majority white mining entrepreneurs and a few of Picher's original inhabitants—the Quapaw Tribe who were fortunate and clever enough to hold on to their land. The boom began in the early 1900s and lasted through the early 1960s. In the decades following World War II the mining began to dry up, the mining companies themselves skipped town and left a literal mountain range of mine tailings covering every surface. Lead was in the roads, the buildings, the streets, people's homes, schools, driveways—everywhere. It poisoned generation after generation until a few citizen activists noticed something was wrong and did something about it. Like many legacy environmental disaster sites, problems begat more problems and compounded over the decades, often made worse by ill-conceived or half-finished remediation projects.

The second half explores my old neighborhood of Greenpoint in Brooklyn, New York—a place I have found continually fascinating. Greenpoint is home to two Superfund sites. Newtown Creek is the local waterway that forms the natural border between Brooklyn and Queens and has been an industrial corridor since the 1800s through to the present day. For 150 years, industrial pollutions were dumped into Newtown Creek where they have settled and remained. That includes everything from oil refining, kerosene, paint chemicals, petrochemicals, copper smelting as well as organic waste like animal rendering and raw sewage. The main pollution events associated with the Creek were the Standard Oil spills. Approximated at 17–30 million gallons, the discharges are thought to have begun with the 1883 Standard Oil fire and continued unchecked throughout the next few decades. The oil mass flowed underground beneath Greenpoint and slowly made its way under people's homes.

That total amount of spilled oil is more substantial than what went into the waters of Prudhoe Bay, Alaska, in the infamous Exxon Valdez spill. It's hard to visualize that amount of oil, in much the same way that Tar Creek's mountains of lead mining waste were imperceptible until seen.

The other Superfund site in Greenpoint is the NuHart Plastics Factory building, which has been leaking cancer-causing phthalates[1], TCE (trichloroethylene)[2], and other chemicals into the ground for decades. Greenpoint was also home to a medical waste incinerator, open sewage tanks, and dozens of other manufacturing businesses producing numerous carcinogenic agents. Like Tar Creek, the compounding effect of multiple chemicals has dire health outcomes for longtime citizens. Greenpoint, unlike Tar Creek, is undergoing massive residential and retail gentrification because of its proximity to Manhattan. But are newly remediated former Superfund sites the best place to invest billions of dollars in high-end development?

---

1. Phthalates are a group of chemicals used to make plastics more flexible and harder to break. They are often called plasticizers. Some phthalates are used as solvents (dissolving agents) for other materials. They are used in hundreds of products, such as vinyl flooring, adhesives, detergents, lubricating oils, automotive plastics, plastic clothes (raincoats), and personal-care products (soaps, shampoos, hair sprays, and nail polishes).

Phthalates are used widely in polyvinyl chloride plastics, which are used to make products such as plastic packaging film and sheets, garden hoses, inflatable toys, blood-storage containers, medical tubing, and some children's toys.

2. Trichloroethylene (TCE) is a nonflammable, colorless liquid with a somewhat sweet odor and a sweet, burning taste. It is used mainly as a solvent to remove grease from metal parts, but it is also an ingredient in adhesives, paint removers, typewriter correction fluids, and spot removers. Trichloroethylene is not thought to occur naturally in the environment. However, it has been found in underground water sources and many surface waters as a result of the manufacture, use, and disposal of the chemical.

I chose these two sites because of their massive-scale, complex intertwined problems, their similarities, and differences. How do federal, state, municipal, and sometimes tribal governments treat a Superfund site that's in the middle of New York City versus one that's in rural Oklahoma? How is a Superfund site handled in a red state versus blue state? How do we value contaminated land? This book investigates the mechanics of power, class, wealth, and race against staggering adversity.

These places could be anywhere in the world. They are unique with specific challenges, but the same could be said for any legacy contamination site. No two are exactly alike. This book is an exploration of the difficulties these two communities have faced and attempts to make sense of why we're facing egregious environmental regulatory rollbacks that will have consequences for the next generation's quality of life, health outcomes, and economic opportunities.

As the decades have rolled on and campaign contribution laws weakened, private interests, polluting corporations and their lobbying machines began to own politicians outright. The mid-century policy restrictions enacted to hinder corporate malfeasance may not have been stringent enough if they could be walked back so easily by a corporatist government with a vendetta for the environmental movement. Bipartisan support for ecological laws has waned over the years. While both parties have accepted campaign contributions and gifts from polluters, analysis shows that the Republican party has taken more direct and indirect funding from the oil and petrochemical companies, who remain the cause of the majority of human-caused environmental disasters.

Words on a page are a map. The words on these pages represent people's lived experiences and told in their authentic voices. The people who suffered are our friends, neighbors, and ultimately, fellow citizens. They are everyone you might encounter when forgotten contamination sites or new spills are discovered. These are cautionary tales. They are also a roadmap on how we can work together to make our environment safer for the next generation of caretakers.

A NOTE ON THE ORAL NARRATIVE PROCESS

THIS BOOK IS AN ORAL HISTORY. I conducted original interviews with all the people included unless noted otherwise. The transcripts are edited to weave individual stories together into a cohesive narrative of the events. Interviews are supplemented with various supporting items including reputable news sources, book excerpts, press releases, newsletters, websites, blogs, academic journals, government documents, television interview transcripts, trade journals, law reviews, and comic books.

In these pages we meet the activists, teachers, citizens, a Governor, a Congressman, business owners, property owners, longtime residents, Native American tribal members, community advocates, environmental attorneys, historians, academics, artists, scientists, community leaders, urban planners, professors, students, archivists, journalists, epidemiologists, and a few others.

There were several people I reached out to who declined to be interviewed or ignored my requests. There were a few people that I wish I could have spoken to, like John Sparkman of Picher, Oklahoma, or Irene Klementowicz and her colleague Elizabeth Roncketti of Greenpoint, Brooklyn. In some cases, it was because I couldn't find them or they were not interested in talking about the old days anymore. I hope this book gets to them.

I sent multiple interview requests to Oklahoma Senator James Inhofe, former Oklahoma Senator Tom Coburn, and to representatives from ExxonMobil as well as any other named company or politicians cited by people as being either responsible for pollution or protecting the polluters. I imagine there was no benefit for any of them to talk to me. The EPA never said "no," but I was unable to get anyone from the agency who was assigned to these sites to commit to an interview. Government documents serve as their testimony as to what was done—or not done.

To put together a concise story about Tar Creek and Greenpoint I could not possibly tell of each instance of heroic insight or perfunctory meeting. This book is for the general reader and paints with a broad brush; I've omitted details that may not be interesting to anyone outside the communities covered here. This fact will inevitably disappoint some of the people involved in the story.

There are inherent problems and limitations when constructing an oral history. The people interviewed here have different accounts of events; sometimes it colors the interviewee in a more positive light, which makes it harder to get at the truth. Every person cited is a real person with a life experience, perspective, and definite point of view, and the words reflect how we talk to each other at the supermarket and in community meetings. Edits were made to the transcript text for brevity and clarity. As the custodian of the trust of the interviewees, I worked to reflect their intention and unique voices which sometimes included "translating" spoken grammar to written grammar. English, as expressed in the United States, is rich with dialect and slang. I've worked to retain that sense of place and individuality in the text.

Early in my research I found that the language of environmental regulation is confusing, filled with acronyms and dependent on internal jargon. There is a glossary at the end of these pages decoding the alphabet soup of agencies, programs, and governmental agencies referred to throughout.

The oral history process is a mess of information that has to be sorted and edited clearly with as little redundancy as possible. I tried to keep the events in chronological order, but timelines were happening concurrently and some overlapping of events is inevitable. I'm incredibly grateful to the people who were generous with their time regardless of how I (or you) feel about what they chose to say.

I'm passionate about saving the environment for my children's future. I tried to correct my personal bias throughout the process of assembling this book by reaching out to many people with a variety of experiences and across the political spectrum. Much of today's partisan rancor could be ameliorated if we leave our personal bubble and actively seek out a diversity of voices. It's important to note that I don't necessarily agree with all of the views expressed here and it's highly likely that you won't either. These are the unvarnished stories from the people who were and are living in these places.

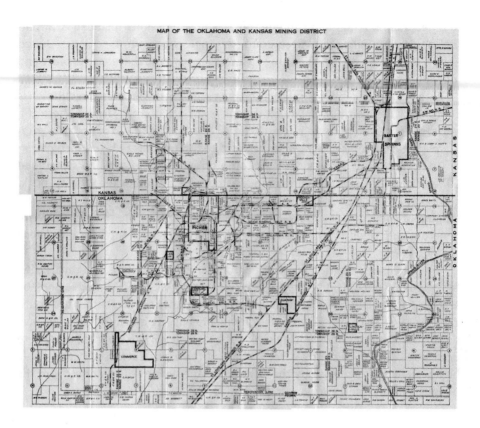

Map of the Oklahoma and Kansas Mining District, circa 1925.
Courtesy of the Fredas L. Cook Archive

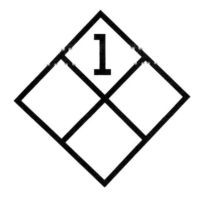

HEAVY METAL

AT THE HEART of what is now known as the Tar Creek Superfund Site, there's a small mining community in the farthest northeastern corner of Oklahoma by the name of Ottawa County. It is part of what's known as the Tri-State Mining Region, which at one time was considered the world's largest Superfund site in the country. The Tri-State Mining Region consists of several small former mining towns in the bordering states of Oklahoma, Missouri and Kansas. Oklahoma's Ottawa County consists of the cities Afton, Cardin, Commerce, Douthat, Fairland, Miami, Peoria, Picher, Quapaw, and Wyandotte. Throughout this story, we cross over into Kansas into Baxter Springs, Treece, and Galena, and then through the Missouri towns of Joplin and Webb City. They have all been touched by the problems associated with mining waste. Our story primarily centers on Picher, Oklahoma, where the thickest and densest lead and zinc mines created a mountain range of heavy metal waste.

When I was there driving aimlessly around, I found myself weaving in and out of these three states' borders. As you read on, the cultures, politics, and problems in these towns have been and remain closely intertwined.

Today I'm known as the [Tribe's] storyteller. I do tell traditional stories. The difference between traditional stories and other stories is that our stories never have a happy ending.

— Ardina Moore, Quapaw Tribal Elder

SUPERFUND SITE

IN 1983, 14 years after the last mine closed, Tar Creek was officially designated a Superfund site by the Environmental Protection Agency. It was one of the first designations of the recently passed Comprehensive Environmental Response, Compensation, and Liability Act (CERCLA), which is known as Superfund of 1980. It went right to the top of the EPA's National Priorities List.

This clutch of declining boomtowns was unique for their overlapping environmental problems and social complexities. Picher, Oklahoma sits on land partially owned by the Quapaw Tribe, which held a high population of unemployed white miners and their families. Add extreme poverty to being surrounded by a toxic moonscape of poisonous, heavy metal chat[3] piles. The lead was everywhere—in the foundations of schools and playgrounds, buildings and houses, driveways and streets.

Coincidentally in 1983, the same year as the Superfund designation, almost as if to illustrate the point, Picher suffered a massive collapse. The ground caved in 75 feet wide by 75 feet deep. Around this time, more subsidence issues began to present themselves in the region. This was not a new phenomenon; a 1967 collapse took four homes into the ground.

Subsidence is the process by which the collapse of mine workings reach the surface. Many mine workings collapse underground without ever reaching the surface. Cave-ins had been happening sporadically since the mining era began. The first public acknowledgment of undermining was in 1950 when the region's most substantial mining concern, Eagle-Picher Mining and Smelting Company, condemned four square blocks of downtown as unsafe.

The town was slowly starting to cave in, occasionally taking houses and streets into the carved-out space below the surface. Iron, lead, arsenic, cadmium, and

3. The term "chat" is applied to fragments of siliceous rock, limestone, and dolomite waste rejected in the lead-zinc milling operations that accompanied lead-zinc mining in Ottawa County. These chats, found as huge human-made mounds in that county, are utilized as construction aggregate, principally for railroad ballast, highway construction, and concrete production.

THE OKLAHOMAN ARCHIVE

Eagle-Picher collapse, 1950. Photo courtesy of the Ed Keheley archive

manganese-tainted water flowed from the cavernous mines and into the creeks, turning the surface waters a bright orange. In the early 1980s, this small mining town's compounding problems become a political quagmire at both the state and local level. Superfund designation means that federal funding becomes available, but how much, for what and for whom becomes the subject of intense, bitter debate.

This is eco-assault on an epic scale. The prairie here in the northeast corner of the state is punctured with 480 open mineshafts and 30,000 drill holes. Little League fields have been built over an immense underground cavity that could collapse at any time. Acid mine waste flushes into drinking wells. When the water rises in Tar Creek, which runs through the site, a neon-orange scum oozes onto the roadside. Wild onions, a regional delicacy tossed into scrambled eggs, are saturated with cadmium—which may explain, local doctors say, why three different kidney dialysis centers have opened here to serve a population of only 30,000.[4]

4. "The Tragedy of Tar Creek," by Margot Roosevelt, Monday, 19 Apr 2004, *Time* Magazine.

DR. ROBERT NAIRN, environmental scientist, researcher, professor Oklahoma University: In the summer of 2015, EPA was doing some remedial work in southern Colorado, and opened up a mine and spilled about three million gallons of mine water that got into the Animas River through Colorado to New Mexico, Arizona, and eventually into Utah. It was on CNN. It was on NBC. It was in the national newspapers that a three-million-gallon spill of polluted mining water contaminated the Animas River.

The reality is that happens every three days at Tar Creek and it has been happening every three days for 40 years.

EARL HATLEY, Cherokee environmental activist, co-founder of LEAD Agency, Grand Riverkeeper: It's big. I knew this when I saw it. I knew if I took it on, I would have to drop everything else. It's going to be my last site. I was going to have to focus everything on it.

MARC YAGGI, Executive Director Waterkeeper Alliance: It was my first time in Oklahoma. I was really looking forward to that trip because I had spent a decade speaking with Earl about it and reading about it, but never actually seeing it. It's hard to prepare. You don't necessarily; I don't know how to put it in words. But it's hard to prepare yourself mentally and emotionally, forced witnessing what kind of struggle people have gone through.

BRIAN GRIFFIN, former Oklahoma Secretary of the Environment, Chairman of the Board at Clean Energy Systems: The interesting thing in Oklahoma is that Ottawa County is not that far off the interstate that goes from Tulsa to Joplin, and finally St. Louis. It's close to the interstate highway, but is just far enough, off five to ten miles up the eastern side that you don't see it from the highway. It's kind of one of those lost quadrants that most Oklahomans had no idea about.

TOM LINDLEY, author, retired journalist, *The Oklahoman*: Tar Creek is a very frustrating thing to deal with if you're a state or federal agency because it comes with a magnitude of problems. The health and environment issues there are unparalleled in the country.

BRIAN GRIFFIN: In environmental regulation, it's always a balancing act. You're balancing the need for environmental protection but also trying to realize that in a modern society, virtually all human activity has an environmental impact, so if you want no environmental impact you virtually go back to the Stone Age.

It's always that delicate balance between doing what is good for the environment and doing what allows us to live in society and enjoy the lifestyle that we all want to live.

FRANK KEATING, former Governor of Oklahoma, attorney, author: I do remember my insistence that this is our problem and our solution and we don't need the Feds to come in here and tell us to step aside because they would never fix it. It'll take them forever.

SCOTT THOMPSON, Director of the Oklahoma Department of Environmental Quality: EPA has an HRS (Hazard Ranking System) model, and it has changed over time, but in the early days, there was an anecdotal story about Tar Creek, that it was the number one Superfund site in the country.

REBECCA JIM, Cherokee, educator, environmental activist, co-founder of LEAD Agency: [Congressman Mike Synar[5]] pulled together a Task Force hearing in 1981. It was held in Tulsa, and it must have been on my spring break because I was able to attend. He invited everyone that knew anything about Tar Creek to come and talk.

WALLACE KENNEDY, retired journalist, *The Joplin Globe*: Shortly after that, Congressmen Synar, Taylor and Whitaker got funding for a USGS (United States Geological Survey) study of the entire Tri-State Mining District—Missouri, Kansas and Oklahoma.

It helped you identify all of the hazardous waste sites, all of the open shafts and all of the problems that existed in the Tri-State district. And about the same time this was happening, Tar Creek was starting to emerge, and Mike Synar decided that he would pitch the Tar Creek area in the formation of the new EPA and the Superfund program.

REBECCA JIM: What Mike Synar did was help us all focus on what we already knew, and what gaps there were. He always had it in mind that it could be fixed. Before he died, the kids at the high school decided to do a Tar Creek project. I called Mike Synar up and told him that we were gonna dedicate the project to him. He probably died three months later, but I did not know he was ill.

A couple of other things that happened at that Task Force hearing. Dr. John Neuberger[6] spoke. I don't know if he shook everybody else up, but he shook me up because he had done a study on lung cancer deaths in Ottawa County and how high the numbers were for us. He excluded miners and smokers from the

---

5. Michael Lynn "Mike" Synar (October 17, 1950–January 9, 1996) was an American politician (Democrat) who represented Oklahoma's 2nd Congressional district in Congress for eight terms. He was an early advocate for action at Tar Creek. LEAD Agency's yearly award is called the Mike Synar Environmental Excellence Award.

6. John S. Neuberger, DrPH, MPH, MBA. Professor, University of Kansas Medical School. Specializing in: Identifying environmental causes of cancer, brain cancer, radon and lung cancer, radon and multiple sclerosis, and the health effects of toxic chemical and physical agents (e.g., lead and ionizing radiation).

study. He had found that we were the lung cancer capital of the country during the 1980s when he did the study.

The other thing he showed was some slides, and none of them were in color, except for that bright red star in Ottawa County. Then he showed a picture of a chat pile, and he said, "This is the scariest thing of all." And everybody in the room, me included, we all looked at each other and said, "chat piles?" but then he used a pointer, and he said, "children's footprints."

He was concerned about children's exposure to lead and the other metals. He had done work in Kansas and across the state line in the counties that are the Tri-State Mining District, and knew that the lead was an issue for children there. Of course, in Ottawa County, it didn't hit the radar until our Indian kids were already lead-poisoned. But he already knew it then back in the early '80s and was worried about the lead poisoning that was occurring.

BRAD CARSON, former Congressman of the 2nd district of Oklahoma, former Undersecretary to the Army: I've often said that if Tar Creek happened in Tulsa or in Oklahoma City instead, it would have been solved in a matter of three years.

REBECCA JIM: If this site were in the middle of Dallas, it would be fixed.

THEY WERE GOOD KIDS WHO COULDN'T THINK

IN 1994 the Tar Creek lead and zinc mining fields had been shut down for two and a half decades and declared a Superfund site for just over 10 years. Despite recognition by the federal government and the money being spent to study the site, little had been done to improve day-to-day life for the citizens of Picher, Oklahoma, and the surrounding towns.

The EPA had launched Operable Unit 1 in 1984, which capped 66 hazardous, open wells to save the local drinking-water aquifer from contamination. OU1 also attempted to divert Lytle Creek around polluted mineshafts to curb some of the polluted mine waters, which was a significant source of surface water pollution. More or less people carried on as usual. Lead poisoning and heavy metal-based diseases were a fact of life here. Still, residents had more significant economic problems on their minds. The end of mining meant there were no jobs, no investments in the town, no income, no upward mobility. It seemed like the modern world was passing them by. It's hard to care about invisible pollution problems when you're worried about how to make the rent or feed the kids.

There were six critical years in the life of the Tar Creek Superfund Site that seemed quiet on the surface. From roughly 1994 until 2000, a diverse set of people working in different capacities threw themselves into the center of the issues to effect change. They ranged from scientists, teachers, journalists, and politicians.

> *"We have a lot of people with kidney disease. We have a lot of people with cardiovascular disease. We have children that are being exposed before they are even born. I have former students that are dead already. It's robbery. It was all preventable. This shouldn't have happened. And now their children will die as well if we don't finish [the cleanup]."*[7]

— educator and activist Rebecca Jim referring to her students

REBECCA JIM, Cherokee, educator, environmental activist, co-founder of LEAD Agency: I was a school counselor, and I had to do an IEP (Individualized Education Program) for students. We knew there were kids with educational problems and learning problems, but I had worked in some other school districts, and when I got here I noticed they were all over the place. They could not sit still. Teachers had to work to keep the kids tuned in long enough to get an assignment. It wasn't cultural. It was uncontrollable. These were good kids that couldn't pay attention. They were good kids that couldn't think.

Then this fellow wrote this letter in 1994. (see page 20)

EARL HATLEY, Cherokee, environmental organizer, activist, co-founder of LEAD Agency: There was this fellow at the Indian Health Services [Miami, Oklahoma] named Don Ackerman. He was working doing a Ph.D. at Oklahoma University, and chose as his dissertation to do a study of blood lead levels in Indian children there. Using the Indian Health Service records at the clinic, he discovered that 34% of local Indian children had blood lead levels of 10 mg per dl which is the CDC (Center for Disease Control) maximum level.

REBECCA JIM: [Don Ackerman] was the field sanitarian with the Indian Health Service. I worked at the high school, and he worked at the Indian clinic which was just across the little highway. He was already volunteering with us. He loved poetry so we would encourage our high school kids to write poetry.

---

7. Quote from Rebecca Jim. Rebecca Nagle. "Toxic Tar Creek Continues to Harm Residents, as Cleanup Stalls." ThinkProgress, 1 Feb 2018.

DEPARTMENT OF HEALTH & HUMAN SERVICES   Public Health Service

Oklahoma City Area Indian Health Service
Five Corporate Plaza
3625 N.W. 56th Street
Oklahoma City, OK 73112

January 21, 1994

Michael D. Overbay
Remedial Project Manager
OK/TX Remedial Section (6H-SR)

Dear Mr. Overbay:

Approximately 34%(66 of the total 192) of the people tested for blood lead
have had a 10 ug/dl or higher blood lead level. Of these 66 children 4% are
above 20 ug/dl. Most of the individuals tested are participants of the WIC
program here at the clinic. Some of these children come from outside the
Oklahoma area.

Location does not seem to be a factor when comparing the levels among these
children. I would say that a small majority of these people live within one-
half to five miles from chat piles and there is a possibility that some of the
older homes and public water systems contain lead in some form as part of the
plumbing. Occupational exposures, debris around the home(items suspected of
containing lead), and hobbies may all be contributing factors to these blood
lead levels.

Two methods are used here at the clinic for collecting blood samples for lead,
venal puncture and finger prick. We have experienced some high readings with
the finger prick method when compared to the venal puncture sample of blood.
I am notified of some of the blood lead levels as they come in, but most of
the time I will go back and pull the charts on these people to gather data.

The mean blood lead level for the entire group is 8.34 ug/dl and for those
children that are above 10 ug/dl the mean is 13.56 ug/dl.

Sincerely,

Donald S. Ackerman

Donald S. Ackerman
Field Sanitarian
Office of Environmental Health
USPHS Indian Health Center
P.O. Box 1498
Miami, Oklahoma 74355

**Letter from Don Ackerman to EPA regarding his research discovering consistent elevated
blood lead levels in the Native American children around the Tar Creek Superfund Site. 1994.**
Courtesy of Rebecca Jim/LEAD Agency

**DON ACKERMAN, Environmental Health Specialist, retired commander in United
States Public Health Service Commissioned Corps, former researcher for Bureau
of Indian Affairs:** That was my first job in my profession. I started there in February
1992.

REBECCA JIM: While he was working at Indian Health Services, he wanted to get a better job in the Public Health Service, and you did that by getting another degree—getting more college education. It was before computers. He had to go to classes, and the state colleges had come up with a method to have a place in Tulsa where they could have a center so people could take classes and get a degree. So he did. He'd get off work at 5 p.m., get on the turnpike and go to Tulsa. That takes about 90 minutes. He'd barely make it to class, then stay in class until 11 o'clock. Then he had to do a thesis paper for his master's, but he couldn't ever go to the library because it was closed when he got back at midnight and then he couldn't go after work because he was going to classes!

DON ACKERMAN: I was driving from Miami, Oklahoma to Tulsa, and then from Miami, Oklahoma to Norman, Oklahoma when I needed to, which I think was over two hundred miles away.

REBECCA JIM: A couple of years before that, parents brought their kids to the Indian clinic and the parents said, "The school is saying my kid is hyperactive. I need something for this kid." And they began to medicate them with Ritalin.

They got a new doctor [Shirley Chesnut at Indian Health Services], and the doctor said, "Why do we have so many of these? Why are so many kids hyperactive?" The nurse said, "I've been reading about lead, lead can do that." Dr. Chesnut said, "How do kids get exposed to lead?" She had just gotten out of medical school, and they had told her that lead poisoning had only occurred in inner cities.

The nurse, who is local, said, "Well, we do have one of the largest lead and zinc mining sites, maybe in the world, just five miles from here."

Dr. Chesnut began to test every child that came into the clinic for lead, and that's how Don was able to find the records.

DON ACKERMAN: I guess Dr. Chesnut was wondering why so many kids were coming in and they were hyperactive. I remember getting the book from CDC, *Elevated Blood Levels in Kids*. I can't remember all the discussions, but I was around head nurse Carol Barnett and Dr. Chesnut when they were talking, and I got the charge and they said, "What are you going to do about it?" So, I started keeping track, as any good environmentalist or epidemiologist should.

I just started keeping track through records and following up with people the best I could as far as if the people were receptive to me coming out; I would do a home evaluation, collect a water sample. Run the water sample at Northeastern Oklahoma A&M college. I found a well-approved method for looking for lead in water at the time. It was a digestive method, using potassium cyanide. I got the potassium cyanide and started going to town. They had a vent that I could use and a laboratory. So it worked out well.

We used Epi Info[8], developed a questionnaire, and just started going to town with it. I would pull charts and when I was done with my workday, I would pull 10 to 12 charts, whatever I needed to do.

And in 1994, I believe we had 192 based on the letter that was written at that time, and I think by 1997 when I left, there were probably six hundred kids that were being followed through the clinic.

EARL HATLEY: He wrote his paper and got his grades in 1994 at the same time EPA (Environmental Protection Agency) came back to do their five-year review. He handed his paper off to the EPA. They passed the paper over to the Agency for Toxic Substances and Disease Registry (ATSDR)—they do health investigations for the Superfund sites for the CDC—and it spurred ATSDR to come back to see if his research was accurate. The ATSDR then commissioned a study with Oklahoma University Health Sciences Center in Oklahoma City to do a survey of the lead levels in the blood of youths six years old in the Superfund towns in Ottawa County.

The results that came of those tests spurred the community into organizing.

REBECCA JIM: ATSDR had to figure out if this was true. The Ottawa County Health Department set up at Walmart and they began to test randomly any kid whose parents they could talk into taking a Pizza Hut coupon. "Want a pizza? Let me test your kid." That's how they found out that it wasn't just Indian kids but a lot of kids were lead-poisoned.

EARL HATLEY: They found that in Cardin, Oklahoma, 68% of the kids had blood levels above 10%. 30% of kids in Picher were above 10% and so forth. It turned out that on average between the five towns it was somewhere around 35% of the kids with above-safe limits of lead in their blood. The Indian Health Service study Don did was more than accurate.

DON ACKERMAN: We know that lead affects the central nervous system (CNS) and has detrimental effects on children under five years old. And at the time in 1994, they were saying 10% was okay. Now they're saying 5%. Currently, that's the action level. The numbers of affected kids would have changed significantly higher by looking at how many kids came in and at what levels they came in.

SCOTT THOMPSON, Director of the Oklahoma Department of Environmental Quality: Lead is one of the few things that we were actually measuring in people, and that

---

8. Epi Info is statistical software for epidemiology developed by Centers for Disease Control and Prevention (CDC) in Atlanta, Georgia.

we have some idea of what it means when you measure it in people. But the focus was on children under six. The belief was that most of their time is spent in the yard or in the house and some of the lead levels in the house could be associated with dust from the yard being tracked in.

REBECCA JIM: I found this study by Dr. Rokho Kim[9]. He was at the Harvard School of Public Health, and he tested teeth because teeth are like a treasure, it records the lead exposure you had as a child because your teeth grow like rings in trees. The little blurb in a health magazine said that he believed that lead exposure between ages seven and 21 led to extreme obesity in later life.

DR. HOWARD HU, epidemiologist, physician, researcher, clinician, University of Washington School of Public Health: Rokho Kim was one of my doctoral students who came from Seoul National University. He was one of the top scholars there— he did his thesis work with our research group on the toxic impacts of lead on the kidneys, and new methods for measuring lead in the body that could then be used for more advanced research studies. That was in the mid-1990s, around the time that we started this conversation with Rebecca Jim.

REBECCA JIM: I had been reading a lot about lead poisoning and how you identify it. I went to an EPA meeting that was held in Picher, and I took this girl with me; she was a big girl who had a hard time in school and made poor decisions. I brought her home, and we're riding along in the dark, and she says, "Do you think I was lead-poisoned?" and I said, "Why on earth would you be lead-poisoned? You're not a child; you're not crawling around the floor, why would you be poisoned?" She said, "Well, I had a chat pile in my backyard where I played. So maybe I might have got exposed." She said, "Then my dad *did* get me a sand-box. He got me that really soft sand, really fine sand."
I said, "Well yeah, you might have got exposed."

DR. EMILY MOODY, pediatric environmental health fellow, environmental medicine and public health at the Icahn School of Medicine at Mount Sinai: If a little girl grew up in Tar Creek and played on the chat piles or had chat in her backyard because it was used for the driveway or as a foundation for her house, she might have very high bone lead levels, which she will pass that to her fetus, both during gestation and then through breast milk. Then that child would have an even higher lead level due to prenatal exposure and environmental exposure. That child is at increased risk.

---

9. Beginning in October of 1995, Dr. Kim, as a member of Dr. Hu's team, published a number of papers on his lead study findings in academic journals. A summary of the Harvard Lab's research was published in the April 17, 1996 issue of the *New York Times*.

DON ACKERMAN: I knew from my undergrad to graduate work that lead was in paint up to 1978. And I knew that lead was used in soldering and most of the homes in the area when it was built. It was just a good assumption to say, *Okay, I know a lot of the homes were built before 1978 in this area, I know that a lot of the plumbing has lead. It can be significant just because of the lead solder.* I would gather that lead in that area has multiple sources and to start to mitigate is probably the best thing that you can do.

REBECCA JIM: Then school ended for that year, and in the summer I read that article, this little blurb. It was like two sentences long; it gave Dr. Rokho's name and where he worked. So, I just called Information and got the [Harvard] School of Public Health phone number, and then I asked for Rokho Kim, and I got him on the phone. I'm telling him the story [of the older girl who lived with the chat pile sandbox] and he said, "Well, you should bring her to Boston and have her bone lead tested," and I said, "I cannot afford to bring her to Boston."

DR. ROBERT WRIGHT, pediatrician, medical toxicologist, and environmental epidemiologist at the Icahn School of Medicine at Mount Sinai: I wasn't involved initially. Rebecca may have seen some of the papers that Howard and Rokho had written on X-ray fluorescence (XRF) and asked if they could do this with the teeth. But the XRF is not a mobile device; it's a pretty big instrument. They couldn't take it with them to Oklahoma. I think Rokho may have suggested that if she could get teeth, we could analyze them inside of the laboratory and then people wouldn't have to travel there.

REBECCA JIM: I said, "If you could test her baby tooth, could you test other people's teeth?" He said, "Yes." So, we gathered teeth together from all sorts of people, four-year-olds to 80-year-olds, and we put them in an envelope and sent them off to Dr. Rokho Kim.

DR. ROBERT WRIGHT: For the teeth that she sent us, we used a technique called Inductively Coupled Plasma Mass Spectrometry which is a laboratory technique used to measure trace elements and can measure lead.

DR. HOWARD HU: It turns out that baby teeth are a terrific medium using advanced methods for trying to understand what the toxic exposures were to the individual and going all the way back to the womb.

One of the scientists we trained came to us from Australia; Manish Arora perfected this new method for doing fine-grain analysis of the layers of dentine. That's one of the chemical matrices of baby teeth that is laid down during growth in the womb and then during the first few years of life before the tooth is shed. His methodology allowed him to measure toxicants in these layers of dentine.

We showed quite convincingly that those measurements represented the exposures that occurred during life in the womb and then after. In fact, he could pretty much understand what the lead exposures were like at every two-week interval during pregnancy. That's pretty amazing.

DR. ROBERT WRIGHT: It was my first day as a postdoc, and I inherited Rokho Kim's desk, and I couldn't get my computer to turn on. I had taken the computer apart to figure that out, and that's when the phone rang, and it was Rebecca. When she said she was looking for Dr. Kim, I told her I was looking for him too and that I would help her find him.

REBECCA JIM: I said, "Can you help me find the teeth and the results?" He said, "Hold on." Then he passed the phone over to somebody else. So, I tell the whole story again. I said, "Who are you?" and he said that he was Howard [Hu] who was like the big guy there.

DR. HOWARD HU: I was a professor at the Harvard School of Public Health from 1990 to 2006. During that time, I led a research team that was investigating the impact of the exposure to toxic metals on human health, and one of the subjects that we were quite concerned about was the exposure of the unborn, and how that might screw up physical and mental development.

During the conducting trials, and publishing of this research, Rebecca Jim got hold of me to persuade me to come and take a look at the situation at the Tar Creek Superfund Site.

I went down there. She and Earl picked me up at the airport in Tulsa, and we drove out to the Tar Creek Superfund Site; as we were driving around, I remarked, "Gosh, I didn't know that there were mountains out here in this part of Oklahoma," and she said, "Those aren't mountains, they are chat piles."

That was my introduction to the enormity of the mining waste problem down there. Over the ensuing year or two, we started gathering information, planning projects, and then successfully applied for funding. Our collaboration began with the funded project as part of the Harvard Superfund basic research program.

REBECCA JIM: Anyway, so that's about how we got Howard. But the fellow that answered the phone was Robert Wright.

DR. ROBERT WRIGHT: After I helped her with that, she called me again looking for a speaker for a conference that she was running with Earl Hatley. I told them that they didn't really want me, I'm too low a rank, but I ended up being the person who went to present at the conference.

I think that was 1998 and I met a lot of folks from the community. I met Brad Carson, who at the time was a U.S. Congressman, and I met a whole bunch of people from EPA. I learned a lot about *Superfundspeak*. They have their own language. I was relatively new to EPA culture and what Superfund site cleanups were about. I learned what a ROD (Record of Decision) was. I listened to talks where people would use terminology like OU1 and OU2. It turns out it meant Operable Unit 1 and Operable Unit 2. So, it's the sites for the cleanup.

I spent a lot of time just figuring out what people were saying and was quite confused much of the time. Quite honestly, they don't teach you a lot about this in environmental health academics. This is the regulatory world.

REBECCA JIM: As these kids got turned on about their own situation, they learned about Tar Creek. Kent Curtis, who worked with the Cherokee Nation, said we have to do something but also to be careful. The high school kids learned things, and then they went to the elementary school, and they taught the elementary school kids about Tar Creek and lead poisoning and how do they protect themselves. Specifics like how to wash their hands, and then they would tell their little brothers and sisters how to protect themselves from the lead. The safety information cascaded from the older kids to the younger kids.

Other teachers took on various pieces because we got a little funding from Cherokee Nation in Oklahoma for education in the schools. Otherwise, there's no money. We had kids in almost every discipline doing something research-related. It's easy for English classes because they can write about it. They wrote poetry and essays and research papers. We put the first batch into a book. Cherokee Nation funded the first printing, and we distributed them. One of them ended up on the desk of journalist Tom Lindley at the *Oklahoman*. He's reading through it, and he couldn't believe it could be that bad, and he didn't believe the kids knew so much about the issue. So, he came up here to find out more.

TOM LINDLEY, author, retired journalist, *The Oklahoman*: It was an open mining field and big chat piles. Ever since the 1980s when it was put on the Superfund list, I had written some clips about the cleanup by the U.S. Army Corps of Engineers over the years and how much money they spent to remediate yards in Picher and Cardin. It wasn't a lot; it wasn't a controversy. There was no real concern about the health implications at all. There wasn't a significant body of work that I was following.

I decided I wanted to go down there and spend a few days and learn more. I contacted Rebecca. The first time I toured this area, it was just four days, and out of that initial visit, I put together a series of articles that ran right on page one of the *Oklahoman* (December, 1999). That's why it all happened—because that little pamphlet the kids published ended up on my desk.

J.D. STRONG, Director at Oklahoma Department of Wildlife Conservation, former Chief of Staff to the Secretary of Environment of Oklahoma: I think I had probably been briefed on the Superfund site in the past by DEQ, the Department of Environmental Quality. It wasn't until Governor Keating had read a series of articles on the front page of the *Oklahoman* by Tom Lindley, and that's where things ramped up for Tar Creek.

REBECCA JIM: He called in the Secretary of the Environment, Brian Griffin, and he said, "How on earth could this be happening in Oklahoma? How could we have these children lead-poisoned? How can we have this mine waste sitting around? How can we have this orange water? How can we have all that? How's that happening? Why is that happening?"

J.D. STRONG: As I recall, Keating's reaction was "We've got to do something about this," and we convened and they decided they wanted to put together a gubernatorial-level task force with Brian Griffin in charge of it as chairman.

BRIAN GRIFFIN, former Oklahoma Secretary of the Environment, Chairman of the Board at Clean Energy Systems: I've had experience in the private sector and in Washington as an official at the U.S. Department of Justice. When Governor Keating asked me to serve in his cabinet, I told him I didn't have direct experience managing an environmental regulatory agency.

He said something to the effect of "Well, I know you, and I know you're a quick study and most importantly I value your judgment. You don't come tainted either way towards industry or tainted towards the environmental spectrum; you come as a kind of a tabula rasa and can analyze these issues independently and arrive at what will be a good solution," for a lot of very intractable problems that Oklahoma was facing at the time in the environmental arenas.

J.D. STRONG: [Governor Keating] appointed a group of folks largely from that area to sit down, meet and figure out what's best to do about it.

BRIAN GRIFFIN: I remember his quote, he said, "Brian, we've got to get a handle on this right at the beginning; if we let it get away from us we may never be able to deal with these issues effectively."

FRANK KEATING, former Governor of Oklahoma, attorney, author: Rodgers and Hammerstein's musical *Oklahoma!* emphatically states that we Oklahomans belong to the land and that "the land that we belong to is grand." [Tom] Lindley's Tar Creek broadside in the *Oklahoman* was stunning, frightening, persuasive, and anguish-stricken. How could generations of our leadership, including our federal representatives, look the other way? The task force that I appointed was made up of informed members from across the academic, business, civic and political spectrum.

BRIAN GRIFFIN: Keating created the task force in January of 2000. We had a very ambitious program with just over eight months to study the issue and try to come up with fresh approaches dealing with the problems.

J.D. STRONG: So, we ramped up this task force and set about developing a set of recommendations. I can't remember exactly what we needed to do to mitigate this disaster, and in particular, protect children's health in that area—which is, of course, the most vulnerable population, the kids that are six years old and under.

SCOTT THOMPSON, Director of the Oklahoma Department of Environmental Quality: He [Governor Keating] was highly motivated. I sat in some meetings in his office, and he was very concerned that the kids' health—the school officials had indicated some of their issues were related to lead exposure. We also had EPA gearing up and getting excited about trying to do some cleanups there. Of course, we were trying to explain to the Governor how the program worked and that we might have to come up with some matching funds depending. He was very supportive of that.

There were a lot of activities. There was a lot of work. Trips back and forth, interaction with EPA and local folks and legislators, et cetera, just trying to work through the analysis of what the issues were overall. It was broader than only the lead in the soil because we had a lot of undermining[10] and people were still concerned about the water quality, about the groundwater services for some of the towns and surface water impact and downstream impacts in Grand Lake. It was quite an expansive effort.

FRANK KEATING: They came up with a plan, but they were promptly stifled by the federal government. Action was required, and all that we got was delay and diddle. So very sad.

EARL HATLEY: By law, EPA had to come back and do remedial action at the site to deal with the path of exposure that was causing the lead levels in children's blood to rise. The EPA determined that the chat was the reason for the high levels. So, the EPA started testing people's yards when they first admitted that the lead amounts in the chat were astronomical. People had been putting chat in their driveways for decades; it had been used in the towns for fill, it was in the gravel and dirt roads. The real fine sand had been used to fill sandboxes; it had been

---

10. undermine: to excavate the earth beneath; form a mine under.

used in the schoolyards, near playgrounds—it was scattered all over the county and spread beyond. The EPA had a colossal cleanup issue on their hands.

WALLACE KENNEDY: Until that moment happened, nobody really cared about the health of the people who were being impacted by the Tri-State Mining District. There was some talk over on the Kansas side, and then when Tar Creek hit and they formed the Tar Creek Task Force.

Nobody thought to check the blood of the children who lived there. Nobody did blood tests. How are you going to give somebody a clean bill of health if you're not going to blood-test? The whole thrust at the beginning of the Superfund designation was the fact that Tar Creek flows into the Neosho River, which flows into Grand Lake O' The Cherokees which is one of the premier recreational sites in northeast Oklahoma. They were concerned about heavy metals and acid water flowing through the Creek down through Miami and into Grand Lake O' The Cherokees.

It wasn't the impact on people. People weren't paying attention to that.

BRIAN GRIFFIN: All of a sudden Tar Creek was identified as the number one Superfund site in the nation in an area of Oklahoma that most Oklahomans have never visited or don't even know about; it made galvanizing the public attitude more difficult. Tom Lindley's story did a lot to help that.

DON ACKERMAN: I think, you know, because of that letter, in the time that I wrote it in 1994, there is no true and identifiable source of the lead. I had to speak in general terms. I think I said that a lot of the people live within a half-mile or so of a chat pile and proximity plays a role. There were some homes I went to and they had the alligator chipping[11] on the outside of the area. Now that we know, keep the kids from playing in the drip zone. And that's why I also mentioned hobbies too and occupational hazards, because Eagle-Picher still had a very viable plant for lead batteries. You might see things more widespread in certain areas, I don't know if they've done a lot of GIS (Geographic Information Systems) work or GEMS work to look at it spatially based on geo-points and proximity of the chat piles or—I think it'd be kind of hard looking at it since we're very mobile as people to say *well, where are you spending most of your time? And then what hobbies do you have? Do you smoke?* At the time that smoking was a big concern for a good lead source just because of the burning of cigarettes. Or people into flint-type of weapons where they use a lot more lead. There was so much happening in that area at that time. I think that's why I wrote the letter as a general

11. Alligator chipping is a term used to describe a type of damage due to the use of an unsuitable base material, or shoddy application of plaster and paint. Often visible in cheaply constructed homes that used lead paint.

point just based on "Well, I don't have any data that shows identifiable sources. All I have is exposures." So, I couldn't at the time and all in good faith say, "It's this or that. Here are the options and because of the age of the homes, because of the age of water systems, because of how ubiquitous lead is in the environment here." It's land of a roll of the dice.

REBECCA JIM: It all began with Don's letter in 1994. They've now spent over $300 million to protect children.

THE DOWNSTREAM PEOPLE: A BRIEF, BRIEF OVERVIEW

TO UNDERSTAND the political dynamics of northeastern Oklahoma and how it became the Tar Creek Superfund Site, we need to go back a few hundred years and look at the region's original inhabitants—the Quapaw Tribe. As is common in Native American cultures, the origin story of the Quapaw people is handed off from one generation to the next in the oral storytelling tradition. According to the esteemed Quapaw historian David Baird, "Unlike other Indian peoples, the Quapaws have not preserved elaborate traditions explaining the genesis of their ancestors. Indeed, they remember only that their Ancient Ones issued forth from the water."

The Quapaws' story started with the Dhegiha Siouan Tribe. Legend has it that the Dhegiha Tribe were traveling around the Ohio River Valley when they came upon the mouth of the Ohio River, which they had to cross. They were having a hard time getting over to the other side of the flooded river. The Tribe first sent their expert swimmers across with ropes to the other side to tie around trees. They made boats out of hides to put their possessions on. As they crossed over the river, they used the rope to pull themselves across.

One group made it across to the far bank. That group became known as the U-mo'n-ho'n, meaning *those that went upstream*. The group that was in the water when the rope broke washed downstream. The downstream people were known as the O-Gah-Pah. The group left on the riverbank was known as the Wazhazhe, *the people of the middle waters*. White settlers anglicized the native names as Omaha, Quapaw, and Osage, respectively.

Historical estimates put the Quapaw living alongside the Mississippi River population at approximately 5000–6000 members during the 1500s. Like many other tribes, diseases brought in by the Europeans, such as smallpox, dwindled the tribal populations. In a mere century, the Quapaw were diminished, with only about one thousand people remaining.

30

The United States has an extensively documented history of exploitation and cruelty to its indigenous people. The Louisiana Purchase in 1803 more than doubled the landmass allocated to the United States, but to rule a land, it must be occupied and so began the westward expansion. The forced removal of America's original inhabitants, the attempted erasure of their culture, and the remaking of the landscape is our country's greatest shame that reverberates in the sociopolitical obstacles still facing Native American peoples today.

During this growth period of the United States, the Quapaw Tribe had been moved numerous times from their traditional home in the convergence of the Mississippi and Ohio Rivers. The last forced exodus took place in 1833 when the Quapaw were pushed to the northeastern corner of what became the state of Oklahoma in 1907. A significant portion of the Oklahoma side of the Tri-State mining complex consists of lands legally recognized as belonging to the Quapaw, who are still very present there today.

> The Indian Removal Act was signed into law by President Andrew Jackson on May 28, 1830, authorizing the president to grant unsettled lands west of the Mississippi in exchange for Indian lands within existing state borders. A few Tribes went peacefully, but many resisted the relocation policy. During the fall and winter of 1838 and 1839, the Cherokees were forcibly moved west by the United States government. Approximately 4,000 Cherokees died on this forced march, which became known as the "Trail of Tears."[12]

LARRY KROPP, East Shawnee Tribal council, Quapaw Tribal member: Prior to air conditioning (laughs), people would come and they'd sit out in the yard and visit. You used to learn about tribes and everything because that's where the stories were told and history was passed on.

MRS. SMITH, Quapaw Elder: They originated in Arkansas. Originally their name is *Ugahxpa*. What they did is they divided off from the Dhegiha Tribe. We used to be the Downstream People. It's because they were together but some went up north and some went south and so that's why we are called the downstream people after the river, you see.

The Arkansas is what some of the French called the Quapaws at one time. I often say that Arkansas is named after the Quapaw people. They were sent to Red River at some time. I think it was Chief Heckaton that took them down there. And then they were to come back to Quapaw because they were sent down there [to

---

12. From: 13th Amendment to the U.S. Constitution - Research Guides at Library of Congress, Indian Removal Act: Primary Documents in American History.

integrate into] the Caddos[13] and Caddos didn't treat them too well and that was down at Red River.

Then they came back and most of them settled around Pine Bluff, Arkansas, I believe, along the Arkansas River. A lot of the French intermarried with the Quapaw people, and this is why you have the Quapaw and the French. They are called Arkansas Quapaws.

EARL HATLEY, Cherokee, environmental activist, co-founder of LEAD Agency: The Tribes are on reservations; these reservations were established back in the early to mid-1800s. Long before there was an Oklahoma or Kansas, or even Texas, which was, I think, the Republic of Texas at that time.

The Trail of Tears in 1838 and 1839 was the Cherokee. They were the first Tribe brought across the Mississippi River from the east, and they were marched through the western boundary of the United States, which was Arkansas and Missouri at that time. The Oklahoma Territory was Indian country and became part of the United States because it was part of the Louisiana Purchase.

The land had been appropriated for the Cherokee, and the reservation was established and then eventually piece by little piece of that was plucked out, and that was divided again for a bunch of smaller tribes to the Quapaw, Seneca, Shawnee, Peoria, Miami, and other tribes that we have in Ottawa County. Nine tribes altogether at the little corner of Ottawa County and Delaware County. They're all Indians, and so these are Indian reservations.

FREDAS L. COOK, archivist, photographer, lifelong Picher resident: Most of the northern half of Ottawa County, Oklahoma, was the Quapaw Nation reservation with restrictions on "blood" Quapaws' ability to sell their land. Quapaw Nation adoptees had no such restrictions, causing much confusion about who owned what. Picher, for instance, is a patchwork of "deeded" and "tribal" land. Cardin, Oklahoma consists of 40 acres belonging to William Oscar Cardin, an adoptee that signed over the 40 to the town.

So many words are misused and I am guilty as well. "Reservation" is the word used most often but "reserve" is the word used at the time land was *given* to the tribes. "Blood Quapaws" is used to differentiate between the people with a Quapaw lineage as opposed to the many people adopted into the tribe prior to allotment time. "Deeded" applies to the land allotted to adoptees since they had no restrictions on the land and could sell it with a title.

---

13. In 1825 Governor George Izard of Arkansas asked the Quapaw to be removed from their land and were sent south to merge into the Caddo Tribe. The Caddos were not given any advance notice of this forced emigration. From "Chapter IV: Into the Wilderness 1819–39," *The Quapaw Indians: A History of the Downstream People*, by W. David Baird, University of Oklahoma Press, 1980, pp. 67–72.

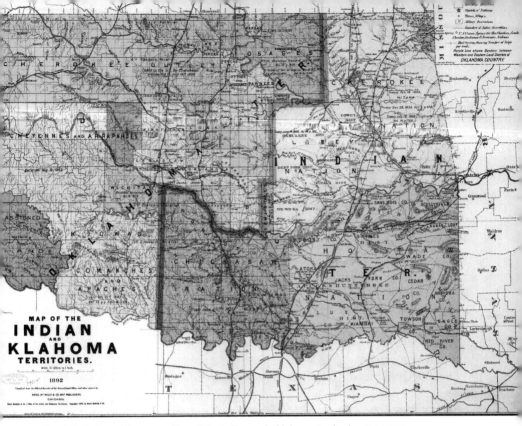

Rand McNally and Company. *Map of the Indian and Oklahoma territories.* [S.l., 1892]

EARL HATLEY: The Dawes Allotment Act was back in 1887. It required tribes to begin allotting certain amounts of acreage to heads of households, to single individuals, and to male orphans on their reservations. On tribal reservations, every household and single males above 18 were all given a certain amount of acreage within the reservation of that tribe. The land allotment was to be finished by 1905 and all the tribes had to register their tribal members.

Within what's now Oklahoma is a checkerboard of land that was homesteaded by whites within the Indian reservations. Indian reservations were never de-established. They're still reservations. But white people are still living on lands that were taken from tribes and allowed to be homesteaded by non-Indians.

When it was all said and done, almost all the tribes had land left over after they had done the allotments. They didn't have enough enrollees to use up all the acreage that they had within their reservation. They think that land belonged to the tribe because it was reservation land, but the federal government decided that extra land left over belonged to them, and they took that land from the tribe and cut it up into 160-acre lots and either put it up for sale for whites or put it up for the Homestead Act.

LARRY KROPP, East Shawnee Tribal council, Quapaw Tribal member: Tribe allotments back then I believe was originally 120 acres apiece rolled out to members at the time. That was my grandmother's allotment.

The Shawnee were never included in allotments. My grandfather on my mom's side got their allotments, but only if you were on the original log roll did you get allotments.

Her allotment was north of Quapaw and my grandmother was able to buy several farms around. And my dad, he farmed all his life. In 1939, he took over a farm; she'd bought east of Quapaw out on Spring River and Grandma moved off the allotment. She'd moved to two or three places on the farms she had. She was able to invest in property through mining and buying other properties.

EARL HATLEY: The Quapaw reservation was the only reservation in Oklahoma where the Indians had a lawyer. This lawyer married a Quapaw woman. He was really smart, and he saw this possibility, and so he drew the allotments times the number of adoptees and figured all of that in. And so, the Quapaw didn't have any land left over. It was all allotted and sent back to the Dawes Commission[14], and it was approved.

So, the Quapaws didn't get any lands stolen *that way*.

LARRY KROPP: There's a lot of intermarriage between tribes. The Eastern Shawnees purchased their allotments from the Quapaws. There's always a lot of respect between the two tribes. There's a lot of intermarriages between the two tribes. There's a number of people just like myself, Eastern Shawnee and Quapaw.

It's very common with a lot of tribes around here. Ottawa County, I think, is the only place in the United States where there's I believe nine federally recognized tribes that have their offices here in Ottawa County.

My raising and growing up—we're Indian people. There're really no specifics as to which tribe; you were recognized as Indian people. You might ask me, I'm Quapaw, I am Eastern Shawnee. I know one individual, he is actually of five tribes.

After the Civil War, [the United States government] brought the Modocs to the Quapaw reservation. Then they brought the Poncas in. Then they brought the Nez Perce Tribe in. They were the tribe that never surrendered. They continued to fight in Idaho until they were eventually starved out. And if you've ever studied

---

14. An act of Congress, approved March 3, 1893, established a commission to negotiate agreements with the Choctaw, Creek, Chickasaw, Seminole, and Cherokee Indian Tribes. The commission became known as the Dawes Commission, after its chairman Senator Henry Dawes of Massachusetts. The commission's mission was to divide Tribal land into plots which were then divided among the members of the Tribe. As part of this process, the Commission either accepted or rejected applicants for Tribal membership based on whether the Tribal government had previously recognized the applicant as a member of the Tribe and other legal requirements. www.archives.gov/research/native-americans/dawes

about Chief Joseph and the Nez Perce Tribe, they've never surrendered to the United States, yet they were removed from Idaho and brought into Oklahoma.

But they were all here on the Quapaw reservation at one time before they were moved out to various parts of states.

I had a lady ask me one time, "What kind of games do you guys play? Did you play cowboys and Indians when you were kids?" I said, "Yeah, but nobody really wanted to be the Indians because they always get beat. Everybody wanted to be a cowboy because they won all the time."

BOOMTOWN, USA

BACK IN New Jersey during the 1980s, when I was taught about the industrial revolution in grade school, it was presented with the clarity of hindsight as though it was an inevitable, linear march toward destiny. It was presented to us as a technology that was willed into being by self-interest, self-reliance, and the conditions of our unique democratic experiment. Some of that's true. History has revealed the industrial revolution was not a linear progression but a series of fits and starts, depending on the region and its resources.

The Tri-State Mining Region began its life as such in 1848 when lead deposits were first discovered in Joplin, Missouri. But it wasn't until nearly 50 years later in the 1890s when lead was found in Peoria, Oklahoma, and more importantly a little later—the massive 1895 discovery of lead in what became Picher, Oklahoma, which was considered the densest and richest lead and zinc veins in the country. The discovery of minerals set off a chain of migration to the area. All of a sudden, homesteaders found something more lucrative than farming, and the rush was on. It led to a lot of conflicts between the local Native American inhabitants and the nascent mining entrepreneurs.

The mining industry went into hyperdrive when Congress passed a law in 1897 allowing the Bureau of Indian Affairs to lease lands for mining, haying, and lumber. Even in the early stirrings of corporate America, people of color were not included in the gold rush. A few savvy Native Americans became very rich, while others got taken advantage of. Some of it can be chalked up to racism, which led to fraud, collusion, and outright theft; there was also a fair amount of the Native American experience that was just missed opportunities due to a sharp divergence in worldview. This created a problem when the white man then presented them with contracts and legal documents.

By 1905 the federal government claimed that the Native American land allotment project was done. In 1907 Oklahoma became a state. Picher had become a peak boomtown during the World War I years when the government demand for lead and zinc use was at an all-time high.

The Downtown, USA has been represented in TV and movies many times. We all have a picture of what it was like in our heads. When you go to the Tri-State Mining Region today, you can still see traces of the Old West in the architectural outlines of some of the buildings, particularly in some of the downtown shopping districts like in Miami, Oklahoma, or Baxter Springs, Kansas.

EARL HATLEY, Cherokee, environmental activist, co-founder of LEAD Agency: In 1897, the Congress passed a law that allowed the Quapaw Agency, which was the Federal Indian Agency for this area that covered these small tribes in that corner of the state, to lease lands for mining, haying, and lumber.

In 1895 or so, lead was discovered in Peoria, Oklahoma. Then a couple of years later, they found lead right where the headquarters for the Quapaw reservation stood, and they discovered lead in Commerce, and so on. That's why the U.S. Government passed that law about mining on Indian land that stated that if the Secretary of the Interior found that any Indian landowner was incompetent to handle these leases, then the Secretary could manage those leases for him. From the beginning, the Indian Agency went to the tribe interviewing the Indians that were on the land where the mining companies wanted to get a 40-acre lease. They determined them all incompetent, and so with the signature of the Secretary of Interior, these guys could start mining on Indian lands. It was as if they were too dumb to read the contract or that they're incompetent—*this dumb Indian.*

The Secretary of the Interior never really conducted interviews to determine competence. It was racist from the get-go, and the tribal owner had the right to get something like a 12 percent royalty, but the money went to the Indian agent, and the agent was in charge of the bank accounts for the owners. Indians at that time were considered non-human. They weren't allowed to have bank accounts, they weren't allowed to sign contracts, and so the money from the royalties that the miners were getting paid went to an Indian agent who put the Indian's name into an account to his [the agent's] name. If an Indian wanted 40 bucks for something, he had to go through the agency and fill out a request for 40 bucks from that agent.

MRS. SMITH, Quapaw Elder: I do have a lot of documents that were signed by the different attorneys and the Indian agents. They were crooked and they would sell, like, a new car to some of the allottees every so often. I heard later that one of the agents, his brother was a car dealer, so they'd even sell cars, you know. It was just a money profit thing for them.

Jumbo blocks of lead weighing 2,500 pounds each at a large smelting operation. From the Eagle-Picher plant near Cardin, Oklahoma, come great quantities of zinc and lead to serve many important purposes in the war effort. United States Office of War Information, Henle, Fritz, photographer. 1943. Library of Congress

ED KEHELEY, retired nuclear engineer, expert on Tar Creek: The Tribe was always eager to say that they owned most of the land, and they say that today. When you go back and look at the record, that was not true. Most of the Quapaws, when the allotment occurred, did not live on the reservation. Most of them lived in central Oklahoma with the Osages. Many others had moved back to Arkansas and lived in other states.

They only came to the reservation for the purpose of getting their allotment, which most of them immediately sold and went back to work where they lived. Most of the Quapaw landowners who retained their allotments, and on whose land mining occurred, did not live on that land.

So, it's not like you have this large indigenous population that dominated the mining field and then mining occurred and people were displaced. The Quapaws were never satisfied with the reservation from day one. They were not farmers as they did not like the prairie.

The point I want to make is, too many authors that I have read tend to want to migrate to this nativist situation where these poor people were so horribly treated on their own lands so on and so forth. And while some of that is true, it did not affect most of the tribal members because they weren't anywhere near—for example, the Kenoyer family lived in California and their allotment ended up being one of the biggest mine areas, but they didn't live here. The Cardins didn't live on the reservation.

MRS. SMITH, Quapaw Elder: The thing of it is, when they were listed out and given their allotments in Oklahoma, some were placed in different areas, you understand. Grandmother and her brothers were put on the prairie in Ottawa County. Some were put out east by Spring River. They were all scattered about in different areas. However, luckily for those put on the prairie, it turned out that all the mines were there. All the mining was under their land. Some of them were quite wealthy at that time.

Quapaw is six to eight miles from here, and the state line of Kansas is not where it used to be, it was further up into Kansas, but the state of Kansas is along a straight line across. Those that had allotments on the Kansas side were told to leave. And I think they were paid a dollar to get off. Now, that's what happened to my grandmother's mother.

ED KEHELEY: The maximum number of Quapaws who were ever restricted, and restricted means they were not capable of handling their own business affairs, which was 65 people, 65 Indians including some children.

The errors of other Indians. And those were the Indians who were considered to be restricted, meaning they couldn't freely manage their own land and sell it and that sort of thing; the government had to approve any sale of their land to make sure that they were fairly treated and get a fair share of value for their land. It was not up to the Bureau of Indian Affairs in Miami to make that determination—that determination of restricted or not restricted, which was not made by the local office. There was a commission that was sent out here from Washington to make that determination. And the local BIA office was simply given the list of names of people who were considered to be restricted and therefore their land had to be managed. Now, all of the other Quapaws, the Kenoyers, Harry Crawfish, who had big land holdings and valuable mines—they were not restricted and they managed their own affairs.

This issue of kind of a welfare state where most of the Indians were incompetent is a myth that's just not true. And if you look at the 1921 act that came out, which set forth leasing regulations and all of that, it's explained in there. In all of these 65 Quapaws are identified by name in there.

And then if you ask me, was there abuse of managing their affairs by the Bureau of Indian Affairs (BIA)? I'm going to say yes there was, and these examples are well documented, but at the same time the lawyers in Miami were also screwing over them, and everybody that could had screwed them over.

EARL HATLEY: You may have heard about the Cobell case, where royalties were being ripped off from Indians for decades by the BIA. It was about the Osage Tribe in Oklahoma's oil and gas, but the Quapaw Tribe was part of that case because BIA was stealing their money from the lead and zinc too.

There was that one case a few years ago, where one family discovered their ancestor had donated $80,000 to an Indian school in Kansas, and they went back to the records from that school and found that only $40,000 was donated to the school. They recorded $40,000 to that name, and the records show that he had signed for an $80,000 payment. The agent got $40,000 in his pocket. And so, they found all kinds of stuff like that going on.

The agent was making out like a bandit. Yeah, he was a bandit.

MRS. SMITH, Quapaw Elder: My grandmother signed leases, but when the time had come, this person that she signed the lease with said, *No, you didn't sign a lease, you sold it to me* and she said, *no I didn't,* but there was a lot of—that's how the forgeries come in. And that's where so much fraud comes in.

Being my grandmother lived in Kansas, they took her case. It even went as far as the Supreme Court of Kansas and she won her case. But then this gentleman that she was filing against, his son, I think became a lawyer, and he re-appealed it. They finally took it over. Then his father who took all of her money left for Florida. And he never did come back. In fact, he died down there. So, his son stayed here and took over the matters. They never could get a way to get him back up here for anything, for another court hearing.

My grandmother ended up here in Baxter in Kansas because she was burned out twice. She knows the gentleman who did it, but her attorney advised her to move to Baxter for her safety and her family. It was a lot of fraud, there was a lot of forgery. There was these lawyers here roundabout, were responsible for this. It just was the way life was at that time.

> *Tar Creek proved to be the deepest reservoir of lead-zinc ore in the world, producing a whopping $1 billion in minerals between 1908 and 1950, according to the Oklahoma Historical Society. Picher, the largest of the mining towns, swelled to a population of 14,000.* [15]

MARY BILLINGTON, director of the Baxter Springs Heritage Center and Museum: Picher had the largest lead and zinc in the area. If you think of a paintbrush and you fill your paintbrush up, and you drag it in, the closer you get, the more you press on it so you can get that heavier paint out. It was like that with the mining field. If you think of Carterville and Webb City and Joplin, they were all nice and thick mines, but by the time you got to Picher, it's heavier and denser. So all of this mining field was there, but Picher had the majority.

WALLACE KENNEDY, retired journalist, *The Joplin Globe*: The thing about Baxter Springs, it was on the cattle drive and it was established because there were actual springs there. And John Baxter set up camp there. Well, there was the cattle would come out from Texas. They would stop there, where there was water—Spring River and at Baxter Springs. And that was all open prairies. There were no trees there. People just don't understand that if you go to Picher today, you see all these trees as the time it was developed. There wasn't a tree in sight, it was the prairie.

MARY BILLINGTON: If you look at the statistics between World War I and World War II, the mines in this area supplied almost 40 percent of all of the lead needed for the war effort.

It created this boomtown, and you've got all of these people coming here to find a better way of life. If you could mine and make money, you were making more money as a miner than you are as a homesteading farmer. Many left the wife and kids and came to work. You had a lot of new immigrants coming here to make more money for their families. People were revamping their life after the Civil War.

---

15. Malcolm Burnley and M. Scott Mahaskey. "The Environmental Scandal in Scott Pruitt's Backyard." *Politico* Magazine, 6 Dec 2017.

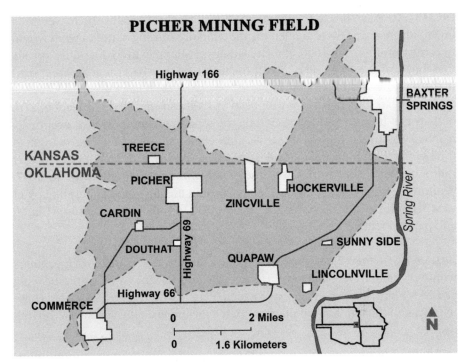

A simple Picher mining field designed by Ed Keheley. Image courtesy of Ed Keheley

It was new immigrants to the country, and it was African Americans looking for a better way of life, hoping to homestead as well. Granted, as far as the lead and zinc mines go, most of the African Americans were kept out. There was one mining company here in Baxter, Kansas, [that] was known as the Estes Mine, that was on property owned by an African-American family, and blacks worked it. Prejudice was there. Obviously, some of it was a higher degree, you know, it all depended on each individual as most things do from a familial perspective.

MRS. SMITH, Quapaw Elder: Because I was raised in Baxter and there was some but not too much [racism]. You can always look back and think, *oh why did that teacher do that* or *why did that person say that?* But to me as a child, I just—I just bypassed it and went on. Years later, I look back at it and I think, *that was a rude thing for them to do.*

MARY BILLINGTON: You saw a lot of money come into Baxter, Kansas—the mine owners in Baxter—and it didn't have a mine in the town per se. It was a cleaner community. It didn't have the dust stirred up in it that the mining towns had. Baxter had big homes that were built by the managers and owners. Not like in Miami, Picher, Commerce, and Quapaw, which were the communities where the mine workers lived.

FREDAS L. COOK, archivist, photographer, lifelong Picher resident: There were very few roads, nor was there a need for them before mining came to what would become Commerce in 1906. The city fathers of Miami figured out pretty quickly that they had the shipping point for the ore since they had the railroad. A road to the mines was immediately built.

A trolley to Hattenville was proposed in 1908 and started on November 27th of that year. It was extended to Cardin and then to Picher in 1916. It eventually reached Columbus, Kansas. The trolley line eventually became a railroad system throughout the mining fields. It went through several owners and names. Another railroad serving the mines was the Miami Mineral Belt Railway. In 1927, Commerce Mining and Royalty Company built an electricity generating plant west of Cardin supplying 25-cycle electricity to its installations as well as to Cardin and part of Picher.

MRS. SMITH, Quapaw Elder: Baxter was quite a thriving town. And all of the miners would come in from Picher and Hockerville and Cardin and it would be a big Saturday night, the town was just crowded. People would visit, they would come in town and the families would sit in their cars and visit. It was really a thriving town.

Miami Record-Herald, **Friday, January 7, 1916.** Courtesy of the Fredas L. Cook archive

Crystal Mine, Eagle-Picher Mining company, 1940. Courtesy of the Fredas L. Cook archive

Picher also had movies and they were a thriving town too. The miners were tough, tough people. My husband is a miner. My husband was 14 years old when he started working in the mines. And I have a picture of him. He was hauling coal and stuff, and of course they used mules underground and I have that picture.

WALLACE KENNEDY: At the time, the Joplin area was one of the most sophisticated places to live in the country because it had so much wealth. You would not know that now. But at one time it was. We had a trolley car system that connected communities in Missouri, Kansas and Oklahoma. Miners could get on a trolley car and go from town to town. They didn't have to live where they worked.

MARY BILLINGTON: There were hundreds of [mining companies], and a mining company might exist at this point, and in six months it would be gone. You see record after record where a company leased the same piece of land, and they mined it for a while. Then it was leased by another company, and then they mined

43

it for a while. Each new lease was to a new mining company, so there are many layers of it. Everybody is trying to get their piece of a better life.

FREDAS L. COOK: Commerce Mining and Royalty Company predated Eagle-Picher and was probably the second biggest. American Lead and Zinc which was originally named Evans-Wallower.

MARY BILLINGTON: Eagle-Picher Industries, they were one of the largest lead and zinc [companies] in the area.

LARRY KROPP, East Shawnee Tribal council, Quapaw Tribal member: My grandmother and grandfather operated mines, north of Quapaw almost to Hockerville. All on the original allotments. They operated a number of mines over there.

MARY BILLINGTON: For the mineworkers it was about creating a way of life for their families. It was about supporting their families at a point in time when there wasn't anything; it was about these new immigrants who didn't have anything and hoping for something in the new country.

LARRY KROPP: Lincolnville reached its heyday in about 1915. The minings where I lived—that's out east of Quapaw in the Lincolnville district—they were very active during World War I. Then they had the Lincolnville mines cease production and everything, it moved over towards Picher mining fields, Picher–Cardin area, that takes you to World War II. The goal during that period of time was to extract as much lead and zinc as possible, as fast as possible, to support the war effort.

That's the reason that they cut it so high and wide. There was really no concern for the after-effects; the concern was winning the war and using the products produced from the mines for the war effort.

THE MINES WERE BEGINNING TO PLAY OUT

FOSSIL FUELS and minerals are finite and take millions of years to form underneath the surface of the earth. When we use them up, that's all there is. The mid-1920s are widely considered the Tri-State Mining District's peak years, but it's the 1930s that were a turning point for the region. The Great Depression led to a temporary halt in mining, and continued market volatility led to fluctuations in lead and zinc production prior to World War II. Small miners went bust as the big mining enterprises consolidated the industry. Some of the old mines went dry while new ones were being discovered. During the 1930s, scientific advancements were revolutionizing the mining industry. Old chat was able to be reprocessed for more lead and zinc content.

While there was continued volatility in metal markets during the 1940s, World War II gave mining a boost just as the previous war effort did, but when the war

Arthur Rothstein, photographer. **Zinc miner's home. Picher, Oklahoma. 1936.** Library of Congress

ended, so did many of the government contracts. The booming postwar economy kept the big mines going for a few decades as consumer products containing lead and zinc were in high demand. In 1957 the biggest mining concern in the Eagle-Picher area shut down operations. By 1958 the mines began to "play out" as they say in Oklahoma. Some of the towns that benefited from mining had cultivated other industries, such as Joplin, Missouri, who weathered the end of the mining rather well, while places like Picher, Cardin, Commerce, and Quapaw had no other industries or exports. Mining was the only game in town.

Keeping a campaign promise, President John F. Kennedy passed H.R. 84 in 1961, which tried to give the mining communities a boost by getting lead and zinc subsidies passed in Congress, but it wasn't enough to keep it going. It seemed like a slowdown at first, but eventually all operations stopped. Everyone in the area felt the effects.

ED KEHELEY: The city fathers in Picher, if you read the whole history, from the very beginning wanted to make it more than just a mining town. They wanted it to be a thriving, vibrant community. But in 1950, Eagle-Picher came in, and [they] condemned the four-and-a-half blocks of the downtown business district of Picher because of the potential for collapse. The city fathers still kept trying to come up with ways of *how can we keep this a viable community? How can we help it grow?* The city of Picher formed an economic development commission for Picher and they called upon the state to help them. The state came in and looked at Picher.

They generated two documents. The first one is a preliminary report on the economic and population data of Picher and Ottawa County. It has a lot of statistics in it, which tells you that basically the town is a mess: undereducated people and very little industry that was really in trouble. This was the first document, then the second document that the Department of Commerce and Industry created was the comprehensive plan for Picher.

WALLACE KENNEDY: You would not know growing up in Joplin that it was—in the time that I grew up in Joplin that would be in the late 1950s. I was born in 1953, so the mining had pretty much ceased by then and it was just a community that was going through a transition from hard rock mining community into a more manufacturing and retail and medical-type community.

VIRGIE CURTIS, owner of Classy Brass Antiques: They were still mining in the 1950s, but it was winding down. At that time, of course, you could still see the chat piles that looked like mountains from here, from Miami, and then it just gradually went down. You can hardly see them now.

CATHY SLOAN, environmental specialist, Quapaw Tribe: I was born in Picher in 1955, and there were three hospitals there at that time. I think they said the population was like 60,000.

LARRY KROPP: Lincolnville was a rural school and it was probably about a mile and a half outside of Quapaw, set in this area around here. Lincolnville was described as being the roughest town in Indian Territory. I've gathered all the newspapers—it documents a lot of things that were in Lincolnville at the time, which was if I remember correctly, there was a hotel, right, three general stores, two stables, and several houses of ill repute.

WALLACE KENNEDY: I'm definitely a descendant of a mining family. My grandfather, Festus Jackson Kennedy, was a miner, a hoisterman at the Federal Brewster mine in 1926, at Picher, Oklahoma. He was Native American, mostly Cherokee. He's a direct descendant of John Baxter, founder of Baxter Springs, Kansas.

Fess was a handsome man. He looked like a gangster. He was a poker player. He had a fedora hat, a vest on with a tie and white shirt, and he drove a Studebaker—a colorful character. And so he managed to do pretty well in regular society, but there was a real issue with people of color, women, and foreigners in connection with the mining at Picher, Oklahoma.

Because Jackson really looked Indian. They gave him a job above ground as a hoisterman, which was a responsible job and he got good pay for what he did, and he didn't get as much exposure as the people who were actually in the mine.

He developed silicosis stage three. They just cut him loose because they didn't want the medical responsibility or financial responsibility for a bunch of sick miners. I distinctly remember going on a trip with my father and my grandfather in about 1958 or '59. My dad was driving. My grandfather was in the front seat and I was in the back seat. And we're on Route 66, and you pass through some of the worst mining in that area between Webb City and Carterville. I remember my grandfather looking out the window of the car and turning to my dad and saying, "I never thought they would leave it like this." And then after that he said, "The bastards."

TOM LINDLEY, author, retired journalist, *The Oklahoman*: In the local culture, miners were pretty noble figures. I think over the years that's something that's lost in this story. This is where Mickey Mantle sprang from, Commerce, Oklahoma. There were pictures of him when he was 17, taking one of those elevators into the ground and coming back up.

MARY BILLINGTON: Mickey Mantle was recruited to play ball. They lived over in Commerce. His dad was a miner; Mickey mined some as well. He was signed right out of high school. He played a year at Independence, Kansas, and a year at Joplin, Missouri, but in that period so many men could have been recruited to play professional ball that turned down the contracts because mining paid more, mining could support their families, whereas playing baseball could not.

TOM LINDLEY: I think that upset a lot of people because they were proud of what they did and they had a right to be. It's tough work. They helped build the country. They were significant contributors. A lot of them died of silicosis or black lung disease at a young age. That's also a part of the tradition and culture there as well as the environmental destruction.

FREDAS L. COOK, archivist, photographer, lifelong Picher resident: The general belief is that the mines played out, causing the closure.

MARY BILLINGTON, director of the Baxter Springs Heritage Center and Museum: Without the subsidies from the U.S. government to continue mining, the mine owners had to look somewhere else to invest their money.

FREDAS L. COOK: It was a time of shock, confusion, and disbelief. In the early 1950s, as best I can remember, the government reduced or rescinded the import tariff on lead and zinc which curtailed mining in the area. Many families moved to Grants, New Mexico in search of jobs in the uranium mines.

MARY BILLINGTON: Just south of Picher, the last mine closed down in the early '70s. It had been a tourist attraction for several years. They would take you down in the safety can and tour the mine.

FREDAS L. COOK: Few mines were dry. Many ran through the water table with the shaft. The hooker [was] the man at the bottom of the shaft that hooked the cans of rock to the hoisting cable; he wore a rain slicker. Some mines were wetter than others while some even ran into underground streams. Some couldn't be worked at first because the pumps couldn't keep them dry enough to work. Advancement in pump technology, from horse-drawn to electric, made more mines operable.

LARRY KROPP: It was costing too much money to keep the water pumps hooked up to continue to mine what little bit of lead that was left in the area.

REBECCA JIM: The mines were closed. The pumps were off. The caverns were filling, but the water didn't start coming out of the ground until 1979.

DR. ROBERT WRIGHT: We added poverty on top of that because there's a lot of unemployment up there. They had a lot of issues that were all tied to the toxic waste site.

All those elements are all bad for your health, but they weren't necessarily directly related to lead. One of the things I learned by going out there was this idea that a toxic waste site could affect your health even if you're not directly exposed because there is this stress that comes with it. The stress might be economic, based on your property values, job security—all those issues.

WALLACE KENNEDY: I don't think they understand the scope of it. I mean, four hundred square miles in the Picher area alone impacted by mining, and then they got equal amounts of that over in Missouri, in Kansas, and what a booming enterprise this was when it was taking place.

ED KEHELEY: When you read the Department of Industry and Commerce summary, what it said was Picher, there is no hope for you, you have too many chat piles, you have too much land owned by Indians, and the rest of your town is a mess. You have too many miles of streets and water mains and all of that. And you ought to shrink the town by at least by a fourth and clean the town up. That was really the death knell, if you will, for Picher. That occurred in 1964 and from that point on, if you read in there the condition of the housing and how deteriorated it was, and just really how nasty and filthy the town was, you can conclude yourself that there was never going to be any opportunity for Picher to recover.

THOSE AREN'T MOUNTAINS, THOSE ARE CHAT PILES

IN MY RESEARCH I've found that when a community discovers an untreated environmental problem, the problems tend to multiply and pile up on one another. In the case of a city approving a dump, it will usually follow up with a recycling center or an incinerator, with a city government claiming there is nowhere else to put the blight. In Ottawa County the eco-problems compounded on their own accord—the abandoned mining waste made its way into the water, the air, and formed the entirety of the landscape.

There was nearly a decade between the last mine's closure in 1970 and the first appearance of metallic, orange water bubbling up from out of the earth. This is 15 years before Don Ackerman wrote his infamous letter to the EPA in 1994 which sparked the community's investigations into their children's learning disabilities and the cascading events that followed. But in 1979 the mines were full of groundwater and the ecological problems began piling up.

But obvious to everyone was the hulking, man-made 750-million-ton mountain range of toxic mining waste that was the unusual town landmark. In the Tri-State

Overlooking Douthat Road. Fredas L. Cook Archive

Mining District, the combined lead-zinc ore mining waste is called "chat." "Mine tailings" is another term to describe the crushed waste rock remaining after the lead and zinc ore have been removed. Tailings range in size from rocks to fine sand and contain a slew of heavy metals. The mine waste was removed from the mines using water, which created a tailings slurry, then dried and placed in large piles over two hundred feet high and a quarter-mile in diameter. It's the varying amounts of harmful substances that make chat so dangerous.

The dry chat of nearly a century of mining is now piled hundreds of feet high behind houses, schools, and in the middle of the prairie.

The Oklahoma portion of the Picher Mining Field produced over 12 million tons of lead and zinc concentrate from mines and chat between 1891 and 1970. These concentrates provided over 1.5 million tons of lead metal and 5.2 million tons of zinc metal worth just under $1 billion.[16]

For every 1 ton of ore extracted, approximately 16 tons of chat and tailings were left behind.[17]

16. U.S. Bureau of Mines Microfilm Records of Lead and Zinc Mine Production Data, Missouri Southern State University, Spiva Library Archives, Joplin, Missouri.

17. Tim Kent. "Quapaw Tribe Remedial Efforts at the Tar Creek Superfund Site." Environmental Justice Forum, 12 June 2018, Dallas, Texas.

MATT MYERS, filmmaker, *Tar Creek*: I'm from a town not far from there called Vinita, which is about 30–40 minutes away. In Picher and Commerce, you would see the chat piles, and that's all we knew about it back then. You would ask what those huge mountains are, and someone would say chat piles and that was kind of the end of the discussion.

DR. ROBERT WRIGHT, pediatrician, medical toxicologist, and environmental epidemiologist at the Icahn School of Medicine at Mount Sinai: At a lot of Superfund sites, it's in the water, it's in the soil, but you don't see it. Everything looks relatively normal. But if you go to Tar Creek and drive down the Will Rogers Turnpike you see these hills in the distance, and you realize it's kind of unusual because the land is pretty flat, because it's a great plain; then as you get closer and closer it looks like the surface of the moon, and then you realize those aren't natural hills—it's mining waste.

MRS. SMITH, Quapaw Elder: Way back when I was a child they looked like mountains.

WALLACE KENNEDY: I went to work for the *Globe* in 1976 and it was shortly after that I was assigned Galena, Kansas. And the people, the city leaders there wanted to promote economic development in Galena, Kansas, but they couldn't because the town was completely surrounded by mining sites. There was no place to go.

School bus in front of chat piles, 1990s. Photo by Earl Dotter.

And these were bad mining sites. Galena was home to Hell's Half Acre.

And the aerial photographs of this site, if you see them, it looks like the moon. It is crater after crater after crater where people were digging the ground looking for lead and zinc. And it was just unbelievable.

BRIAN GRIFFIN, former Oklahoma Secretary of the Environment, Chairman of the Board at Clean Energy Systems: It looks like a moonscape if you see it from the air.

BRAD CARSON, former Congressman of the 2nd district of Oklahoma, former Undersecretary to the Army: It's a moonscape up there, I remember thinking when I first traveled through all the chat piles and stuff, and it was pretty vexing from a political standpoint.

BRIAN GRIFFIN: It just blows your mind. When I was told by the EPA that if you loaded a unit train—that's a hundred-car coal train that stretches a couple of miles—if you loaded a single unit train every day for a hundred years, the chat wouldn't be gone. It took us so many statistics to realize how much chat was there.

LARRY KROPP, East Shawnee Tribal council, Quapaw Tribal member: The Old Eagle-Picher Central Mill over between Commerce and Quapaw used to cover over 60 acres and at one time it was classed as the largest man-made object in the United States.

SCOTT THOMPSON, Director of the Oklahoma Department of Environmental Quality: It consists primarily of some of the bedrock which is chert, a flint-type rock, or dolomite which is more like a limestone kind of rock. Then you had the ore that has been ground up multiple times. As the ore was ground, it became finer and finer. Then you had mill ponds where the ore was actually leached out and processed, so the finest material is in the mill pond sand.

TOM LINDLEY, author, retired journalist, *The Oklahoman*: Chat was the big issue. Chat had some economic significance to the Tribe and some intrinsic value, that's all that was left there. It was also imposing a danger.

EARL HATLEY, Cherokee environmental activist, co-founder of LEAD Agency, Grand Riverkeeper: Under the roads, you lay a base, and then you pour the road on top of the base. So [chat] can be used for the road base and it can be mixed into the asphalt, and that's it. That's all you can use it for.

DON ACKERMAN, Environmental Health Specialist, retired commander in United States Public Health Service Commissioned Corps, former researcher for Bureau of Indian Affairs: Lead is going to be ubiquitous out there. As far as some of the stories I had heard, some of the chat was used for roads. It was used for railroads at the time, for the foundation. I even heard that it was used for some home foundations. Instead of gravel, people use chat, and that's when everything starts to deteriorate.

BRAD CARSON: There were economic demands for it. Chat is quite useful in road construction. I think that was the debate, and sure, they would dump it in the roads in southeast Kansas and northeast Oklahoma, but the idea of transporting it across the country seems less viable. Part of the issue was economic, especially at that time, before we had widespread Indian gaming[18] in Oklahoma. The Quapaw had no real source of revenue at all. There was some stew bubbling about who had title to this material. They knew this stuff was valuable, but should the Quapaw sell it?

I think the Quapaw had title to it. But the question was the Bureau of Indian Affairs had to approve it because these things would always seem to be tossed to the BIA. So, they were always going through these legal disputes. How can you use this stuff and sell it?

LARRY KROPP: The BIA came in. I said a lot of the tribal members weren't receiving royalties off of the land that was mined off of their allotments and the BIA was likely shorting them.

BRIAN GRIFFIN: One of the inequities we saw early on was the Bureau of Indian Affairs that administered that area had put a moratorium on the sale of chat. So the Quapaw Tribe were restricted from being able to sell or deal with any of that chat, while at the same time the EPA had no restrictions and they actually encouraged the use of chat. It seems a bit patently unfair that one U.S. agency is saying, *you can't even touch your chat while you're over here* and the EPA is saying yeah, *use the chat for road-building material and asphalt and things like that.*

That was something we identified, that first and foremost. We had to come up with a workable solution that dealt with the chat that was to the benefit of the Quapaw and everyone else in that area, and it needed to be done in a fair manner that treated everybody fairly so that the Quapaw weren't disadvantaged.

---

18. Mr. Carson is referring to the Native American casinos that many of the Tribes own, which have become a steady revenue source for many tribal governments.

CATHY SLOAN, environmental specialist, Quapaw Tribe: When we came to work here, we moved to Miami, and then we went to Picher, and we would haul truckloads of chat in for our driveways. Everybody did it. When my dad moved to Peoria, he had like eight dumptruck loads of chat hauled in his yard. It's just what everybody did. It wasn't like, *oh that's harmful.* It was plentiful. It was just something you grew up with, never realizing that it was as bad as it was. I think when you grow up around something you don't really think about the effects.

LARRY KROPP: As a kid I got run off several of the chat piles.

SCOTT THOMPSON: Of course, kids were going to play in them. I would have. Adults would play in them. It was a popular recreation for off-road vehicles. Some people just slid down the chat piles on old car hoods and stuff. But when you start taking samples, it showed pretty quickly that the lead measurement numbers of the soil in the yards were a concern. The health outcome is not lethal. It's more potent in the development of some intelligence or behavioral issues and stuff.

DR. ROBERT WRIGHT: There is this visual representation of what is happening that's sort of a daily reminder of the toxic waste that I don't think you get in most Superfund sites. Things like cave-ins where kids have been injured. People have also been hurt while playing on top of the chat piles because sometimes it would cave in.

If you can imagine, all those over two hundred to three-hundred-feet-high chat piles on the surface become what's missing underground. This means there is a gigantic hole in the ground with these enormous caverns that occasionally cave in and people have been killed.

FREDAS L. COOK, archivist, photographer, lifelong Picher resident: Obviously mining caused the current contamination. No one ever considered what it was doing to the environment while it was happening.

TOM LINDLEY: I can't prove this, but I think the mining companies and the government were aware of the risk posed by going down several hundred feet in the ground and all the dust all the time.

MARY BILLINGTON: [Mining companies] have proven that they knew much earlier than many people did that serious exposure to lead contamination was detrimental to people's health.

THE HOUSE OF BUTTERFLIES

BY THE 1980s lead poisoning had been scientifically and conclusively proven as detrimental to child development. Lead had been banned from paint manufacturing since 1978 but is still commonly used in heavy industry under strict regulation. This remains an active area of research as the body of knowledge about lead's health effects continues to grow.

In Picher, there is always lead surrounding you. It's not just the mountain range of mine tailings. Every single structure in Picher used a form of lead in their construction materials: paint, roads, schools, hospitals, institutional buildings of all kinds, people's homes, driveways, and sandboxes—everything. The amounts of lead exposure residents and visitors experienced during Tar Creek's peak mining years is hard to fathom.

Lead's toxicity in human beings has been known as far back as ancient Rome. According to the EPA website[19], in ancient Rome, lead had been employed in multiple everyday objects such as face powders, rouges, mascaras, paint pigments, spermicide for birth control, a "cold metal" for chastity belts, seasoning for food, and a wine preservative for stopping fermentation in wines. Its malleability made it ideal for pewter cups, plates, pots and pans. Lead was also a partial ingredient in Roman money and plumbing. The Romans were aware that it causes "madness" and sterility, but the threat was often ignored because of its versatility. Workers both free and enslaved bore the brunt of high exposure through smelting and manufacturing operations. The upper classes didn't get off easy as they were exposed through their diets and their utensils.

In the 20th century the United States became the world's largest producer and consumer of lead. In 1921 the invention of tetraethyl lead created the first high-power, high-combustion engines that kickstarted the modern automotive industry. By the late 1920s, the damage in humans caused by lead began being studied, and in 1925 the Surgeon General put a temporary stop to lead use in cars until further study. But due to pressure from the auto industry and the Calvin Coolidge Administration, the Surgeon General issued voluntary standards on lead's industrial uses in 1927. Eventually the industry did put in more safeguards to protect workers and lead poisoning cases in the workplace decreased.

By January 1971, EPA's first Administrator, William D. Ruckelshaus, declared that "an extensive body of information exists which indicates that the addition of alkyl lead to gasoline...results in lead particles that pose a threat to public health." The EPA began more studies and in 1973 the agency was advocating for a

---

19. Jack Lewis. "Lead Poisoning: A Historical Perspective." *EPA Journal*, Environmental Protection Agency, May 1985.

Family in front of chat piles, 1990s. Photo by Earl Dotter.

phase-out when it became obvious that the lead in car exhaust was in violation of the Clean Air Act. In 1975, all cars were manufactured with catalytic converters so they could run on unleaded gasoline. In the 1980s lead was phased out of general usage wherever possible. By the time Tar Creek's multi-generation toxic exposure was brought to light in the 1990s, scientists knew a hell of a lot more about the effects of lead. Known pathologies of lead exposure include neurodevelopmental disabilities such as autism, attention deficit disorder, hyperactivity disorder, dyslexia, and other cognitive impairments including dementia. Lead poisoning is not limited to diseases of the brain, and when combined with exposure to other metals such as cadmium, arsenic or manganese, the symptoms can be numerous and quite complicated.

KIM PACE, former school principal Picher Elementary School: Many of our children's eyes were not working together.[20]

ED KEHELEY, retired nuclear engineer, expert on Tar Creek: I began to think about my own upbringing. I can remember from the time I started school there were kids who just could not learn, and this is in the early 1940s and 1950s when there were no remedial classes available in a small mining community. There was no way to provide special help for these kids. Teachers recognized those traits, and they would just pass these kids off to the next grade. That's all they could do.

In some cases, they would hold them back. Often, they would just let them go ahead through the school system all the way through the twelfth grade to graduation. They gave those kids high school diplomas, but they had some severe learning difficulties.

There were some, I don't want to say 30%, but it was a good percentage of those kids had learning difficulties.

WALLACE KENNEDY: And now the prevailing theory is that there is no safe level for lead exposure in children because of the incredibly damaging effects it has on brain development. You can lose three to five IQ points and never get them back from lead exposure. It's that serious. There were great teachers there, but the kids just—some of the kids just couldn't get it, and they definitely know what's causing that. And that is without a doubt what was happening at Picher, Oklahoma.

DR. EMILY MOODY, pediatric environmental health fellow, environmental medicine and public health at the Icahn School of Medicine at Mount Sinai: Exposure to lead early in life is very critical to childhood development. Lead exposure during

---

20. *Making a Difference at the Tar Creek Superfund Site*, edited by Rebecca Jim and Marilyn Scott, 2007, p. 119.

pregnancy and young childhood are most detrimental to the behavioral and neurodevelopment of our children. And we know that children absorb lead at a higher rate than adults.

Lead is absorbed into our system through our gastrointestinal system. There's a transporter in your intestine that actively transports calcium across the gut and into the bloodstream. Lead is what we call bivalent, meaning it is a +2 ion; so is calcium, which is also +2. Kids are set up to absorb a lot of calcium when they are growing because they need it for building bones and so they absorb lead at a higher rate too. Kids are also exposed to lead via food, water, house dust, or lead being on things that they put into their mouths.

DR. HOWARD HU, epidemiologist, physician, researcher, clinician, University of Washington School of Public Health: Lead and calcium are both bivalent cations[21] chemically, and it turns out that a lot of calcium-related processes in the body are affected by lead. Or lead will substitute for calcium and of course, make whatever molecule that results behave differently than the calcium-dependent molecule.

One of the processes affected is when calcium is incorporated into the hydroxyapatite mineral structure of bone, and everybody knows that calcium is essential for bone growth and is a mainstay of the bone architecture. Lead will essentially substitute for calcium in the chemical structure of bone, and then it will sit there for many years. We used to think the skeleton was kind of a sink for lead, that lead was being incorporated into skeletons. But now we know with much better understanding of the behavior of bone and calcium in bone over the lifespan that in fact, bone is a very dynamic organ.

DR. EMILY MOODY: [Lead is] absorbed at a very high rate in kids and then we also know that lead is transported across the blood-brain barriers. It means there's a little bit of a higher protection for chemicals to get into the brain and the other organs of the body. But there are transporters, like calcium, that will carry certain essential nutrients across the blood-brain barrier to the brain, and lead follows one of the transporters. Lead is equally transported into the brain and causes neurotoxicity.

Once it's in the brain, I don't think we know exactly which cells are targeted or why it causes those effects, but we know that it does, and we as a society, or in ancient societies, brilliant societies, probably saw a lot of dementia and cognitive thinking problems in adults due to their high levels of lead. It is well established.

---

21. Cation: atom or group of atoms that bears a positive electric charge.

Lead's impact on adults—I think I will divide this up into what we call acute effects and then chronic effects. Everything that we've talked about so far with the health effects on children are chronic effects. Even if a child has a short period of high exposure or they have a high exposure for a period of months, you might not notice any change because there's no immediate acute effect, but down the road you would notice that effect.

In adults, because we have learned a lot about lead because of occupational exposure, we know that there is a handful of what we call acute effects or symptoms somebody can experience from one day to the next. That's a pretty significant effect. For example, we know that one acute effect in adults targets the brain and central nervous system, and so in industries that have had really high levels of exposure, they had people who come down with psychosis. They start having hallucinations; they have trouble concentrating, memory problems, and depression.

There are actually stories about the lead plant which produced what they call tetraethyl lead, which was the anti-knocking compound that used to be added to gasoline. It was a volatile agent so it would evaporate on its own and people could breathe it in, and they called it "The House of Butterflies" because there were so many people who became very acutely intoxicated with lead that there were a lot of those neurologic symptoms, including hallucinations, sometimes leading to seizures and coma; a lot of people died from those exposures.

The other acute health effects that people might have experienced was gastrointestinal so a lot of constipation or vomiting or diarrhea. But then the other category of health effects are chronic. Those could be caused by either or environmental occupational exposure—meaning anybody getting exposed just from the environment. Those chronic health effects can also include some of the memory loss or earlier onset of dementia.

DR. HOWARD HU: I have spent 25-plus years researching the effects of lead poisoning on middle-age adults and young adults, and women in the peri-pregnancy period to understand the health impact of cumulative exposure to lead. For pregnant women, we learned how much lead gets mobilized[22] from mom's skeleton during pregnancy and how it becomes an independent risk factor for exposure to the fetus.

DR. EMILY MOODY: There are reproductive issues. Some men might experience decreased sperm count or decreased sex drive. Women might have more trouble getting pregnant.

---

22. Mobilize (medical use): to release (something stored in the organism) for bodily use.

DR. HOWARD HU: During pregnancy, a woman's skeleton is literally dissolving to help feed the enormous demand for calcium of the fetus as it grows its own skeleton. Beginning in the 1990s, our research group worked hard trying to figure out whether mobilization of lead from mom's skeleton during pregnancy constitutes a major threat to fetal development. After a couple of decades of research, we have shown that's true, and so true that National Institute of Health funded our team to conduct a randomized, double-blind, controlled trial of calcium supplements vs. placebos of women during pregnancy. The goal was to see if we can inhibit the reabsorption of mom's skeleton by providing an outside source of calcium. We did show that calcium supplements reduced the amount of lead that's circulating in mom during pregnancy by at least a third. That protocol has now gone on to become one of the recommendations made by the Center for Disease Control for pregnant women exposed to lead.

Later in life is when women experience osteoporosis, which is bone demineralization, and their risk for osteoporosis is when they experience menopause. That is the time when lead leaches out of bone at a heightened rate which is not so good for elderly women.

DR. EMILY MOODY: There are also kidney abnormalities. Reduced kidney function, that also might be related to hypertension, so you would see higher cases of high blood pressure in adults who lived with lead in a community or were exposed occupationally.

Rebecca Jim reached out to the epidemiological researchers at the Harvard School of Public Health and received an EPA grant. Dr. Howard Hu, Dr. Robert Wright, and Dr. James Shine conducted a study on the impact of lead, arsenic, cadmium, and manganese and their impact on the health of children of Tar Creek. Released in 2007, the study was the result of years of research and informs much of what is known about the health effects of these heavy metals on children's development.

At the Tar Creek Superfund Site (TCSS), one of the nation's largest such sites, over 40,000 residents live in a 50-square-mile area filled with mining waste containing lead, manganese, cadmium, and other potentially toxic metals. The TCSS has been the subject of two major ongoing studies undertaken by the authors and colleagues with support from the Superfund Basic Research Program and the Center for Children's Environmental Health and Disease Prevention Research at the Harvard School of Public Health. We will use the TCSS as an example to discuss issues related to the multiple pathways through

which toxic waste mixtures may gain access to the immediate environment
of children (or fetuses); factors that may influence absorption of mixtures
once ingested or inhaled; the vulnerability of children's developing organs to
mixtures; lessons for clinicians; and research needs.[23]

DR. HOWARD HU: We know how extensive the contamination was, but the some-what happy finding from the study is that it luckily didn't translate into off-the-scale lead absorption in the residents. There were clearly higher lead levels in the offspring who were born in that region than one would expect from folks in a non-mining community, but it wasn't at the magnitude that would have been a total disaster.

The less happy circumstance is that it looks like the residents were also exposed to other toxic metals, manganese among them. One of the unknowns in toxicology and environmental health is how the mixtures of metals interact and the unexpected, untoward effects from mixtures, as opposed to predicting the effects of just a single agent exposure. That's still the subject of ongoing research from the work that Bob Wright and colleagues are continuing.

DR. ROBERT WRIGHT, pediatrician, medical toxicologist, and environmental epide-miologist at the Icahn School of Medicine at Mount Sinai: There's also a stigma. I learned from some of the parents in Picher that some of the neighboring towns make fun of their kids. They call them "chat rats" and other derogatory names because there is a certain assumption that they were exposed to lead and weren't very bright. There is a stigma attached to being from that area. There are other things that happen from living near a toxic waste site, and you might never get exposed to lead, yet it influences your health and your life. That's just as important. We don't seem to study that, and that to me was the most interesting and important question of understanding sort of holistically how toxic waste sites affect health. We tried to incorporate all those ideas into the study, and the study got funded. I think the reviewers clearly liked it. Unfortunately, all those social-political issues that I talked about became barriers in some ways to the study.

EPA tried very hard to stop the study, which was a bit paradoxical because there were different sections of the EPA that were both partly funding it and partly trying to stop it. There is a part of EPA that does research. They were funding half the study and NIH was funding the other half, and then there was the part of the EPA that was doing the cleanup; they wanted us to go away and tried to kill the study. I think I'll leave it at that.

---

23. Dr. Howard Hu, et al. *The Challenge Posed to Children's Health by Mixtures of Toxic Waste: The Tar Creek Superfund Site as a Case-Study.* Pediatric Clinics of North America, 14 Feb 2007.

Lead, at what is called lower levels, between, say, one microgram per deciliter to five micrograms per deciliter, caused controversy because of what were the assumed toxic effects. I think now it's very well accepted that the kidneys have a low threshold for toxicity. But at that time it wasn't widely accepted, so we proposed that if you had low-level exposures to lead in combination with the other metals present in chat (which included manganese, arsenic, and cadmium) that the combined metals are synergistically more toxic than lead alone. We also proposed that the mixture of metals is more toxic than an individual metal, and if all you did was measure one metal you would actually miss the mixture effect. We proposed to measure all four.

The other hypothesis we wanted to test was that if you were a person who experienced additional stressors from living in a Superfund site, whether that stress was because of potential exposure, or economic stress or other emotional stressors, that lead and heavy metals would be synergistically more toxic for you versus somebody who was emotionally and psychologically resilient. We put forward a new idea that people could be susceptible to lead poisoning, but you would only see that vulnerability only if you measured both stress and lead simultaneously. There have been some studies that have come out since then that have actually proposed some more ideas about the relationship between stress and toxic poisoning, but we were unique in that we focused on Superfund sites rather than a sort of general urban or rural population.

In Tar Creek, we were up against a lot of barriers to doing this study. Our follow-up in the study wasn't as strong as I'd hoped, which limited our ability to look at interactions. We primarily focused on what epidemiologists call *main effects*. We did publish a paper that showed that higher levels of arsenic were associated with lower birth weight in babies. We had about six hundred to seven hundred kids enrolled in the study at birth. When we started to do the follow-up, our numbers dropped to about 250 kids at two years of age. We needed more statistical power with more participants to look deeper into those of interactions of stress and exposure.

I conducted a second and third study in Mexico City where we actually were able to follow enough kids to look at those interactions. What I alluded to before—the issues about EPA wanting to kill the study, and also some of the issues around people in the community being wary of us because they were worried we were going to hurt their economic situations, so awful—I think that made it harder to enroll and retain people in the Tar Creek study.

It was difficult, but we did publish several papers. We published a paper looking at manganese in birth weight; that higher levels of manganese is associated with lower birth weight. We published, but we didn't have good enough numbers to look at the interactions that we had proposed in the study, not in Tar Creek. Most of the published work is based on Mexican studies because we had better retention in Mexico.

DR. EMILY MOODY: The other mechanism other than just directly passing the lead from one generation to the next, these intergenerational effects, is that many different kinds of toxins are passed through epigenetics. Epigenetic refers to the information that is on top of the gene. It also refers to modification in these methylation[24] patterns or the normal changes that happen to DNA that change its expression pattern.

We know that even if our genes are the same, that a family that has exposure to lead or other toxins or maybe they've had an extremely stressful psycho-emotional experience, like a refugee experience or other violence, or if they've been exposed to a high level of air pollution, will be affected. Their epigenetic profile, meaning how well and at what rates they express certain genes, will be different.

Those patterns are hereditary, and they are passed from one generation to the next. And that's one of the newer areas of research. It's ongoing, but it's teaching us a lot more about how the intergenerational effect of certain types of exposures can be passed down.

DR. ROBERT WRIGHT: I thought it would be very cut-and-dried: there is toxic waste, let's clean it up. I understand the perspective of the people in the community and those against the cleanup plans. In a sense, they feel that if all you're going to address is the cleanup and you're not going to address the poverty, you're not going to reduce social stresses that come with the poverty, all of which were caused by in some ways being a Superfund site, then are you really helping us? Or are you hurting us?

The lead levels weren't super high, statistically. Something changes in the environment so that one day there is massive contamination that had to be cleaned up. The cleanup, I think, helps the community, and I think it's the right thing to do, but it's all the other issues that aren't resolved, and don't get addressed. People don't think of the corollary issues as being related, but in my mind, they're very related. They have just as profound an effect on child health and development as lead poisoning would, but it's not within the EPA's mandate. I don't know how to get that better across so we can start to address it, because the poverty and the social stressors absolutely are part of living in a Superfund site. That's why the people who live there are so emotional about the issue. The other problems get ignored even to this day. I would like to see more research on that.

---

24. A common type of epigenetic modification is called methylation. Methylation involves attaching small molecules called methyl groups, each consisting of one carbon atom and three hydrogen atoms, to segments of DNA. When methyl groups are added to a particular gene, that gene is turned off or silenced, and no protein is produced from that gene.

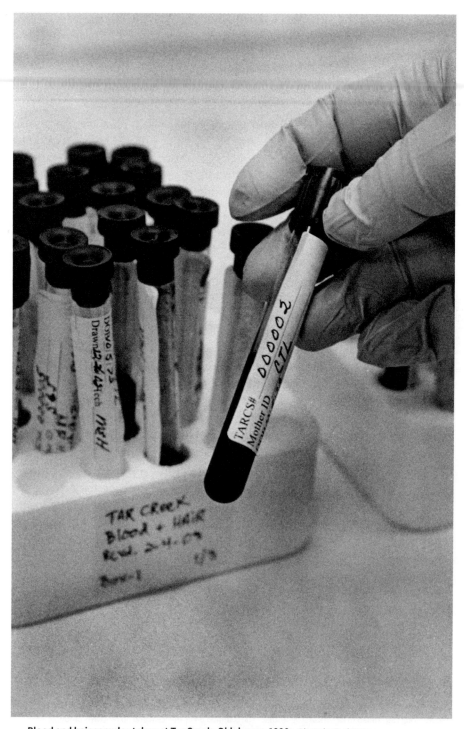

Blood and hair samples taken at Tar Creek, Oklahoma, 1990s. Photo by Earl Dotter.

A RARE CONDITION

DURING THE boom years, miners unsurprisingly contracted diseases such as tuberculosis and silicosis at staggeringly high rates. In 1934 the highest incidence of tuberculosis in the United States was in Ottawa County.

After Indian Health Services researcher Don Ackerman wrote his letter to the EPA uncovering the patterns of lead poisoning in Native American children, the thrust of the cleanup focused on getting children out of harm's way. Throughout the course of my research and interviews, I came across all kinds of anecdotes about other types of illnesses throughout the Tri-State Mining Region beyond lead poisoning in children. Like most places with high amounts of toxic waste, cancers and leukemias are common and compounded by socioeconomic conditions of poverty, lack of education, access to medical care and proper nutrition.

Prior to the passage of the federal Superfund laws, it was accepted that diseases were a fact of life in a mining town. That all started to change when the orange-colored acid water appeared.

"All the kids had to have a chest X-ray," he said. "Tuberculosis still existed in this area. At one time, Ottawa County had the highest tuberculosis rate in the nation. The miners would develop silicosis from breathing dust in the mines, and that would lead to tuberculosis, which they would give to their wives and sometimes their children. Cases of tuberculosis were found in kids."[25]

Karen Harvey, 53, lived in Picher from 1960 to 2002, and as a kid she played on chat piles and swam in tailings ponds. "We'd go swimming in them, and our hair would turn orange, and it wouldn't wash out," she said. At age 18 she had surgery to correct bone growth in her ears that interfered with hearing. Noting that she's also dyslexic and was recently tested with an I.Q. of 65, she said she's starting to wonder if her childhood in Picher contributed to her health problems. "I don't know if that has something to do with it or not," she said. "I'm just figuring it out as I get older."[26]

LARRY KROPP, East Shawnee Tribal council, Quapaw Tribal member: Well, basically, I've said that you had the miners that had consumption or what they call the

---

25. Wally Kennedy. "Business Hub of Former Mining District Center Burns." *Joplin Globe*, 15 Apr 2015.

26. Dan Shepherd. "Last Residents of Picher, Oklahoma Won't Give Up the Ghost (Town)." 26 Apr 2014, NBC.

black lung back then. They had the cough and everything. And as far as cancer goes, I'm sure that cancer was a problem back then, but they didn't know the means of treating it like they do now.

TAMMY ARNOLD, environmental grants manager, Quapaw Tribe: We have always known Tar Creek was bad. I grew up knowing Tar Creek was bad. Not to get in it.

JAMES GRAVES, former school board member, chairman of Governor Keating's Task Force Committee: I put in a home filtering system. It would turn brown when it needs changing, and when I would jerk it out, the water would just be bright red, just like Tar Creek.

REBECCA JIM, Cherokee, educator, environmental activist, co-founder of LEAD Agency: George Mayer was at a public meeting. It was one of the meetings that had the court reporter present, and they recorded everybody. Lots of people spoke, and George was one of the last ones to speak. Some years ago now—1979?

He started asking everyone to do something about these boreholes that were ruining his property and harming his horses. He's saying, "I've talked to the Bureau of Mines, I've talked to the Health Department, I talked to EPA, I've talked to everyone, and no one will fix this. No one will help me." And he says, "Isn't there anybody out there that'll do something about this?"

> *Water boiled out of a red wound in the pasture and spilled across the grass. It flecked the ragweed with rusty foam. George Mayer knew in an instant what it was. "The damn mines," he said to himself. "The mines are full, and the water's finally coming out." It washed around the ankles of his purebred Arabian horses, stained the ends of their tails and splashed against their roan-and-tan bellies when they ran. Their hides turned orange. The hair burned off their legs. They developed open sores. Not far away, water gurgled out of another hole in the ground. Then it surged from another. And another. It belched from a mineshaft and gushed out of an old cave-in. It splashed down ditches and gullies and into a stream called Tar Creek. It turned the stream blood-red, and it killed the fish.[27]*

---

27. Richard E. Meyer. "Acid Water Drowns Tar Creek as Cleanup Delayed." *The Oklahoman*, NewsOK, 6 Feb 1983.

CATHY SLOAN, environmental specialist, Quapaw Tribe: I don't think any of us knew what the lead, zinc, and cadmium effects were. I think it's just because either we didn't want to be involved or we just didn't know.

WALLACE KENNEDY, retired journalist, *The Joplin Globe*: I remember at one point as the situation was developing, that the ATSDR was to come in and do a study of the health of the people in Ottawa County and Picher, Oklahoma. I did my own survey in Picher.

I think I may have gotten one or two streets over from the main street and just went door to door asking people if there were any medical issues in their households, and if their neighbors were at home, I would ask them, "Well, are these people okay over here? Do they have any medical problems?" They would tell me. I had a notebook and it was filled with notations by the time I got down the street. There were a lot of interesting cases: a lot of hypertension, children needing special attention and tutoring, children with asthma problems because of dust, diabetes and lung disorders and kidney issues. You just go right down the list.

Now the question becomes this: Picher was a very inexpensive place to live. These people were battling medical conditions. They may choose to live there because they could live there inexpensively, and it may not have anything to do with where they live, the fact that they live in the middle of the hazardous waste site, once declared the worst in the nation—but it seemed to be striking to me that there was so much illness there, so many problems.

And of course the ATSDR—I don't want to say it was a superficial look, but they just looked at the records and I don't think they did any kind of door-to-door survey of people. They came back and said, "Well, there's nothing special about Picher." I beg to differ on that.

REBECCA JIM: Once we established LEAD Agency, everywhere we went people would say, "You know, people on my block have this, and my sister has that," and they began to say all these illnesses, and so that's why we did the health surveys in 2004.

What we did was we looked at the ATSDR tox profile[28] for every known element that we could be exposed to in Ottawa County. Then we looked at what those substances were, and then we looked at what diseases they caused, and that's the survey we did. And yes, we've got every kind of disease caused by these exposures we're having, and we had too much. We really have a sick community.

---

28. Toxicological profile: An ATSDR document that examines, summarizes, and interprets information about a hazardous substance to determine harmful levels of exposure and associated health effects. A toxicological profile also identifies significant gaps in knowledge on the substance and describes areas where further research is needed.

MARY BILLINGTON: There's a condition called Chiari malformation[29] and I know three people in this area that have Chiari. It's a condition when your cranium is not formed properly, and so your brain instead of sitting up in your head has a tendency to slide down and put pressure on your spinal cord. It's a very rare condition.

I know three people, two of whom are in my daughter's age category, that have this condition. Too many people have different things like this and they are the second, third, fourth, and fifth generation in the community. To me that all points to something more, because when you see that many instances, you don't have to have the medical proof to suspect that this is a genetic mutation created by generations of lead contamination.

REBECCA JIM: It just keeps happening. The ones that didn't quite make it. Things have been hard all their lives. They just struggled, struggled through all their lives because they can't think as clearly as they want to. Things are hard for them to figure out, and there was no help for them through school. If you were lucky enough to be designated learning disabled, then you got some help at school, you had some allies in school, but you also felt put out, and you felt stupid, and that doesn't go away. It changes their lives forever.

29. Chiari malformation is a condition in which brain tissue extends into the spinal canal. It occurs when part of the skull is abnormally small or misshapen, pressing on the brain and forcing it downward.

MISHANDLED

UNDER CERCLA, when people live near a Superfund site, the EPA is required to take steps to remediate the area. EPA employs project management organization techniques and identifies smaller and easier to manage sub-projects called "Operable Units" (OU). The EPA then conducts mandatory five-year reviews to determine what has or hasn't worked, with the ultimate goal of achieving full remediation. In the case of Tar Creek there have been multiple sources of contaminants and the resulting damage to remediate: the mine water, the chat piles, subsidence, and the creeks in which orange, metallic mine waters flow into the river.

In 1984 EPA launched Operable Unit 1: Surface Waters (OU1) which was the first such project to come out of the Superfund process, and it involved plugging 66 deep wells of the 150 that were drilled. All of which were headed directly into the Roubidoux aquifer which supplies clean water to the area. Plugging those wells could have potentially averted a drinking water catastrophe for the area. The Boone Aquifer also runs beneath the area and is contaminated with mine water. The other half of OU1 was rerouting Lytle Creek around the contaminated site. Two mineshafts were plugged to prevent mine water from draining into Tar Creek.

The timeline becomes convoluted as the EPA has had several Operable Units running at the same time since the 1980s. Operable Unit 2 was begun in 1997 and continues today. It was designed to remove contaminated dirt from the "high traffic areas" where children play and replace it with fresh, uncontaminated dirt. This program ultimately extended to people's yards throughout Picher, Cardin, Quapaw, Miami, Joplin, Galena, etc. But because of the myriad issues surrounding Tar Creek, this seemingly simple task turned into a living nightmare for the people involved.

> *Operable Unit (OU): During cleanup, a site can be divided into a number of distinct areas depending on the complexity of the problems associated with the site. These areas called operable units may address geographic areas of a site, specific site problems, or areas where a specific action is required. An example of a typical operable unit could include removal of drums and tanks from the surface of a site.*[30]

---

30. EPA Superfund Glossary epa.gov/superfund/superfund-glossary

Polluted with mine water. Photo courtesy of Rebecca Jim/LEAD Agency.

TIM KENT, environmental director of Quapaw Tribe: There are three components to consider about these sites: politics, science and policy. You have to have all three present. One without the other two doesn't get it done. If you have politics without the science, you're not going to get it done.[31]

DR. ROBERT NAIRN, environmental scientist, researcher, professor Oklahoma University: As a scientist, one of the things that I teach at university, when we talk about how we address these problems, is that everything is driven by risk. If there's no risk, we're not going to commit resources, whether those are financial or human resources, to fix a problem. There's got to be some risk that we deem to be unacceptable and that's going to trigger our action.

In very simple terms, if you break it down as simply as you can, in a lot of these environmental and human health risk assessments, there are two very general options. You have a source of contamination and a receptor, whether that be the human population or an ecological system. You can either address the source, clean up the problem, remediate it, or you can remove the receptor. If you remove the receptor, the fact that the source is still there "doesn't matter" because now the risk has been alleviated because we no longer have the receptor.

EARL HATLEY, Cherokee, environmental activist, co-founder of LEAD Agency, Grand Riverkeeper: I got there around winter '92–93. There were no cleanup efforts at all. Actually, EPA wasn't doing anything. They had done Operable Unit 1 (OU1) which is the surface and groundwater, which was also taking care of mine water.

The remedy that they chose didn't work. They had gone away; they did the remedy, got money and did the work, plugged a few wells and went back to Dallas. That was in 1987.

DR. ROBERT NAIRN: In 1997 they had Operable Unit 1, the surface water and groundwater. That Record of Decision had been issued in the mid-1980s.

TOM LINDLEY, author, retired journalist, *The Oklahoman*: They had done the public school, they had done the school area and all that stuff around downtown and they got rid of it. Some mineshafts were being filled and stuff like that but there were still thousands of areas, maybe hundreds of mineshafts that hadn't been touched.

DR. ROBERT NAIRN: Our focus has always been more water-oriented. We immediately got involved in some of the data collection, filling some data gaps on the waterside that really had kind of fallen by the wayside after the 1984 decision in Operable Unit 1.

31. *Making a Difference at the Tar Creek Superfund Site*, edited by Rebecca Jim and Marilyn Scott, 2007, p. 127.

Once the Record of Decision was issued by EPA, as it was on OU1 back in the mid-'80s, that kind of is a turning point. They'll follow through on their cleanup if they chose to do one. In that case, they used a Fund Balancing Waiver that said these waters are irreversibly damaged by past mining practices. So, we're going to continue to do some *after-action monitoring*. We're going to have the state collect data, but we're not actually going to go in there and clean up the water.

BRIAN GRIFFIN, former Oklahoma Secretary of the Environment, Chairman of the Board at Clean Energy Systems: I recall the first ever real direction of the Operable Unit 1, as they called it, was looking at the water quality issues and some drainage issues due to the mine acid drainage impacting the aquifer there. They had two aquifers as I recall in that area: the shallow Boone aquifer, and the deeper drinking-water aquifer, the Roubidoux.

CATHY SLOAN, environmental specialist, Quapaw Tribe: The city of Miami gets water from an aquifer called the Roubidoux. It runs from Arkansas and I don't know how far it goes, but it runs right through here.

BRIAN GRIFFIN: The Boone, at the time, it already had become contaminated, but there was great concern about the danger to the deeper aquifer, the Roubidoux, that we believe would have been catastrophic if it had become unaided, because then that would have impacted all the drinking water in that area of the state.

EARL HATLEY: The berm that they made to divert Lytle Creek over to Tar Creek so that Lytle Creek would not flow into a cave that the mine water was coming out of, they thought that was causing the mine water to surface, but the mine water was coming out of the mines because the mines had filled up and it was coming out of the mines anyway.

Nothing had changed at Tar Creek. It was still orange.

WALLACE KENNEDY: They built a dike to divert some water and they did some other things, and it really was ineffective because they didn't ever have a grasp of the complex geology and hydrology that was taking place there, and because the thing was so mammoth. But what they did do was plug 66 abandoned wells that connected the mine to the Roubidoux aquifer, below which was the primary source of drinking water in northeast Oklahoma.

By capping those wells, those abandoned wells, they prevented groundwater contamination into the aquifer. So that was important.

DR. ROBERT NAIRN: Operable Unit 2, the residential remediation work, had kicked off a few years earlier, and the real focus in the late 1990s was on the residential property soil remediation work. There was still a lot of yard cleanup going on.

The thing that drove Operable Unit 2 was the Indian Health Service study in the mid-'90s that identified 35 percent of the children in the watershed with elevated blood lead levels. That was really the driver for the residential cleanup, was the fact that you had kids with elevated blood lead. That was linked directly to soil lead levels.

SCOTT THOMPSON: The quickest thing was to go clean up the yards because EPA had no interest in purchasing of properties at that point at Tar Creek. They had been through that with Times Beach, Missouri[32] and some other sites, and they were not interested in going down that path again. The quickest thing to do was to start cleaning up yards.

VIRGIE CURTIS, owner of Classy Brass Antiques: I was in here one day working and a guy came in and said his job was to clean up the lead in the yards. They were going in and grading or going down deep and taking the soil out and I saw part of that. I was over there a couple times buying merchandise. People would call, they were going to be moving out, so they would want to know if I would want to come and buy some of their stuff, their antiques.

TOM LINDLEY, author, retired journalist, *The Oklahoman*: The scope of it, it was this huge problem. We were not remediating yards. How could we address it when we had all the chat piles still remaining? The wind still blows, and as long as that happens nothing is going to really change. It was interesting. There was a lot of work going on when I got there.

ED KEHELEY, retired nuclear engineer, expert on Tar Creek: When I came in '99, I began to get involved; people were very upset with the EPA because of the problems associated with the Yard Remediation Program. For example, they did not come in and remediate a street at a time. They just kind of hopped around. There was no requirement that the contractors check the elevation of the yard after they finished the remediation to make sure that the water would run away from the house and not to the house. Then by doing a couple of yards and going across the street and down, and doing another yard, they upset the drainage system in a rather flat town. There was a lot of flooding and stuff that the community did not have previously. They were busting a lot of sewer lines, water lines and that sort of thing, and so the people were complaining.

The EPA would sometimes listen and sometimes help with those issues, but the crowning blow was in February of 2000: the FBI raided the remediation contractors' office amidst some whistleblower who complained that they were

---

32. Times Beach, Missouri is a Superfund site ghost town—a town that was destroyed by dioxin poisoning.

removing contaminated soil out of one yard and taking it across town as clean backfill and dumping it. It precipitated enough pressure that the FBI raided it and that shut the remediation down.

The EPA has spent more than $176 million over the past 25 years on cleanup work inside the 42-square-mile area, on projects from plugging mineshafts to removing contaminated surface soil in people's yards. Though the amount of money sounds large, it hasn't been nearly enough to remove the toxic dangers, and many residents insist the cleanup was mishandled from the get-go. In some cases, the removal of soil resulted in sloping yards, which, during bouts of rain, caused flooding and mold inside houses. The company later settled a lawsuit brought by the federal government alleging false representation of billing and progress reports for a sum of $1 million. In the settlement, the company made no admission of wrongdoing.[33]

REBECCA JIM, Cherokee, educator, environmental activist, co-founder of LEAD Agency: [Contractors Morrison-Knudsen] were absolutely awful. They did fraudulent work. They were mean and inefficient. They didn't care, and they got away with it. We knew that they were doing bad work because we had a whistleblower that came and told us. I had no idea who I was meeting, but I meet him and they were telling me that they [Morrison-Knudsen] were digging up dirty dirt and they were driving around the block and putting it back. Or they would dig up dirty dirt and go get dirtier dirt to put on to put back in.

ED KEHELEY: When this occurred, this yard remediation issue, in 2000, I received a call from the Army Corps of Engineers Inspector General's office. They said, "We understand you're a former government executive. Do you know anything about contracting?" And I said, "Yes, a little bit, you know I just spent a lot of my career contracting." And they said, "Will you come to Tulsa and will you read the contract for the yard reclamation work? Advise us." And I said, "Sure." I drove to Tulsa and I went to the Inspector General's office and they gave me a contract and said, "Would you just take it in the room and sit down and read it and then give us your thoughts." I went in and it only took me about 15 minutes. It was a half-an-inch-thick contract with the Morrison-Knudsen Corporation. They were the actual contractor at the time.

I looked at the contract and I say for about 15 minutes and quickly found the important parts. I came out and they said, "Well, what do you think?" And I said,

33. Malcolm Burnley and M. Scott Mahaskey. "The Environmental Scandal in Scott Pruitt's Backyard." *POLITICO Magazine*, 6 Dec 2017.

"This contract was dead on arrival. It was never going to work." And they said, "Oh, why is that?" And I said, "Well, the Environmental Protection Agency was experimenting with a new method of contracting that has never, to my knowledge, proved of any value and was discounted a long time ago." They said, "What do you mean?" I said, "Besides the award fee that they were giving the contractors and paying all their costs plus the fee? They also had an incentive element in the contract." They said, "Well, can you explain that?" I said, "Sure. They have about $943.00 that Morris and Knudsen can make extra on each yard if they do certain things. When they go in and test the soil in a yard and find it to be contaminated, if they removed the soil within two weeks of their sampling they get four hundred and fifty-something dollars."

That was just half of the incentive contract, and the next part of the incentive was backfilling it, grading it, et cetera. In other words, they were decreasing amounts. They would get the $943.00 if they expedited things. I explained to the Inspector General's office that was the answer as to why people were complaining so much about the yard remediation effort. For example, during fall Morrison-Knudsen Corporation would go in and just scrape out hundreds of yards and take the soil out.

Then in December Morrison-Knudsen Corporation would shut down for the winter and then not start up until February, so they were leaving these yards open. It was called open; the ground was as deep as 18" so people had to lay boards from the street to get to their homes. In the meantime all the old-growth tree roots were exposed. And so what Morrison-Knudsen were doing is they were going in and opening up all of these yards and then removing the soil but they weren't backfilling. Because the incentive was not as great to backfill as it was to remove the soil.

They were leaving these homes stranded all winter. There literally were people who had water all around their homes. It was a nightmare. That's partly why these people are complaining—they don't understand why they're removing soil and then going off and leaving it for months instead of going back and finishing their yard.

LARRY KROPP, East Shawnee Tribal council, Quapaw Tribal member: We went through the whole process. When they first came out and proposed cleaning these sites up, it was explained to us that "if you allow us to clean it up, we'll do it at our expense. But if you don't allow us to clean it up, you'll have to pay for cleaning them up." So what's a landowner to do?

On the side of the house here, they started testing for cadmium after the lead test and everything. And they came right up to my yard, and they actually came into my yard and they said my yard is contaminated with cadmium, but we don't clean the yards up, we're just doing the outlying areas. They took right up to my yard fence and stopped, it's kind of funny. My wife asked them about the contamination that showed. "Well, you're contaminated but it won't hurt you." And I asked him, "Why are you cleaning it up if it doesn't hurt you?"

"Well, we're supposed to clean it up." You couldn't get a straight answer out of him.

On the other side, the farm side, the agreement on that was that they can clean them up, but they can restore them to a useful purpose. Where we are as far as the useful purpose? If it grows grass, we can use it for pasture. And they went in there and it was ridiculous. All that they're after is moving out and every time they moved a pile of brush within the contaminated site, they'd get paid for it. It would be a two-day process to shift. And they knew everything we went through to try to plant and restore to a useful process.

When I went to complain and then sit in on meetings and everything, and they had one lady who was a joke. She was a representative of the EPA. It was her job to smooth everything over. I accused her of being on the payroll of the construction company and that didn't go over too good—accusing that girl. I just sat down listened to them. They tried to run me out and I said, "no, you're talking about my property. I want to find out what's going on." That didn't go over too good. I'm kind of hardheaded on stuff like that, I guess.

According to them it was contaminated and you cannot set foot on the property. Oh, they were stringing it up, a tape line with a little red flag on it. *That's contaminated; you can't set foot on that property.* I been walking on that property for 70 years! I said, "What's gonna hurt me now? What difference does that make when it's been contaminated for 70 years."

I can do what I want to on it. It was just fiasco from day one on the contractors. If it would've been done and done right it would have benefited the area, but the contractors came in to make as much money as possible and to leave the country and they could care less the shape the land is left in and anything else.

REBECCA JIM: They got caught. We were driving by the EPA headquarters which was in Picher. There's these people coming out and crossing the road carrying stuff out of the EPA office, with great big FBI letters on the back of their jackets. Everything got confiscated from their office. All their computers, all their files that said Morrison-Knudsen, and so they were caught doing fraudulent work.

ED KEHELEY: The EPA fired Morrison-Knudsen and the story just went dead. Just completely dead, you couldn't find out anything about it. What happened to Morrison-Knudsen? They declared bankruptcy and then started a new company. If you look at the EPA Inspector General's 2007 Annual Report to Congress, you will find on page nine a very brief article which congratulates the EPA for settling the Morrison-Knudsen case. The EPA agreed to a million dollars out of court in a no-fault settlement.

REBECCA JIM: The EPA celebrated all the lessons they learned and so they're nicer now, you know, they're all nicer, and they finally just gave that program to DEQ (Department of Environmental Quality) and they're funding the state to do it.

SCOTT THOMPSON, Director of the Oklahoma Department of Environmental Quality: We thought okay, we are done with OU2 and we are going to advertise one more last chance to get your yard cleaned up.

REBECCA JIM: Most of those houses have already been torn down and people have moved on. They got an ombudsman payoff from EPA and got some compensation for the damage that was done. The damage is still happening because people are not getting their yards done. We still have, probably, could be six thousand more yards to check, and the line is not very long ever because people are reluctant.

SCOTT THOMPSON: I had some folks who worked for me who spent a lot of time on that site. I was at some public meetings with them and some of the locals thought they lived there. I mean, it was just a part of the fabric of the whole thing and there were different characters that had their own little agendas or whatever. You couldn't help but get burned out after a number of years sometimes on the site. I saw a lot of folks with EPA or our staff or even other players get kind of burned out. Some of us, we kind of re-energized and got back into it. But it was just because it was such a big project. Had this been a normal-size property, it wouldn't have been anywhere near as difficult to implement things.

There were a lot of issues with the contractors and some peripheral stuff that went on with that and some of the costs, but bottom line is, in short order, the percentage of kids that had elevated blood lead dropped from, I think the whole area overall was around 12 percent or so. It was dropped in just two or three years, I believe, or maybe a little longer, down into the three or four percent range and then lower. It got to where it was lower than the state average in that area.

They are still cleaning up yards in Ottawa County so OU2 is still going on.

ED KEHELEY: The rate EPA was paying our contractors for the yard remediation was rapidly escalating. It went from $20,000 a yard to $70,000 a yard in just three or four years. Seventy thousand dollars was higher than the value of most of the homes but they were still remediating the yards. The people in Picher kept saying to the EPA, "Look, you're spending more money on my yard than my house is worth. Why don't you just get us out of here? Why are you keeping us here and screwing us over? Why don't you just buy us out and get us out of here?"

IT'S IN MY NATURE TO SAVE THE COBRA

IN THE LATE 1990s Operable Unit 2 tore through people's yards and lead exposure continued unabated; the EPA's plans for the next Operable Units were in the beginning study phase. For obvious reasons not everyone in Ottawa County was eager to embrace the federal Environmental Protection Agency, or the local eco-warriors—LEAD Agency. Many of the residents of Picher didn't see anything wrong with their town and were happy to carry on as if outrageous environmental problems weren't endangering anyone. If you can't see it, then it's not there.

Oklahoma is a state where antipathy toward government programs runs high. Driving to Ottawa County from the Tulsa International Airport you see American flags waving everywhere, a Confederate flag here and there, and "proud gun owner" bumper stickers. You can understand why people don't want the government to interfere in their lives, especially when the residents' experience is with the crooked contractors Morrison-Knudsen.

OU1 was a partial success in which fewer than half the wells that went into the Roubidoux aquifer were plugged. It was enough to prevent the Roubidoux from total contamination. During the EPA's five-year review in 1994, they declared the OU1 rerouting Tar Creek and Lytle Creek around the contaminated sites a failure. The water in the area was running red and people's yards had been dug up and destroyed by corrupt contractors. People throughout the county were angry at these do-gooders, bringing nothing but problems. The 1990s and early 2000s were a particularly difficult time for the activists who fought desperately to live without toxic waste.

DR. ROBERT WRIGHT, pediatrician, medical toxicologist, and environmental epidemiologist at the Icahn School of Medicine at Mount Sinai: I think when I first started going there, I naïvely assumed that everybody would want to clean up. *Here is this Superfund site, why wouldn't you want it cleaned up?* and then later discovered that that's actually an overly simplistic view. Superfund sites come with problems.

ED KEHELEY, retired nuclear engineer, expert on Tar Creek: One of the big factors is that the people of Picher, even when I was living there, refused to accept the seriousness of what was going on. There are still people today who will argue ad nauseam about the impacts of lead on small children. They argue that there is no evidence of that, and yet the results are overwhelming.

EARL HATLEY, Cherokee, environmental activist, co-founder of LEAD Agency, Grand Riverkeeper: It's their legacy. There is nothing wrong with it. They are just lead-headed, you know? Everyone was convinced the EPA, Rebecca and I, and people like us were all just troublemakers. There were threats, and there was a lot of meanness.

People in town said that I had EPA in my back pocket and I was getting paid for pretending that this was a Superfund site, and that lead wasn't the problem. There was a Congressman [former Representative and Senator, Tom Coburn] that said that lead was no big problem at the Superfund site. Here was a Congressman telling them exactly what they wanted to hear, and [Senator James] Inhofe[34] wasn't helping either, and the doctors out of the corner of their mouths saying how bad it was, but in public would never say anything and the agencies would not say anything.

They were mad at me because when I was hired as Quapaw director, I was also Rebecca's new organizer, meaning her expert and gunslinger. So here I was hired by the Quapaw Tribe and they saw Rebecca as having the EPA in her pocket, and that she dragged EPA over there and now me and that *we were going to steal their chat,* and that we were getting paid by EPA under the table, bringing EPA there and we were getting money off of EPA and we're getting fat off of this whole thing, and then I always said, "Well, then why do I drive such a clunky car now?" Anyway, and that was the whole rumor that circulated around the Quapaw Tribe.

I've been practicing organization since 1968 and so I have an analogy about the Quapaw Tribe. Two yogis are sitting on the banks of the Ganges and they see this cobra get caught in the river and was about to drown. One of them jumps up and runs out into the river to grab it to save it and the cobra bites him, and they get back to the shore and the other yogi looks at him and says, "Didn't you know the cobra was going to bite you, why did you do that?" He says, "It was in the cobra's nature to bite me and it is in my nature to save the cobra." On every project I end up taking a lot of negativity and I take too much seriously and knowing what I know, but I'm human, but you know, I'll still keep going. I have been all over the country and I have worked with organizers all over the country, and I see what I deal with and I don't think anybody would ever want to do it in Oklahoma. To try to bring change to a place like that is just like walking into hell and saying, "OK everyone, open up your Bibles."

---

34. Senator James Inhofe's office ignored several requests to be interviewed for this book.

Since the Operable Unit 2 yard remediations was a project fraught with corruption and incompetence, OU2 has been passed on to the Department of Environmental Quality which is an Oklahoma state agency and is still humming along today. But the question that remains is what good is removing the lead-based dirt without removing the mountains of chat everywhere?

EPA's Operable Unit 3 was a single contaminated site—a former office and laboratory complex located in Cardin and operated by the former mining goliath Eagle-Picher—the largest mining company in the area. They closed their doors in 1970. Approximately 120 containers of chemicals were removed as part of a removal response action in 2000.

KEATING'S TASK FORCE AND "A WORLD-CLASS WETLAND"

DURING THE 1980s, Oklahoma's Governor at the time, George Nigh, took an interest in what was going on in Tar Creek. He formed the first Tar Creek Task Force in 1980, which was one of the forces that led to the Superfund designation in 1983. When Frank Keating got elected Governor of Oklahoma in 1995, not much had really happened aside from the EPA plugging the 66 wells during Operable Unit 1 and diverting Lytle Creek. There were two Governors who served between Governors Nigh and Keating, who did little on the Tar Creek Superfund site issues.

In 2001 a young Congressman named Brad Carson was elected to the same seat which had previously been held by Congressman Mike Synar. Synar, who grew up in the area, was defeated in a primary election in 1994 and died in January of 1996, with his former seat going to Republican Tom Coburn. Synar was the politician who had done the most to bring a positive change to the area.

The Tar Creek Superfund Site had by 2001 become an extended headache for politicians as well as local and state agencies for at least a generation. Politicians who did address the issue were interested in trying some out-of-the-box ideas and approaching Tar Creek with a bit of creativity.

As you would imagine, a plan that's radically different and wildly consequential would invite many different takes on its feasibility and popularity with the stakeholders. After Keating's term was up, the 2004 World-Class Wetland idea that came out of the Governor's Tar Creek Task Force Report gained a lot of traction among Oklahoma's political class, but not from the scientist whose work it was based on.

BRAD CARSON, former Congressman of the 2nd district of Oklahoma, former Undersecretary to the Army: For me, I remember sitting down with some of my staff and putting together a list of about one hundred questions that we wanted answered: the causes of Tar Creek, possible remediation that could be done, the alternatives. Just trying to really understand the problems in a very clear-headed way. We were kind of bringing ourselves up to speed on it, answering these questions.

Governor Keating, someone you would say is not a political ally of mine, like lots of Republicans in the state; I was the only Democrat. It was a delegation and they made it their mission to try to defeat me at every turn, but I found working with Governor Keating on Tar Creek to be really refreshing.

FRANK KEATING, former Governor of Oklahoma, attorney, author: From the time I was a young boy, I always was interested in the land. What could we do to improve the water projects that were for a water-starved state like Oklahoma? Back in the '50s and '60s we were building these mammoth lakes. I thought that was just incredible, I mean, because now we have habitats, we have flyways for geese and ducks and other migratory waterfowl. Something that simply didn't exist in the past.

BRAD CARSON: [One of the things] that was always bedeviling about it was that we might agree about the situation at Tar Creek. It was a complex, social, economic, ecological matter and you can find people who you may say, "Hey, I grew up with it. It's in this community, if there's lead here, I grew up with it. It's perfectly fine." There are people who had homes remediated from Synar's days and they were upset with it or they were happy with it, but there was no consensus, seemingly, about what to do about it.

BRIAN GRIFFIN, former Oklahoma Secretary of the Environment, Chairman of the Board at Clean Energy Systems: [We] basically started with a kind of comprehensive approach where we say, "Okay, we're not coming into any preconceived notion to how to go about this, let's try to look at it from 30,000 feet and see if we can figure out solutions that hadn't yet been explored," and that's what we did on the Tar Creek matter.

ED KEHELEY, retired nuclear engineer, expert on Tar Creek: I was asked to co-chair one of the subcommittees under Frank Keating's Task Force that he established. Not only was I on the co-chair of the subsidence subcommittee when I was on the mineshaft [subcommittee], the drainage subcommittee and the chat use subcommittee, I wanted to be on a whole bunch of them because I wanted to learn.

The eight subcommittees of Governor Keating's Task Force were: the Health Effects Subcommittee, Subsidence Subcommittee; Mine Shaft Subcommittee; Chat Use Subcommittee; Drainage/Flooding Subcommittee, Water Quality Subcommittee, Native American Subcommittee, and the NRDA (Natural Resources Damage Assessment) Subcommittee.

DR. ROBERT NAIRN, environmental scientist, researcher, professor Oklahoma University: I served on a couple of subcommittees under Governor Keating's Task Force to address the water side, but in terms of the kind of higher-level political discussions that were going on, I certainly wasn't privy to any of that.

ED KEHELEY: The Task Force of Keating's was a real eye-opener I think for everybody, because there were eight subcommittees and all of them found some serious concerns. That was sort of the door-knocker or the opening kind of a shadow role, that *hey, the subsidence issues are for real.* Nobody on the Governor's Task Force understood subsidence and the history of it. Nobody really was familiar with all the letters that were written in the '60s and '70s about how bad it was, and so that kind of brought this to the forefront. What that did was look beyond the concern about yard remediation and public health. It added a new dimension to the equation of public safety, and so we started looking at solutions that would address both problems.

Governor Keating and Brian Griffin, again I say I was impressed in that they wanted to try to solve the problem. Both began to propose doing these wetlands concepts where instead of having residential areas, you would just try to convert as much land as you could to wetlands.

SCOTT THOMPSON, Director of the Oklahoma Department of Environmental Quality: How can we turn it into an asset? Is there anything that we can do? Okay, we have to fix this, but what else could we do?

BRIAN GRIFFIN: To us, the main issue was that it was putting Band-Aids on enormous problems and there was no assurance that it was a permanent solution, so you could keep doing this for the next five hundred years and maybe not really ever address the real root of the problem. Until we got rid of the chat which was the source of the problem, until we figured out a way to fill all of those mineshafts and caverns and help deal with the mine acid drainage and subsidence, nothing that was going to be done would be a permanent solution.

SCOTT THOMPSON: Some of the stuff Dr. Nairn is doing is trying to reverse that process and lock these things back up in sulfite. His project is pretty impressive really. But at Tar Creek you had this potential that maybe the thing to do is put the stuff back underwater and whatever oxygen exposure you had would then begin to stop. You would have some leaching early from the stuff that is oxygenated, but as that surface is essentially washed off that should stop and it would be more protective in the middle. The problem is, when you have a fluctuating water table, you are going to get that upper layer getting oxygenated periodically. But if you could maintain it in a flooded state, you could essentially stop that process and the system would flush out. That was kind of the basis of it.

Then Fish and Wildlife Service had some concerns about leaching stuff because there are two sites in California where we have had some leaching of things and getting into the biota. But my attitude was half the place, at least, is wetlands already. What are you doing about that?

DR. ROBERT NAIRN: I think one of the important things is to first define what we call active treatment, which is the more traditional engineering approach. That would be building what is essentially the same as a wastewater treatment plant: a concrete 24-hour operation, maintenance, seven days a week labor. Typically adding refined chemicals using a lot of energy off the grid to improve water quality. That's a technology that works very, very well for mine drainage.

Active treatment works very well, but obviously it's expensive and it requires a long-term commitment from whoever is paying for that. With that background, passive treatment is the idea of using natural processes—things that happen that Mother Nature does in the environment: physical, chemical, and biological processes to improve water quality. Really, all we tried to do is create the right conditions for those passive mechanisms to help us treat water. So, what that has evolved into is building parks and wetlands and what we call bioreactors which are a little bit more engineered to force the water to flow certain ways where we can promote some specific purposes. That's where we are building ecosystems to improve water quality.

In very general terms, the two processes that are most important in our passive treatment systems are oxidative, where we're trying to get air into the water to oxidize the dissolved iron and really create rust, create this iron oxide sludge. That has a great affinity for some of the trace metals—sort of pull some of those trace metals out of solution as well. The other mechanism is reductive. One is oxidative and one is reductive. There we are using naturally occurring microbial populations. Microorganisms that are there. If we create the right conditions, they'll do their job.

In that case, the right conditions means giving them something to eat and that is a waste organic material. We have used mushroom compost which is locally available in Ottawa County as an organic matter source, which we then flood in those naturally occurring microorganisms. We use that compost as an organic source and we'll use sulfate in the mine water, and their metabolism will create the right conditions to again sequester the metal contaminants within the substrate.

In the processes in these passive systems, the idea is that once we build it, if we do it right, we can kind of step back and let Mother Nature do her thing. That's the passive component. If we do it right, there's very little intensive operation and maintenance. The design lifetime on the system is 20 to 25 years. So, it's not as if there is no maintenance. We know we are going to have to come back in there in a couple decades and remove some of the sludges and we are going to have to do some refurbishment, but we get 20 to 25 years of water quality improvement with very little energy input.

BRIAN GRIFFIN: That's when it started dawning on us that maybe the better approach is to think about relocating these people, and then coming in and creating a world-class wetland here and creating an area like a National Wildlife Preserve, and I think that was the final statement in our Task Force recommendation.

I have it up here right now; I thought it was a very good summary:

> Pursue development of a world-class wetlands area and wildlife refuge within the boundaries of the Tar Creek Superfund Site that will serve as an ecological solution to the majority of the most pressing health, safety, environmental, and aesthetic concerns identified by the Task Force.[35]

FRANK KEATING: The thought of a Superfund site being addressed by turning it into a wild, flyway, basically wildlife habitat and a wetland seemed like a pretty good deal, and then about the time I was leaving office, Brian said "Well, EPA is fighting this, they think you have to spoon it all out." I said, "That will be a hundred years." There's huge costs.

J.D. STRONG, Director at the Oklahoma Department of Wildlife Conservation, former Chief of Staff to the Secretary of Environment of Oklahoma: The outcome, as I recall, was what we need to do is move everybody out and turn this into a giant wetland that would essentially attenuate over time the contamination that was welling up from the ground through acid mine drainage or contaminated mine drainage.

We brought in Dr. Nairn from University of Oklahoma, who's one of the nation's experts on using constructed wetlands to remediate contaminated mine water.

---

35. "Governor Frank Keating's Tar Creek Superfund Task Force Final Report." Documents.OK.Gov, Oct. 2000.

DR. ROBERT NAIRN: What we recommended, what the subcommittee had looked at and came up with, was this idea of targeted passive treatment which is the kind of work that we're currently doing right now under other funding mechanisms. The systems that we have in the ground right now range from about two-and-a-half to three and a half acres. We are treating about four hundred gallons a minute on a regular basis, which is not inconsequential, but it's a fraction of the bigger problem.

At that time, when the idea came out we expressed some concerns about that idea.

J.D. STRONG: I mean, it's already naturally a wetland [because of the flooded mines] so you may think it's crazy but if you move everybody out and just walk away from it? It's going to be a pretty large wetland area on its own.

DR. ROBERT NAIRN: The passive treatment systems are particularly designed to not promote wildlife use. We designed it with water levels, water depths, kind of the vegetated habitat to not necessarily draw in waterfowl, et cetera. What they were talking about was flooding a very large portion, turning it into this "world-class wetland" for public hunting and fishing on contaminated lead- and cadmium-contaminated soils.

I think that the idea that we were proposing was certainly taken and raised to a different level than we had never proposed raising it to. There was never a discussion amongst the technical folks on the subcommittee of building this, however many acres it was, that proposed world-class wetland. That was something that was never discussed in any serious manner.

It can get pretty chemistry-intensive and microbiology-intensive and it's hard to relate to the public. But I think when you talk about a dam and building a big reservoir and waterfowl habitat that a lot of people go, *Oh yeah, okay, I understand that. I like to hunt, I like to fish. What a great idea.*

FRANK KEATING: My view was that that was never going to be cleaned up a spoonful at a time and it still hasn't. I mean, 20-plus years later it's still a mess, but if in fact a wetland could have been done—I think the native people are very, very much focused on the land from a spiritual standpoint, and to say to them, *All right then, why don't we condemn it. We'll own it, the state will look and then we'll buy it from you.* But we did have to do something. We can't have people living out there. That would just be terrible.

DR. ROBERT NAIRN: I hope what happens is that we target the treatment of particular sources of bad water and focus on recovery of the receiving streams. That those creeks, that Tar Creek, Lytle Creek, Beaver Creek, Elm Creek, all those small drainages in that corner in northeast Oklahoma, are able to come back. If we could address the water quality concerns, and certainly address the habitat concerns in some of those creeks, we're going to see recovery of the ecological system.

BRAD CARSON: Just go back a second to look at the political dynamics of all this, because [Senator James] Inhofe was a major player in the story too, and Keating and Inhofe don't like each other. In some ways it's where I was kind of in between them all.

It was a bold solution, that everything else was just incremental and kind of not going to really solve the remediation of yards, which had been kind of a quasi-fiasco. In the end the people like Brian Griffin and Governor Keating and I more or less agreed on kind of the general direction to take things at Tar Creek. That was where Inhofe proved to be a big obstacle.

FRANK KEATING: A huge amount of money has been spent. I knew it. Before Scott Pruitt left,[36] I talked to him a couple times and I said, "You know, that's something that is unfinished business." You know, if what was proposed by the Oklahoma scholars and academics and wildlife and the wetland experts was quackery, then okay, I can see we better look for plan B.

I just thought when Brian told me and the others that EPA was like, "No, you guys don't know what you're doing," or maybe they thought we knew what we were doing but they didn't agree with it, I don't know, but if science since then has determined that a wetland was simply not possible, it wouldn't work—well, that's a different answer. But that was not what I was hearing at the time I left office.

ED KEHELEY: The EPA was quizzed about it, and the EPA said well, let's go to ATSDR (Agency for Toxic Substances and Disease Registry) in Atlanta, and have them look and see what they think. They're funded by the EPA. The ATSDR formed a committee that came out here. There's a report on this that exists; they came out and they went around and held committee meetings and played like they were interested and all that sort of thing. In the meantime, Brad Carson was getting involved—Junior Congressman, but he had a lot of guts.

This idea of getting people out of here, all of these things began to gel sort of at the same time. There were a couple of people that were very knowledgeable of what was going on and asked to be on this ATSDR Committee.

---

36. During this time Scott Pruitt was the Oklahoma Attorney General. In that role he famously sued the EPA 14 times and was tapped by the Trump Administration to be EPA chief because of his pro-business deregulatory positions. He has since resigned from that post amid several ethics scandals.

As I recall, they threw out the wetlands concept and without that being agreed to by the committee, and that only could have come at the insistence of the EPA. Brad Carson jumped on it like a dog on a bone.

BRAD CARSON. I'm not an ecological scientist, I don't know enough to know exactly whether it would work, but it seemed to have indications that it could work. It was enormously expensive.

I think what Governor Keating did, that was interesting in that proposal, was there was not only a solution to Tar Creek, but it was possibly something that could transform a rather challenged region of Oklahoma. Over time this could or would change fundamentally in terms of the economic basis of the region. In 20 or 30 years it might even become a tourist place. It was incredibly ambitious, enormously expensive. I think the science suggested it probably would work. There were no good approaches to the problems at Tar Creek. I think it was provocative, whether to be implemented or not, and getting the money to do it. They are asking good questions as I recall thinking about it now.

FRANK KEATING: Two hundred million dollars to do whatever. It was a very reasonable cost and the state, certainly on my watch, we would have been willing to make the investment to do it. You know, forget EPA. If we could turn that into a wetland we could create a state park there. It would be a proud moment that we took one of the worst Superfund sites in the history of the United States and turn it into something that people could actually celebrate.

DR. ROBERT NAIRN: It was a really bad idea and I think they needed to have a big—I don't know, something innovative and new and different, and this certainly was innovative and new and different. It never happened. I hope it never does.

ED KEHELEY: I don't think it would be feasible to build a large wetland; one, because of the topography. What I liked about it is it had everybody thinking, and the Corps of Engineers did a concept plan for wetlands but the EPA kept torpedoing it. Behind the scenes there were these federal issues going on; politicians weren't interested because it would take money and they would have to go to Congress and get the money. It didn't have any real viability but it got everybody thinking, that's what I thought was the important part about it.

TOM LINDLEY: Having wetlands is a nice idea. It sounds very wholesome. You know—scraping it off and tossing it all off and leaving sort of a scarred ground.

Tar Creek reflects what America does. We find a resource, we mine it, integrate it into the population, so to speak, and we don't worry about the consequences at the time. Later on we say, *Oh my gosh, what have we done? We got to do something about it.* It's a cycle we tend to repeat.

QUESTIONS ABOUT EQUITY AND
THE SANCTITY OF THE LAND

PERHAPS THE most consequential takeaway from Governor Keating's Tar Creek Task Force Report of 2000 was the overwhelming evidence of subsidence in the Tri-State Mining Region. The towns were sinking and needed immediate attention, and couldn't be ignored any longer.

Subsidence has been an issue throughout this story, but what the Task Force's Report showed was how undermined the region actually was. From the report, "As of 1986, 59 'major' collapses were identified that disturbed approximately 47 surface acres." It goes on to say, "At least eight more collapses have occurred since 1986." The report was tangible proof that verified some of the local legends and disproved the Pollyannas. This subsidence subcommittee was co-chaired by retired nuclear engineer and local Tar Creek expert Ed Keheley and Maryann Pritchard, who was and is still the director of the Oklahoma Department of Mines. Keheley brought in renowned geologist Dr. Ken Luza. Dr. Luza knew what he was talking about. In 1986 he released his report, *Oklahoma Geological Survey Final Report: Stability Problems Associated with Abandoned Underground Mine Workings in the Picher Field Northeastern Oklahoma.* Most of Ottawa County's residents didn't need a report to tell them that their towns were sinking. There have been cave-ins since the mining era. Despite vast, overwhelming evidence of lead poisoning in Picher, there was still some debate as to the merits of how poisonous Picher actually was from those who were dug in and refused to believe the science. It was harder to deny the reality that the ground was caving into the earth in front of your face. According to the report this was a fairly common occurrence. Everyone knew about it.

Add the threat of subsidence to the fact that many of the mines were full of toxic, acidic, reddish-orange water. The thought of sleeping in your bed one night and being plunged into your dark, watery grave is a terrifying thought. No matter where you go in this country, people are understandably concerned about their property values. In many cases every cent a person earns is invested in their home, and a risk would have to be life-threatening to get someone to consider leaving. But what if you can't just pick up and leave? What if your home isn't worth much and there's not enough money to move? What if everything in life you've ever known is eventually going to cave in to the earth?

People never welcome life-altering disruptions and will compartmentalize threats of all kinds. It's how we survive. The fact that we smoke cigarettes or

Cave-in June 10, 2003. Photo by Ed Keheley.

debated climate change all these years when we should have been active are perfect examples of how we compartmentalize threats.

Year after year, generations of children were exposed to a toxic cocktail of heavy metals through no fault of their own. The times were changing in Picher and it had become a humanitarian crisis long overdue for relief. In the 1980s Governor George Nigh, and into the 1990s and early 2000s Governor Frank Keating and Congressman Brad Carson, worked in an admirable bipartisan manner that you rarely see today. Because of the heavily politicized bodies like EPA and small-government conservatives in Oklahoma, the people of Picher were stuck until the perfect storm of political will and allocated capital could be accessed so that such an enormous home buyout project could take place.

"Well, I'm right here to tell you, mister, ain't nobody going to push me off my land! Grampa took up this land 70 years ago. My pa was born here. We was all born on it, and some of us got killed on it, and some died on it. And that's what makes it ourn—bein' born on it, and workin' it, and dyin' on it—and not no piece of paper with writin' on it! So just come on and try to push me off!"

—Muley Bates quote from the film *The Grapes of Wrath*[37]

MIKALYA KELLER, college student, Northeastern Oklahoma A&M College: If you go through Picher be super careful, because the thing is, the roads will cave in. It's happened here in Miami. There have been places, because they go deep into different towns in the area.

ED KEHELEY, retired nuclear engineer, expert on Tar Creek: When the miners first started in Oklahoma it was just a rich bonanza like the California Gold Rush. The mining companies then began to trim and remove pillars. The mining technique used here is called *room and pillar.* There were no tunnels that were used as people think of mines. There was a series of giant rooms with one or two access points.

After the rich ore was gone, because of the height of these mine workings, they had to leave pillars like every 50 feet. Well, in doing that, initially they had to leave pillars that contained a lot of lead and zinc. That didn't bother them, because they were making lots of money, but as the ore *played out* as they call it, the game was to go in and start trimming pillars and removing those they could remove safely. It was not gougers who did that. It was all of the main mining companies. This went on from the 1930s through World War II until the mines closed in late 1970, They would, for example, go through the mine and make one path and remove all the ore they thought they could safely take out of the pillars. Then they would often sell that mine or lease it to some other company that would come in and repeat the same process. They did that until 1970 when the mines closed.

In later years, in particular in the 1960s, the government was becoming concerned because the number of surface collapses in the mine working were causing some problems. For example, in the 1960s, the little town of Hockerville east of Picher had three major collapses which basically destroyed the town. It became a ghost town. Those kinds of events were very common.

---

37. *The Grapes of Wrath.* 20th Century Fox, 1940. Director: John Ford. Script: Nunally Johnson. Adapted from the 1939 novel of the same name by John Steinbeck.

In July 1967 a large collapse occurred across the street from Picher High School. Four homes were involved. They dropped 25 feet and there were some minor injuries but no one was killed because the collapse settled very gradually. One of those areas is Highway 69, south of the town of Picher. They warned of the dangers of Highway 09 and they continued to authorize pillar removal and trimming right up to 1970 when the mines closed. If you follow the documentation of correspondence and letters, even the State of Oklahoma was complaining about the collapses that were occurring.

There was another one in 1974 on the east side of town. A mineshaft collapsed beneath the kitchen of a home. The kitchen went into the hole so deep that it was irretrievable. They could not salvage anything out of it. Fortunately, there was no one in the room at the time. In 2008 another mineshaft collapsed in Picher, and since they were in the middle of a buyout they just left it. It's still open today. I could keep reciting those kinds of things.

J.D. STRONG, Director at the Oklahoma Department of Wildlife Conservation, former Chief of Staff to the Secretary of Environment of Oklahoma: Over time, as long as they've been mining up there, which dates back to before the late 1800s, there'd been problems with cave-ins, subsidence, and as the mining stopped and water filled those caverns, that subsidence issue, the subsidence risk, anecdotally we knew [had] continued to increase.

DR. ROBERT NAIRN, environmental scientist, researcher, professor Oklahoma University: If you read the report that drove the relocation buyout, that based upon the risk of collapse—it is about the risk of the ground caving in under the towns of Picher, Cardin, and Hockersville. It is not about the risk of lead contamination. It's about the risk of collapse, and the risk of collapse is real.

WALLACE KENNEDY, retired journalist, *The Joplin Globe*: If you want to know the truth, Picher was on the downhill run as soon as it was declared a hazardous waste site—number one on the list of hazardous waste sites in the United States. And the problem was, who wants to move to a hazardous waste site? But the bottom line is you can't leave. You live there, you've got your house there, you've got everything invested there—but you'd put your house for sale, nobody's going to buy it.

DR. ROBERT WRIGHT, pediatrician, medical toxicologist, and environmental epidemiologist at the Icahn School of Medicine at Mount Sinai: You can imagine, if you own a house and all of a sudden your land is designated as a Superfund site, your property values plummet. Then it can have adverse effects on the economy and cost in a lot of areas. A company that may have caused the toxic waste might be the biggest employer in the area. People worry about the company going out of business, and so there's all the economic and social issues that go along with it. Then Tar Creek had some unique aspects about it. One of the things that's really unusual is sort of the visual aspect of it.

WALLACE KENNEDY: Oklahoma was much more involved in what was going on in Picher as a state and the politics associated with it than in Missouri or in Kansas. It was an important issue politically in Missouri and Kansas, don't get me wrong, but it was like EPA comes to these areas and says, *we want to do this, we need your help to do it, let's get it done.* And we got it done. Down in Oklahoma, it was just a whole different approach.

Big corporations became involved and local politicians thought this is what should be done. And people weren't really paying attention to the fact that Picher is totally, almost totally undermined. And it's going to cave in someday; it's caving in right now. There were signs. You get reports all the time. Another cave-in over there at that place. And one day it could be catastrophic. It's no place to be cleaning up anything.

J.D. STRONG: The Keating administration's approach was "look, you are already spending upwards of $60, $80 million on this project by spending roughly $70,000 a yard to dig out contaminated topsoil and replace it with clean topsoil. For less than $70,000 you can probably buy most of these people out—they'd gladly take that check and leave their house. What a waste of money that is." That was sort of the push of the Keating administration.

BRIAN GRIFFIN, former Oklahoma Secretary of the Environment, Chairman of the Board at Clean Energy Systems: I remember we started thinking like *wow, this really is the most cost-effective way to go about this?* Sometimes maybe the homes weren't even worth, from a fair market value, what we spent to remediate the yard. I think it quickly became obvious to all of us on the Task Force that maybe a better approach would be to offer a buyout to these people and see if these people might want to be given a fresh start somewhere else. Well, of course I fully understand, some people jumped at the chance, other people resisted it because this was home and they've grown up here. It was one of those things where that was going to be controversial, no question about it.

J.D. STRONG: [Keating's] Task Force delivered its report in 2000 as I recall. Fast-forward a couple more years to 2002, nothing has really changed. At the EPA level, delegation is still not really engaged, Governor Henry comes into office.

At some point in maybe that first year or two the new Secretary of Environment Miles Tolbert [comes in]. I'm still working there as Chief of Staff to the Secretary of Environment and we're briefing Governor Henry on this issue and his response essentially was "Well, instead of waiting on the Federal Government to save us, which apparently isn't going to happen anytime soon, let's just go to the legislature and see if we can get enough money to at least move out the families with kids six and under which are most susceptible to permanent neurological damage and devastation the rest of their lives, and to get that done and see what happens."

Lo and behold, we were able to get I think it was $3 million out of appropriative state legislature.

We got that through and we set about propping up the Tar Creek Trust to kind of help us make recommendations, and hire companies to do appraisals and everything that's involved in getting better offers to the local families with young children and hopefully get them bought out and moved out.

WALLACE KENNEDY: Brad Henry, then the Governor of Oklahoma, he went in and bought out all of the families that had children so they could relocate, so they wouldn't be exposed to lead. There is Jim Inhofe who was opposed to any buyout at Picher; he thought it could be cleaned up. And so when Henry did this, he really undercut Inhofe, and these families jumped at the chance to get out of Picher with their children.

I remember standing at a chat pile in Picher when the Governor, Brad Henry, made this announcement that he was going to do this. And the people who were standing there, the families and the townspeople who were there to listen to him, when he finished they started singing "For He's a Jolly Good Fellow." They were so moved by the fact that something was happening to protect their children. It was a powerful moment, the most powerful moment I've seen in my career. It was really touching.

> *The first efforts to buy out families in the Picher area were less successful than hoped.*
>
> *The state appropriated enough money to buy one hundred families' property and help them move to safer places; only 52 accepted. Gov. Brad Henry held a press conference on the issue in front of one of the chat piles. [Rebecca] Jim said no one photographed the children still playing on the pile.*
>
> *Volunteers even organized "toxic tours," taking people through the area in buses and on bicycles so they could see the damage for themselves. "It was very shocking to people. It was almost fun to watch their reactions," Jim said.*[38]

38. Betty Ridge. "Protesting Pollution at Tar Creek." *Tahlequah Daily Press*, 20 Apr 2009.

BRAD CARSON, former Congressman of the 2nd district of Oklahoma, former Undersecretary to the Army: The idea that you could ever make this place a lead-free community seemed increasingly remote. Now the Tribe had been doing it for 15 years or longer before I came in there. I think that it was in the mid-'80s. So, they have been doing it for a long time. They said it was not going to work. There were still children who you could see with all these lead-induced infirmities. This is just not going to work.

So they would be like, *what should we do?* We looked it up first. Part of the one hundred questions were, "Have we ever done buyouts like this before in the country?" We researched it and I think there had been six or seven buyouts like this that we could analogize ourselves to another place in the country—I forget, in Montana there was some zinc mine or something, but it was like that.

New things are required, and the buyouts, the relocation idea seemed to be that if people were moved, you'd have more flexibility to do more remediation or a world-class wetland or whatever you wanted to. I said, "You know, this seems like the right idea."

After measuring twice it's good to cut once. Yeah, it probably is the right idea.

In 2003 Governor Frank Keating's second term ended. The state of Oklahoma inaugurated Democrat Brad Henry as its Governor. That same year Oklahoma Congressman Brad Carson brought H.R. 2116: The Tar Creek Restoration Act to the 108th Congress. This resolution's purpose was to lay out the legal foundation for the EPA to begin a federal land buyout program at Tar Creek: "To direct the Administrator of the Environmental Protection Agency to provide relocation and other assistance for residents at the Tar Creek Superfund Site."[39]

Twenty-two years ago, Mike Synar represented this area of northeastern Oklahoma in Congress, and he blasted the EPA for inaction. Decades and millions of dollars later, current U.S. Rep. Brad Carson (D-Okla.) has called for a buyout of 1,800 residents in the center of the site. "I don't think it is much of an exaggeration to say that no other Superfund site in the nation has as many distinct problems as does Tar Creek," Carson said during the buyout announcement in May. Problems "stand largely unchanged and unimproved despite 25 years of remediation and the spending of nearly $100 million by federal and state agencies."[40]

39. United States, Congress, House, Committee on Transportation and Infrastructure, and Carson Brad. Congress. gov, 2003. 108th Congress, 1st session, resolution 2116.

40. Shaun Schafer. "Part Three In A Five-Part Series: Superfund: Damage Control." TulsaWorld.com, 14 Dec 2003.

BRAD CARSON: I don't recall exactly the genesis of [H.R. 2116], but we had done all of this work and thinking it through, and another actor in this was the Army Corps of Engineers. One of the things that was a part of this larger story was the Corps was very active in the [Keating] Task Force in keeping it set up to investigate this world-class wetland idea, and they had done a lot of work on it.

There was a report of that group [Army Corps of Engineers] and I think Fish and Wildlife [Service] was involved and some groups like that, and it wasn't being released. The EPA had jurisdiction, I guess; I think the EPA owned this report and it wasn't being released. They tossed it out, they wouldn't do it. EPA wouldn't hear it. I think that there is no doubt that they weren't going to do it at Inhofe's request. He was chairing the Environment and Public Works committee at that time, as I recall. He had jurisdiction and wouldn't release this report.

In the end, it was leaked out. Jim Myers at *Tulsa World* had done a huge front-page story about what this report said. The basic gist of the report was that it's doable and it's the best solution and stuff like that. That's what led to the bill, so we should fight to get this done.

J.D. STRONG: As I recall there's the report that highlighted the huge risk from cave-ins that got [Senator] Inhofe engaged and motivated to do something about it. Plus we had a little bit of experience at that point with proving that buying people out of their homes was cheaper than cleaning the topsoil out of their yards, especially when you got all these chat piles laced with lead still piled up around you so every time the wind blows it back into your freshly cleaned-up yard.

SCOTT THOMPSON, Director of the Oklahoma Department of Environmental Quality: His [Senator Inhofe's] first point was, "You've got to clean it up anyway, why buy it out?" At the same time EPA was not favoring buyouts. But as the subsidence study got done, Senator Inhofe recognized that you had to look at the whole thing and it didn't make a lot of sense to try to keep these towns in a place that has a substantial chance of subsiding at some point in time. Nobody could say exactly how long it had, but I think that was the pivotal thing that swayed Senator Inhofe to be supportive of the buyout.

ED KEHELEY: State Senator Littlefield and Larry Roberts met with the local Mayors of Picher, Quapaw, Commerce, Cardin, and North Miami and so on and convinced them that the wetlands would not be the right thing.

The Mayors sent a letter to the Governor saying they didn't want the wetlands, and that just pulled the rug out from under Governor Keating. He just basically backed off. He was prepared to try to solve this issue and then he turned around and he left. I thought he was very courageous as a Governor in what he was trying to do and then also what Brad Carson was trying to do.

BRAD CARSON: [Inhofe] disliked Keating and he disliked me. It was still acrimonious between him and Keating. They didn't like each other and obviously Inhofe wasn't a fan of mine.

J.D. STRONG: I think that [Senator Inhofe] philosophically has always been more interested in local control and not expecting the government to bail everybody out of their problems. This is a general philosophical matter, so I think it was tough for him at least initially to embrace the fact that the Federal Government might have to pick up the tab of $80–$100 million or whatever it was going to cost to do this—move everybody out and have a world-class wetland space.

MATT MYERS, filmmaker, *Tar Creek*: Inhofe was the one who turned on the faucet, but he is also the one that kept it off. He had that power and he gathered all the people in power there from Tar Creek and said, "Look, if you want this money to flow, I'm going to get the credit for this. I'm going to say that this is going to be a part of my legacy and that's the way we are going to do it." Who was going to fight that? Who is going to turn $50 million loose?

ED KEHELEY: When we were catering to the Congressional delegations beginning in 2000, Senator Inhofe, for example, he wouldn't give us the time of day, and really, neither would Senator Coburn. Tom Coburn, he was out there trying to save the government money, he didn't particularly care about the issues on the Tar Creek site.

SHUT THIS THING DOWN

THE LOCAL BUYOUT was largely successful. The state found enough money to buy out the families with children six and under. We can only hope they are living better lives today as a result. The arrival of Ed Keheley and Mary Ann Pritchard's Subsidence Subcommittee Report for Governor Keating's Tar Creek Task Force in 2000 began the spark for a federal buyout, but also likely is that Governor Henry's locally funded buyout in 2004 proved that there was political capital in the buyouts. Throughout the life of the Tar Creek Superfund Site, Senator James Inhofe remained immovable on releasing federal funds for a federal buyout.

Inhofe is a small-government ideologue. Inhofe and his cohort have not been a friend to the environment. One can assume that Inhofe's relationship with the oil industry explains why he's been one of the Senate's steadfast climate change deniers. He once famously brought a snowball to the Senate floor to illustrate his willful ignorance about global warming, failing to understand basic grade-school science—the difference between weather and climate. Inhofe has been on the Senate Committee on Environmental and Public Works for decades and, based on his advocacy and voting records, is on the side of his big oil donors as an agent for the oil and gas industry deregulation.

I called Inhofe's office three times and sent six emails and have received no reply to my interview requests.

DR. HOWARD HU, epidemiologist, physician, researcher, clinician, University of Washington School of Public Health: Of course, there's always these questions about equity and the sanctity of the land, and whether that's fair and everything else. It gets very complicated.

J.D. STRONG, Director at the Oklahoma Department of Wildlife Conservation, former Chief of Staff to the Secretary of Environment of Oklahoma: Folks on the outside said it sounded crazy. Why would you ever do something like that? It's never going to work, this, that and the other. Of course, I think the key priority was making sure, you know, the relocation aspect of it—let's get these families, especially the families with young children, out of here, regardless of what you want to do with it next. That was priority one.

SCOTT THOMPSON, Director of the Oklahoma Department of Environmental Quality: The Henry administration supported at least a partial buyout of the people with children. That was the biggest event that occurred. J.D. [Strong] had worked on it for a number of years and remained in the Henry administration. J.D. was tireless in terms of being out there and trying to work through all these issues. Really, I would say he was instrumental in making the buyout happen. Both buyouts.

J.D. STRONG, Director at Oklahoma Department of Wildlife Conservation, former Chief of Staff to the Secretary of Environment of Oklahoma: What I recall, we had two phases of the buyout. We had the state-led effort and then that tapered off, but I was essentially the manager of all of that.

I dropped most of everything else we were doing in the Cabinet Secretary of Environment's office, and then focused a lot of time and effort on going up to, I think it was at least monthly, meetings at the site with the *Lead Impacted Communities Relocation Assistance Trust* (LICRAT), and as I recall we kind of went through the standard state bidding process to accept bids and proposals, requests for proposals, and accept bids on who would do the appraisal work, who would separately review appraisers. I would collect all of that information and summarize it, and the Trust members would openly make decisions at their

Picher, Oklahoma. Photo by the author, 2018.

meetings about what to offer who, and then we would make those offers to people. And for the most part—in fact I don't even recall if we had anyone not accept their offer in that first phase of the buyout.

REBECCA JIM, Cherokee, educator, environmental activist, co founder of LEAD Agency: Anyway, the boy's in fifth grade and can't read, and what he learns today can't remember tomorrow, and so he's really affected. [The mother]'s got two other kids, one is like three years old and maybe one's a little older, I forget. They're kids. She could have taken the first buyout.

I was so excited. I ran into her after that and I said, "How are you?" and she just would not even look at me, and I said, "What's up?" And she said, "I didn't take the buyout." And I said, "Why on earth not?" She said, "There'll be another buyout and it'll be better. I'll get more money." She kept her kids there, exposing them longer when she didn't have to. So I think that happened to a bunch of these folks that were not happy with the second buyout—because they could have taken the first one and probably gotten a better deal and they didn't do it, and then they're angry because they didn't get a good deal, but they're also ashamed and not saying it because they could've got the little children out.

SCOTT THOMPSON: That first buyout kind of set a strong precedent, and it was primarily done by the state because EPA still did not support it. If you are a federal Senator or Congressman, when EPA is sitting there telling you there is no justification for a buyout, it's hard to think that there is, but then as time passed, and we got more of the subsidence studies done, Senator Inhofe recognized that even if you cleaned it up, you are still going to have this potential subsidence problem in some of these key areas. It just made more sense to go ahead and start getting people out of there.

WALLACE KENNEDY, retired journalist, *The Joplin Globe*: What happened was that Ed Keheley and others pointed out to the Senator that if you take a map of Picher's streets and you lay it over the mining maps, that you could pretty well see that the whole town is undermined and that it's caving in. It could cave in at any time. So that became the emphasis: buying out Picher and getting everybody out of there.

ED KEHELEY, retired nuclear engineer, expert on Tar Creek: I was out mowing the pasture one day on my tractor and my cell phone rang and I picked it up. I just didn't recognize the number and so I said, "Hello?" All I could hear was "Brrrrr..." I said, "Hang on, let me shut this thing down." I turned my tractor off and I said, "Who is this?" The person says, "This is Jim, Jim Inhofe." I said, "Hello sir, so nice of you to call." And I said, "What's up?" He said, "I think you and I need to meet." I said, "I think that would be a good suggestion." I said, "I couldn't agree more with you, Senator, I'd be pleased to meet with you." He said, "I'll arrange it and get back with you." I said "Great."

We met over there, myself and a couple of people from Picher, and then Inhofe brought some of his staff down from Tulsa and even one of his guys from his office in Washington. We met at this office around a table.

The Senator said, "Well, what is it that you want?" And before I could say anything, this filthy rich Republican supporter of Inhofe who is a friend of mine said, "No, Senator. Before we start, I want to agree we're not going to talk about the past. We're going to talk about the future, but I want Ed to share with you his background."

Senator Inhofe said, "Well, I'd like to hear that because I've checked him out and I want to see if what he says is what I know." So anyway, I briefly went through my history in government, all that sort of thing. Inhofe said well, that's consistent with what he found out.

He says, "What is it that you want?" And I said, "Senator, my want is simple.

"I have been preaching for some time that no matter what you do to the Superfund site to clean up the surface, it's still not going to be safe to live there because of the public safety issues, and if the site is going to be addressed, both the public safety and public health issues have to be addressed if you're going to ever come up with a solution."

Then he said, "What do you propose?"

I said, "I would propose to put together a *scientific team*. Every time there's a citizen team or committee, everybody and their brother wants to be on it, so you end with 35 people on a committee and nothing happens. I'm talking about a technical team to look at the mining field, the underground mine workings, and determine if we can estimate the probability of what the future looks like for the mining field. He said, "That sounds reasonable."

Then we drove to Picher to give him a tour, which he didn't necessarily want, but we gave him a tour anyway. When the tour was over he said, "Ed, why don't you and I just take off together, you can give me a ride back to Miami to my airplane." and I said, "Sure."

We got in the car, just the two of us cruising around and heading back to Miami. He said to me when it was just the two of us, "Ed, I'm not opposed to a buyout." I almost hit my brakes and fishtailed the car. That's the way we set it up with the Corps of Engineers in charge, and then I worked with the Army Corps of Engineers and we brought in some experts from all over the country. We did something that had never been done before, with people that could contribute, and the hangers-on were kept out of it. We spent a year and a half before we issued our report, and when we finished with it, the results actually turned out much worse than we thought with respect to how badly undermined the field is. We also calculated probabilities of future collapses.

I think in Picher 133 areas had a probability greater than 20% of collapsing. Some of them were as high as 50% probability of collapsing in residential areas.

We presented the report to the Senator. The results of the report were presented to the residents of the area in a big meeting in the Picher High School gymnasium. Even the school buildings were affected, they were undermined.

That was in January, and then in May the Senator made the determination that there would be a buyout on the basis of public safety, not public health. In other words, the EPA was still opposed to the buyout. He went ahead and declared the buyout in May 2006 without the EPA's approval, and the buyout basis was public safety, not public health. The reason I'm saying that is if you read the EPA's documents today, they say that it was on the basis of public safety and public health, which is not true, they're trying to take credit. What the Senator did, and I helped him too, as they were trying to figure out—we're not in the budget cycle so how do we get the money? He started pulling that money back and then reprogramming it so that we could get the buyout started. When we started the buyout we didn't have enough money to finish but it was enough to get us into the next budget cycle. The reason I am so high on the Senator is he never faltered on any commitments he made. He followed through on it.

There was considerable discussion behind the scenes. He also inserted language into the 2007 Water Resources Development Act, stipulating that the EPA would select relocation as the best responsive action for OU4.

> **(e) Consideration of Remedial Action.**—*The Administrator of the Environmental Protection Agency shall consider, without delay, a remedial action under the Comprehensive Environmental Response, Compensation, and Liability Act of 1980 (42 U.S.C. 9601 et seq.) for the Tar Creek, Oklahoma, National Priorities List site that includes permanent relocation of residents consistent with the program currently being administered by the State of Oklahoma. Such relocation shall not be subject to the Uniform Relocation Assistance and Real Property*
>
> —excerpt from Water Resources Development Act of 2007

At that time the EPA was working on a new Operable Unit 4 which was to get rid of the chat piles. What Inhofe did was he inserted in that Water Resources Development Act Bill that the EPA would decide the most reasonable action would be to buy the residents out of their Superfund site. This was against their desires and wishes and required them to have to pay for the remaining amount.

That's why this story about Inhofe is remarkable, if you can get him in the right setting. You try to take him on publicly and he's going to fight you to the death. But like any politician, if you can do it in a way in which he can take credit without a big fight, then that makes everything go smoothly and you avoid a lot of fights and acrimony and all that sort of thing.

A bill allowing federally approved funds for a buyout of Tar Creek-area residents and businesses awaits Gov. Brad Henry's signature. Senate Bill 1463 unanimously passed the Senate on Wednesday and the House 95–1 on Thursday. The legislation was written by Sen. Charles Wyrick, D-Fairland, and Rep. Larry Glenn, D-Miami, whose districts encompass the Tar Creek-area buyout towns of Picher and Cardin and the community of Hockerville.

The bill also sets up a trust authority to oversee the federal buyout. Funds will be channeled through the state Department of Environmental Quality. About $12 million is available immediately for the state to use in implementing the buyout. The remaining $8 million requires a change in the language of federal law before it can be used for this purpose, U.S. Sen. James Inhofe, R-Tulsa, said earlier this month.[41]

PICHER, Okla. — In a move sure to be bittersweet for some Picher, Cardin and Hockerville, Okla., residents in the Tar Creek Superfund Site, an announcement was made Friday that will move ahead the planned buyout of these former mining towns.

Oklahoma Gov. Brad Henry on Friday announced the names of those who will serve on a trust authority, which will oversee the relocation of a majority of residents living in the Tar Creek Superfund Site.

The new trust, which includes several members who had served on a previous relocation panel, will oversee and administer the new program.

Peggy Rhoades, a longtime resident of Picher, reacting to the naming of the trust, said: "I think it's wonderful that we're finally going to get to go, because of the danger here. And I think they'll do a good job, especially those who served before."

Those appointed to the new trust are Larry Rice (trust chairman), assistant to the president of Tulsa University and a resident of Pryor; Ed Keheley, vice-president of Keheley and Associates and a resident of Quapaw; Dr. Mark Osborn, a physician and Miami resident; Bob Walker, superintendent of Picher-Cardin Schools and resident of Miami; Tamara Summerfield, deputy tribal administrator of the Quapaw Tribe and a resident of Miami; Mike Sexton, senior vice president, 1st National Bank and Trust, and a Miami resident; James Thompson, attorney and resident of Miami; Janell Trimble, Miami Public Schools principal and a resident of Picher; and the Rev. Charles Clevenger, pastor with Tri-State Faith Center and Picher resident. Osborn, Walker, and Summerfield served on the first relocation trust.

41. Staff Reports. "House, Senate Pass Tar Creek Buyout Bill." *The Oklahoman*, NewsOK.com, 27 May 2006.

"We're one step closer to ending the long nightmare that families in the Tar Creek site have endured for decades," Henry said on Friday.[42]

J.D. STRONG: We got the federal funds. I think there are a few people that dropped off and a few new people added back on the Trust. At that point, it was pretty clear that I wasn't going to be able to operate/manage that from our offices in Oklahoma City, especially given all the other things we've got going on, and so the Trust ultimately hired a manager at the local level.

So, you've got the Trust, you've got a staff of one, and it's their manager's job to kind of try to replicate the process that we had done in phase one. That's bidding, hiring appraisers, review appraisers again, setting about making offers and getting folks out, and because it was a much more scaled-up effort, a lot more people involved; you're talking about at that time the complete population of that town.

There were a number of folks that were unhappy, thought they should get more for their house than what the Trust was offering; even though it was a voluntary buyout, they really didn't have an option. You have to take this money that they're offering or you're stuck here for the rest of your life.

DEATH SPIRAL

THE 2006 federal buyout of Picher turned out to be a lot more complicated than the earlier and narrowly focused state buyout. The company that was in charge of handling the buyout faced problems that didn't exist when they were buying out the homes of families of small children. What do you do with all the sick and older people? How would they start over in a new town? How much money do you give people when their home's market value is considered worthless?

Further issues were emerging with the new buyout, and there was no oversight of the Trust to make sure these issues were handled fairly and without favoritism. There was no authority beyond the Trust that the homeowners could appeal. In April of 2007, the first few buyout offers were rolled out. But in May of 2008 the community was blindsided with new disasters that caused more chaos and would delay the buyout process even more.

---

42. Carla Short. "Buyout of Tar Creek Progresses." *Joplin Globe*, 15 July 2006.

Picher, Oklahoma during the 2008 tornado. Photo courtesy of Ed Keheley.

MIKALYA KELLER, college student, Northeastern Oklahoma A&M College: The lead itself took out quite a bit of people. Then once the tornado hit, the government pretty much paid people to get out of the town because of how bad it was.

VICTORIA WARREN, college student, Northeastern Oklahoma A&M College: There is only one road that goes through Picher that is deemed safe.

J.D. STRONG, Director at the Oklahoma Department of Wildlife Conservation, former Chief of Staff to the Secretary of Environment of Oklahoma: I think what precipitated the litigation more than anything was the fact that right in the midst of the second round of buyouts, tornado hits south side of Picher and wipes out...

I mean it was a significant tornado that did significant damage. There were some fatalities, and that of course in some ways accelerated the buyout effort. Now you've got a lot of folks that are homeless and they're really anxious to get out of there. But it also complicates things because now we're still having to appraise what the value of that property would be worth so they can get a value for the house that they can actually pocket and go actually buy something somewhere outside of the Superfund site.

Picher, Oklahoma after the 2008 tornado. Photo courtesy of Ed Keheley.

WALLACE KENNEDY, retired journalist, *The Joplin Globe*: Cinnabar was the primary [appraisal] company, and the lawyers representing these families managed to secure about a million dollars from an insurance policy that Cinnabar had, and that ended up being a couple of thousand dollars maybe on average for these 161 plantiffs in 2015.

The story I was told is that once the guy who was in charge of Cinnabar realized what had happened in Picher, he was ashamed and said that he wants all of the insurance money to go to the people of Picher, but the lawyers involved had to take their take. So, in the end, they don't get the full amount. It was terrible and some people were right on the money, on the terms of their appraisal.

ED KEHELEY, retired nuclear engineer, expert on Tar Creek: The tornado came in May of 2008, a year after I resigned from the Trust. I could see this thing from my house 10 miles away from Picher. It was heading directly towards my home and then it began to slowly turn to the southeast; it missed us by a mile and a half, and as soon as it passed us I jumped in my truck and ran to Picher. I got there just a few minutes after the tornado, and people were cut up and walking up and down the street. I was helping rescue people, you know, lifting up, moving debris and... there were people there who came up to me... and said, "Eddie, I don't really know what to do, my house is totally ruined... couple of months ago, because of the buyouts, since I had already been appraised I canceled my home-owners insurance."

I said, "I don't have an answer for you, I really don't, I just don't." Some people came up and said, "My house hasn't been appraised but it's destroyed, what do I do? I said, "I don't have an answer for you, but I will find out for you."

It's really interesting because when I went home that night, by 10:00 my phone rang. It was Senator Inhofe's office: "Hey, the Senator is here in Grove at his lake house and he'd like to know if you would like to give him a tour tomorrow morning," and I said "Sure, I'd be more than happy to."

I invited John Sparkman who was head of the Tar Creek Basin Steering Committee. I knew that the Senator would want to talk to the media, I invited Wally Kennedy, a reporter from the local paper. We picked up the Senator and on our way to Picher he said, "I tried calling Governor Henry on the way down here from the lake and they refuse to awaken him."

Just before we got into town I told the Senator about these people who came up to me and said what do we do? I gave him the circumstances and he said, "Boy, that's a tough one. What do you think we ought to do?" And I said, "Senator, I think we can go ahead and buy these people out," and he said "How would we do that?" And I said, "Well, some of the homes have already been appraised, that's not a problem; for those homes that aren't appraised we can go to the county assessor's office and get the records. It will tell how many square feet, when it was built, et cetera." And I said, "The other thing I have is a series of aerial photos of Picher as recent as 2006, they're high resolution and we can zoom in on these properties, we can figure out what's an outbuilding, fences, et cetera." I said to compare property with what the county assessor's office has, and with aerial photos we can reconstruct and make offers. He said, "Ed, I like that. If you think that's doable, let's do it."

I said, "Senator, we're coming to town now and I've already been over here once this morning." I said, "Every national TV network is here, the Tulsa stations, Oklahoma City stations, Joplin, all these people are here. I know you're going to want to talk to them." He said, "Yeah Eddie, I guess I'm going to have to." I said, "What would be helpful, Senator, is if you could announce to the media that you made the decision to go ahead with the buyout and buy these people out, that could be the best thing you can say," and he said, "Okay, I'll do it." We took him around to, I think it was 22 different spots for him to talk to the media. Anyway, he would have been on CNN, FOX, all the networks. He talked about how bad it is but it looks like we can continue with the buyout. That really made him some excellent press.

He was there for like three hours. On the way back to his car in Miami he called the Governor on a cell phone. Governor Henry and Inhofe didn't get along. Henry was a Democrat and Inhofe was a Republican. I only heard one half of the conversation where he said, "Governor, this is Senator Inhofe, you and I are in this together," and then there was silence and then he said, "I thought you would agree with my decision that we were going to go ahead with the buyout of the people. We've worked out how to do it and I just want to make sure that you're on board." And then there was more silence and then Inhofe said, "I thought you'd understand." He said goodbye and hung up the phone.

Later that afternoon the Governor came up in his Blackhawk and did his tour talking to the media. He said, "Senator Inhofe and I talked this morning and we both agreed to continue with the buyout." The Trust had an emergency meeting the next night with the trust members. Mark Osborn was the Chairman at the time and Mark said, "The Trust has decided that we're going to go ahead with the buyout."

The Trust had decided... you know, I just had to laugh, they've been in on the game all the way through, but it didn't make any difference—the main thing was to go on and give these people some sense of relief.

J.D. STRONG: If a property was reduced to rubble it's going to make it exceedingly hard to appraise it. So, we did the best we could on that. I think the Trust and its manager did the best they could do on all of that and in a lot of the litigation that was brought... especially class action suits, as I recall, brought against the insurance companies for their failure to adequately compensate people for the loss and damage to their properties.

I think the litigation that occurred was over some of the folks that were disgruntled about their offers and were making allegations that there were collusions, and favoritism, and those that were on the Trust, that if they liked you, you got more for your house. Those sorts of things.

WALLACE KENNEDY: The Trust said that insurance money belongs to us and they would take the insurance money and then if their appraisal was higher than the insurance money, they would give them some additional money from the Trust. But that was it. I mean they are kind of heavy-handed if you ask me.

DR. ROBERT WRIGHT, pediatrician, medical toxicologist, and environmental epidemiologist at the Icahn School of Medicine at Mount Sinai: It actually did affect our study. Our poor retention was driven by the fact that a lot of people moved out. We couldn't track them because they left the area. Picher existed when we started. Picher didn't exist a few years after we started. The town was completely bought out. People left. After the tornado, there was this enormous ice storm that closed our field office for about a month because there was no electricity for two weeks and quite a bit of damage. There was a 150-year flood that actually destroyed our field office in another year, and we were actually closed for six months because the building was destroyed. It had to be rebuilt.

There were these almost biblical weather events that happened on top of all the social-political issues. We've got to remember Senator Inhofe is kind of famous for wanting to close EPA, and this study is in his home state. There are all kinds of political issues that were happening kind of simultaneous to this that also made it difficult to operate. Also, I was young and naïve at the time, and I think this was my first attempt at doing a big study like this. I also made mistakes because I was relatively new at it. All those things kind of came together.

The idea that there were stressors involved in this sort of situation was something that hadn't occurred to them, and I think understanding what's happening in some ways is a step towards addressing these issues. I think that helped them as well.

WALLACE KENNEDY: The appraisal company was doing a horrible job and it was totally inconsistent. And upwards of two hundred families, at least, got lowballed by this appraisal company. And for reasons I do not understand—I don't know, I think somebody was trying to do it as cheaply, most cost-effectively, to look good regardless of how it impacted the people who were being bought out.

My very first story about this was about a woman who got a house bought out, and she lived in such a small, dilapidated house in Picher. She only got maybe $20,000 at the most for her house. She could not have enough money to go move into another house. And so she had to go to the bank in Miami, Oklahoma, and take out a loan to help her get into the new arrangement.

Well, it just so happens that many of the people who serve on the Trust are employed by the bank in Miami. And so if the houses are priced low, then the bank stands to make money for making loans to people to buy houses. And it seems to me obvious, apparent conflict of interest. And that issue was raised and nothing happened because the Trust had immunity from all scrutiny. It could pretty much do whatever it wanted to do. And it did.

MARY BILLINGTON, director of the Baxter Springs Heritage Center and Museum: When you've got pride in a community and we've got such a large area that is damaged by the mining industry, it's hard to find a place nearby that you could have relocated a town. And by the time that the buyout actually happened, much of the town's population had already started to drift away. It was just—not only was it on a death spiral, it was on a poisonous death spiral.

MARC YAGGI, executive director Waterkeeper Alliance: There are still a couple people that decided living next to lead mountain was preferable. That was sort of hard to watch too, people living in there.

FREDAS L. COOK, archivist, photographer, lifelong Picher resident: There are four or five homes in Picher that didn't sell out. Consider yourself age 25–35. You bought a house in Picher for $10,000 because you could get a better house for that amount in Picher and that's all you could afford. You find out that if the buyout occurs, you can get $25–35,000 for it, perhaps more. Considering what a similar house in Miami is worth, how are you going to vote? Now, consider yourself 70–75. You live in a house that was paid off years ago. You have it fixed up the way you like it and it is really comfortable. You know everybody in town and all your neighbors are friends. How are you going to vote?

MATT MYERS, filmmaker, *Tar Creek*: They extended the deadline a little bit because they thought they could get a few to move and they did. There ended up being just 12 who stayed after they turned the lights out. I'm sure people have told you that it was like a war zone there. People would show up and then fire off M-50s and who knows what other heavy artillery there. Because there were no police. There was no fire, there was nobody. People just came there and raised hell.

People were wanting them to pipe water to some folks. It was just like, we can't do it. We just spent $50 million getting everybody out of here. We can't spend money making the people who stayed have a better life. As tough love as that is, that was just the way it was. It was a pretty rough place. You wouldn't want to be there at night after they had shut everything down. It was rough.

LARRY KROPP, East Shawnee Tribal council, Quapaw Tribal member: It had to be done. I did see a lot of good people in Picher that was upset. A lot of elderly people. Use yourself as an example. You own a house, if somebody comes in and says you lived there half all your life, chances are that you were born in that house. If somebody comes in and said, *well, you're gonna have to go find you another place to live. Here's x amount of dollars, we'll find you another place to live.*

MATT MYERS: When you are told the only place you can't live is home, that is a tough pill to swallow. The pride that people have there, they still feel like mining is happening, and they still want to talk about the mining as if it's not over and it's still so real to them. It's tougher than in most towns that don't really have like a cultural center the way that place did. Just how huge it was. Just how enormous that field was. So, they grow up on generations of that, and then here's the place you can't go. Then when you have to go, you are moving into places that have been making fun of you for generations. As simple as those things are, that is what I would come into when I would go speak at universities or wherever. People knew not to ask that question, I think. It's kind of indirect and stated a little bit directly also in the film, but you could see people really wrestling with that.

"Why don't you just leave?"

It's just right there in front of you and you don't want to leave home and you can't. People who were living there, they weren't working tech jobs from home. It was a very impoverished area. I said to somebody when I was in New York that at least if you are panhandling in New York there are people to panhandle to.

There are people with money walking around. This is one of the poorest places, if not the poorest place, I've ever been in my life. The poverty there goes so deep and it goes down so far. It's beyond comprehension.

DR. ROBERT WRIGHT, pediatrician, medical toxicologist, and environmental epidemiologist at the Icahn School of Medicine at Mount Sinai: I think it was a good thing. I think it was not a good place to raise kids. There is lead everywhere. This is a very poor community. They didn't have a lot of resources. I think they were so poor they didn't have trash pickup and things like that. There were also these issues of being stigmatized by the surrounding communities because they were these poor kids that grew up around mining waste.

They got teased a lot for that and I think it was better in the long run. It's sad because it once was really a vibrant, wealthy place, but it wasn't anymore and I don't think that was ever coming back. I think it was the right thing in the end.

THE AUDIT

IN 2007, after decades of struggle, it appeared that the homes of the people living within the Tar Creek Superfund Site were finally being bought out by the federal government. At the time, it seemed that the end was in sight for this decades-long nightmare. For some, it was, and hopefully they are in a better place today. But for many, what came next was a continuation of the poor treatment they had unfortunately become accustomed to. Instead of closure, many of the residents were being taken advantage of by the Lead Impacted Communities Relocation Assistance Trust (LICRAT).

A bizarre twist in the town buyout drama developed when former Oklahoma Attorney General Scott Pruitt ordered a financial audit of the Trust due to a whistleblower complaint.

DANIEL STEVENS, executive director Campaign for Accountability: Essentially, what I understood at the time is that there's this big Superfund site in northeastern Oklahoma that the federal government was pumping all this money into to clean up. And so, this local agency [LICRAT] was created to do two things.

One—to buy out people from their homes. To pay the people money so that they can leave the area that was affected by the Superfund site.

Then two—demolish the homes and get rid of all the waste and take it to a landfill site so you don't have impacted houses like just hanging out in the area.

ED KEHELEY, retired nuclear engineer, expert on Tar Creek: Anyway, these three whistleblowers got an attorney out of Tulsa, who is an excellent attorney and he took their claim and put it in the form of a lawsuit. It contained something like 58 or 59 accusations of the Trust being in collusion with this guy Jack Dalrymple. They filed that in Federal Court and as soon as they filed that lawsuit, the EPA had gotten wind of it and they put one of their gophers in the Inspector General's office to do a quick little audit of that lawsuit. If only 10% of these accusations were true, there were some serious things happening. In the meantime, the State Auditor's office had gotten wind of it through [State] Senator Culver, who was sent this lawsuit and basically all the records that these three whistleblowers had. Anyway, he took this over to the Attorney General's office to Pruitt's for investigation. Pruitt's office then turned around and sent a letter to the State Auditor's office asking the State Auditor to investigate these wrongdoings.

DANIEL STEVENS: Is it that the person doing it knew some of the real nitty-gritty issues here? Some people think it's kind of a whitewash. We sent a lot of FOIAs to get to the bottom of that EPA/Attorney General investigation to see what happened.

ED KEHELEY: They started their investigation and one of the first people they called was me, to see what I knew about it. Then they kind of explained the case, and the concerns they were finding was that Mark Osborn, who was Chairman of the Trust, had hired one of his best friends to manage the demolition of the homes that had been purchased by the trust in Picher and other towns. They single-sourced, selected this guy without competition because he had extensive quality assurance experience. That was the basis under which they hired the guy.

WALLACE KENNEDY, retired journalist, *The Joplin Globe*: It was problematic. It was sad because some people got preferential treatment from the Trust. Some people just got bad treatment from the Trust and from the appraisers. And it created a real bitterness between the people and the people on the Trust who are overseeing this buyout. And there was a lot of resentment because a lot of these people were from Miami, Oklahoma, and there's been a long-standing look-down-your-nose attitude involving Miami and Picher, Oklahoma.

There's been a long rivalry for years. Picher was once a rich mining town. Miami became the town it is because Picher was nearby. And the wealth in Miami is directly connected to what happened in Picher, Oklahoma. So, there was this tension, and then it really got bad because it was apparent the evidence was pretty strong.

ED KEHELEY: The [LICRAT] Trust was given legislative immunity from lawsuits by the Senate Bill 1463. Therefore, they could pretty much perform as they chose without any legal liability. When the lawsuit was filed these attorneys took it all the way to the State Supreme Court to see if that was really legit. Well, it turned out to be legitimate. The State Supreme Court says, yes, *the legislation can in fact be given legislative immunity from lawsuits.* In this lawsuit, a Trust could not be sued. Anyway, they sued the Appraiser Contractor and the Appraiser Review Contractor.

The Appraiser Contractor and the Appraiser Review Contractor were named in the lawsuit and so was J.D. Strong, and so was Larry Roberts for colluding with the appraisers to keep the values low on people.

> *One appraiser, Curtis L. Roberts, said appraisers are being pushed to assess as many homes as possible each month and to report their value at the highest amount legally possible. That means that appraisers are making more errors and judgment calls that could result in appraisals being somewhat uneven, he said. In addition, many homes in Picher and Cardin are substandard houses and trailers, yet appraisers are expected to base their assessments on comparable homes that are worth more than the buyout home, Roberts said. This is allowable under the legislation governing the buyout. Also, Ottawa County land records are often in error on lot sizes, deed transfers and other pertinent information, Roberts said. "You have to understand that Tar Creek is not your typical place to do the kind of consistent appraisal work that is done elsewhere," he said. "It is one of the most difficult places to get accurate records, find comparables and then make the final assessment." Strong said two appraisers are primarily responsible for conducting 50 appraisals a month.* [43]

WALLACE KENNEDY: The real problem with the buyout and LICRAT was the appraisal company who was pulling their strings. Why were they undervaluing people? And then afterward there was evidence to suggest that the company that would do the demolition would come in and say, *hey, this is a 1,400-square-foot house* for demolition purposes, and get that much money for it, when the people who lived there actually lived in an 800-square-foot house, and that's what they got their appraisal on, not 1,400 square feet.

Now the other side of that is Kansas; when it came in and bought out Treece, Kansas experienced the same problem with the appraisals. The appraisals were too low for these people to move. They had to have more money for their shacks

---

43. Omer Gillham. "Errors Trouble Buyout." *Tulsa World*, 20 Jan 2008.

and their houses, and whatever property they own. And so these were mining shacks that were built, so let's make no mistake about that. So what did the state of Kansas do? They came back and appropriated more money in order to get these people out. The same could have happened in Oklahoma; there was no reason why it couldn't have been done down there.

J.D. STRONG: Are there going to be mistakes made when you're dealing with people that are appraisers, people that review appraisers, and people that are demolition contractors? You know, you're dealing with humans, and humans are going to make mistakes, but despite the rumors reported from some, I'd say there wasn't collusion and favoritism, at least from what I could see. From where I sat there certainly... as I was managing the first buyout, which as I said was hugely successful, as I recall 100% acceptance rate, very few complaints—of course it was a much smaller scale, I was much more hands-on on that one. You know that one went really well.

No intentional wrongdoing being done. No experience to learn from others how to do it right, and so you know for all litigation and complaints that may have come out of it, the fact of the matter is that a group of mostly local leaders did volunteer to do the thankless job of spending a large part of their lives working to try to provide this opportunity, once-in-a-lifetime opportunity for these people to get out of harm's way.

WALLACE KENNEDY: I remember getting incredible thank-you notes from J.D. Strong about my coverage of Brad Henry's decision to do the buyout of the children of the families with the children in Picher. I just don't know what happened when the chemistry of this group got together, but it changed and it's too bad. It could have been so easy to do; there was plenty of money. I just don't understand.

J.D. STRONG: At the end of the day the goal was basically accomplished. I mean, people complained that they should get more, but at the end of the day there were only a handful of people that decided to stay behind; everybody else took their offers and moved out and hopefully are leading better lives as a result. It also affords the state and federal government opportunity to take a little more time on the remediation effort because you aren't as concerned about a new generation of Oklahoma children being lead-impaired.

WALLACE KENNEDY: It was made to order to be abused, and I think that's what happened. And I think in time the evidence will come out completely.

ED KEHELEY: The State Auditor's people really did a very good job on the audit. I saw what they did, and the level of detail they went into and all of the things they found were really significant. I mean, when you take an engineer who's involved in quality assurance and the first year he makes over $305,000 dollars on a government demolition job? Come on, man. That's crazy.

(State Auditor) Gary Jones took their charter from the A.G.'s office. When the A.G. wrote the letter to Jones and listed these 19 areas to look at, that was not included, therefore the State Auditors can't go out and audit something that they are not directed to audit, let me put it that way. In other words, they can't go on fishing expeditions.

THE COVER-UP

IN ONE of the final turns in the drama of the LICRA Trust buyout, its cover-up and audit is another cover-up at the highest levels of Oklahoma's state government. The audit was finished in 2011 and remained unseen by the public until 2018, when the statute of limitations ran out on all the implicated parties.

On a whistleblower tip, the Campaign for Accountability (CfA), a nonprofit watchdog organization in Washington, D.C., made an Open Records Act request to the Oklahoma State Auditor's office seeking all documents on LICRAT to be made public. Throughout 2017 and 2018, there's a back-and-forth of legal motions between CfA and Oklahoma Attorney General Mike Hunter's office.

Tar Creek is also part of the environmental legacy of one of the state's—and nation's—leading politicians, Senator Jim Inhofe, and his longtime ally Scott Pruitt, the former Oklahoma Attorney General who is now head of President Donald Trump's Environmental Protection Agency. After the EPA struggled to clean up the area, in 2006 Inhofe endorsed a plan in which a trust overseen by local citizens would use federal dollars to purchase homes and businesses in the toxic region so residents could move elsewhere. Then, when the plan proved so problematic that it spawned more than a half-dozen civil lawsuits and an audit into possible criminal wrongdoing, Pruitt, as the state's Attorney General, invoked an exception to state freedom-of-information laws to keep the audit from being an open public record.[44]

DANIEL STEVENS, executive director Campaign for Accountability: If I step back for a second and take a look at the overall project, I think that there are a few Superfund sites and Inhofe wanted to create a way for him to be able to tell the

44. Malcolm Burnley and M. Scott Mahaskey. "The Environmental Scandal in Scott Pruitt's Backyard." *POLITICO Magazine*, 6 Dec 2017.

people of Oklahoma that he helped these people get out of their homes, get out of the secluded area and make the problem go away. And then they set up a local agency to do that, that's just full of problems. I think all these guys wanted to make the audit go away because they didn't want to tarnish their legacy of what they were trying to do here. They were making this Superfund site get cleaned up and go away.

And I think it really undercuts their conservative philosophy that local government is best. They wanted to be able to blame the EPA for everything, but it's really the small state agency that was causing the problems here.

WALLACE KENNEDY, retired journalist, *The Joplin Globe*: Politically speaking it would be a negative for Jim Inhofe. I think that is the real issue. And as I remember it first came to the attention of [Senator Tom] Coburn and then Inhofe became involved, and then there was no more problem because Pruitt wasn't going to do any kind of prosecution for what was found in the State Auditor's report about what happened there.

That's how it happened. And then Scott Pruitt gets named the head of the EPA! Just think about this for a second: an Attorney General from Oklahoma became head of the EPA. It helps that you have ties to the oil industry, which is part, which the Trump Administration clearly does. It just seems very, very unusual. Somebody looks the other way and then just says, *no, I'm not going to prosecute anybody associated with this* and then the next thing you're named head of the EPA.

Picher, Oklahoma. Photo by the author. October 2018.

ED KEHELEY: As soon as he did that, one of the few men of integrity that I've ever met in my life, Gary Jones, the State Auditor, went to the *Oklahoman* and said, "I couldn't disagree more with A.G. Pruitt. We did find activities there that are criminal in nature and should be prosecuted. Therefore, I don't agree with Pruitt basically hiding our report."

DANIEL STEVENS: I think that [Scott Pruitt] was just trying to stir up a lot of smoke to make people scared and to give them some quasi-legal reason for why these audits shouldn't be released. If you back up and think about what is actually here, the audit showed exactly in detail how these guys essentially pocketed a whole bunch of public money through this public agency. So that's what's going on. You know the people who are the board members of the LICRAT, you know there was the contractor involved, you know the money is going out. The public agency, just like the government office, has to keep track of all its expenses and its transactions.

And so, the audit is the document of the abuses by this public agency. Pruitt's claim that these were unsubstantiated and undocumented is just hogwash, right? Gary Jones put it all in writing, and here are the receipts, here are all the payments.

He was really fighting the good fight on this issue. Just to be clear, we never really talked to him, we never met him. Like I said, this tip turned up in the mailbox for a records request and then we filed a lawsuit against the state. So, it's not like we were interacting with any of these people or working with them or anything like that. But, from afar, reading through the court filings and anything else, you see him acting in a very honorable way. When we asked for them to file, he said, "Yes, I would like to but I can't because they're telling me not to." And then we filed a legal brief to that effect; he even attended the proceedings about this in the lawsuit. He constantly was pushing to get this audit released, which I think was really commendable—in a state where almost the other half of officials were trying to make this go away, he was the one who was saying no, no we need to get this out there, this needs to be public.

ED KEHELEY: In the meantime [Mike] Hunter, who was acting A.G. for Pruitt, also would not release the audit report. In particular, they got a lot of publicity from the *Oklahoman*. They just ripped Pruitt routinely and A.G. Hunter just unmercifully. It still didn't cause anything to happen.

DANIEL STEVENS: It is unclear to me why Hunter was carrying water for Pruitt after he took over the office. Maybe it was just a professional courtesy of carrying out what he had started. Also, Hunter could have kept fighting it too.

We had one hearing that he was going to release these records. Hunter could have kept fighting it and could have gone all the way to the Oklahoma Supreme

Court and try to really keep this private for a couple of years, but after that initial hearing kind of didn't go his way he did decide to release it. He didn't fight as hard as he could because he realized that that wasn't a good strategy. We did send a FOIA to Pruitt's office and EPA looking into all the communications with Hunter or Hunter's office. We couldn't find anything about this.

Every state has some public law that governs how public records are treated in the state. And they vary extremely widely. So, a state like Florida has a really good Open Records Law and you can ask for and receive all kinds of public records. Oklahoma is somewhat in the middle of the states that I've seen. They are supposed to give them to you. Knowing the problem with Oklahoma and their Open Records Law is that the appeals systems aren't great.

Say I FOIA [Freedom of Information Act Request] the EPA and they say no, they are not going to give it to you or that there's a fee. You can appeal it within the EPA. And say, *okay, they are not giving it to me, can I visit an appeal process?* With the Attorney General's office, we filed a bunch of FOIAs in the fall of 2017. We still haven't received some of them. They are working on it, is what they tell us.

Senator Inhofe was closely involved in all of this. And one of the reasons that LICRAT was set up as it was in that weird unique way, was that he really didn't believe in federal government, and critically, local government figured that if they could keep the people running this buyout process local and overseen that it will be free of corruption and waste.

We see that it was totally wrong. But I think that is probably the unique characteristic of this whole agency, and it stems from Inhofe's mistaken belief that this could be run by this one-time local agency rather than by a more established agency.

The Oklahoma newspaper asked every living State Auditor about whether they could remember a situation like this, and they all said no. That there wasn't a similar situation where an audit like this hadn't been released. It seems super likely that somebody would be able to do this—not release an audit like this. But definitely, if somebody's misusing public money, that's something we should all know about.

WALLACE KENNEDY: The thing is, I don't really care about what happens to anyone associated with the Trust or anyone associated with the buyout or the demolition project afterwards. I don't really care about those people, the politicians who were involved in all that, I don't care. But the people who were impacted, the families, the people who tried to make a go of it in Picher, but couldn't, the people who were trapped and trusted the government to help them get out of there. Those are the people that I feel for.

COMMUNITY

PICHER OFFICIALLY closed down its city hall and municipal operations in 2009. That same year, Picher's last high school class graduated a total of 11 students. In 2015 Picher's last remaining citizen, pharmacist Gary Linderman, died. Throughout Picher's final few years, the press loved talking to the pharmacist who would remain until there was no one else who would need his services. When you drive through Picher today, you can see a few ghosts of its vibrant past here and there amongst the remaining chat mountains.

Of the various personalities who have shaped Tar Creek's legacy, several continue to carry on the fight. Most of them moved on to other challenges, retired, or are no longer with us. There are a lot of people I couldn't find to interview. Like any decades-long event involving a large population, there are so many more sides to this story. The testimonies presented here only outline its broad contours.

In 2019, 36 years after Environmental Protection Agency recognized Tar Creek as a federal Superfund site through the CERCLA program, the Quapaw Tribe hums away at reclaiming their land as well as non-tribal Picher with EPA funding, implementing the remediation through their Operable Unit program. Who knows how many generations it will take to reclaim their land and remake it as nontoxic. On the trip I took to the area, I took in a "toxic tour"—as countless politicians, policymakers, artists, journalists, and gawkers have before me. Our guide worked for the Quapaw Tribe's Environmental Department. She showed us fields of crops such as winter wheat growing alongside the chat piles. It was inspiring to see some life happening there. In 2013 the Quapaw brought a $175 million lawsuit against the Department of Justice for the mismanagement of their lands that were being held by the government in federal trust. The case is still ongoing today.

Rebecca Jim and Earl Hatley are still running LEAD Agency, pushing for environmental justice in the area. They recently won a decision in the D.C. Circuit court suit alongside the Sierra Club and Waterkeeper Alliance against the Trump Administration's EPA for kneecapping an already weak coal ash rule in Oklahoma. (Coal ash is a highly toxic by-product of coal plant production. It's full of arsenic, lead, mercury, and selenium, as well as, but not limited to, aluminum, barium, boron, and chlorine.) Oklahoma was the first state to acquire an EPA permit to dispose of its coal ash under the Trump Administration's plan to let polluters regulate themselves. There's going to be a need for the likes of LEAD Agency and the environmental movement at large to continue holding these industries and our government accountable.

The indispensable and tireless Ed Keheley is currently working with investigators trying to solve a tragic cold case from 1999 regarding two missing teen girls, Ashley Freeman and Lauria Bible, from Welch, Oklahoma. Ed told me that it's a strong possibility that their bodies are in one of the abandoned mines. Because of Ed's research locating and mapping all of the mineshafts with his friend, the late geologist Dr. Ken Luza, he is one of the only people who may be able to crack this case.

Dr. Robert Nairn and his University of Oklahoma students are continuing to experiment with ways to remediate the polluted mine water using organic, passive treatment techniques. Teams of researchers and reporters check in on Picher now and then because it's still so shocking, and frankly, interesting, to be in a ghost town. You can't help but gawk a little bit.

Scott Pruitt resigned as administrator of the EPA in 2018 amidst numerous ethics violations allegations. Pruitt was the subject of at least 13 federal investigations.

It's hardly a happy ending or even an ending at all. Picher is no more, but all those surrounding towns are still there, still going about their lives. It's not over though. The people of the Tar Creek Superfund Site continue to fight one of the most extraordinary pollution events in the history of this country.

"A total of 4,061,580 tons of source material has been removed from the Tar Creek Superfund Site, 163 mineshafts and subsidences capped, 125 cased borings have been plugged, and a total of 896 acres of land have been remediated. A total of 21 projects have been completed, and three are now progressing with six more projects currently in the planning stage for ongoing remediation projects and three are now progressing with six more projects currently in the planning stage for ongoing remediation projects."[45]

Every day, a steady stream of trucks haul away more than 2,000 tons of soil saturated with cadmium, lead and other metals at the site. Each patch of earth requires years of passive soil treatments before it tests clean enough to plant row crops like winter wheat. Half-acre by half-acre, the hope is that Tar Creek can be put into productive agricultural use decades from now.[46]

45. *The Miami News-Record*, Friday, 28 Sept 2018, p. A3.

46. Malcolm Burnley and M. Scott Mahaskey. "The Environmental Scandal in Scott Pruitt's Backyard." *POLITICO Magazine*, 6 Dec 2017.

Somewhere in the Picher area. Photo by the author. October 2018.

Picher isn't simply another boomtown gone bust. It's emblematic of what happens when a modern city dies: A few people stay behind, trying to hold on to what they can. They are the new homesteaders, trying to civilize a waste-land at the end of the world.[47]

LARRY KROPP, East Shawnee Tribal council, Quapaw Tribal member: I got into such a confrontation with all the old boys at the EPA because the contractors were treating the landowners like they were ignorant. Like we didn't know what we were talking about. And their only concern was how to make a buck on this and get out of the country.

I finally met with the gentleman out of Dallas, Texas. He was the head of the EPA for this district. I explained the situation, what was going on and everything. And I had already talked with Quapaw services in regard to taking over the remediation on our property, and they agreed to take it over and shot me a price of what they would charge to do it. I actually worked out a deal between the EPA

47. Ben Paynter. "Take a Tour of America's Most Toxic Town." *Wired*, Conde Nast, 30 Aug 2010.

and the Quapaw services to get the EPA contractors plumb off of the site and bring Quapaw services in to continue the remediation, and they did an awesome job at it.

MARY BILLINGTON, director of the Baxter Springs Heritage Center and Museum: There's still this community, I mean people living there. The school district is still there, the Quapaw Tribe still uses the school building. They use it as a meeting center, a resource center. The hundreds of thousands of dollars the Quapaw Tribe is investing into that land to reclaim it as part of their agreement with the U.S. government is impressive, but it's also daunting in the fact that it is such an overwhelming job to be done to try to reclaim that land.

DR. ROBERT NAIRN, environmental scientist, researcher, professor Oklahoma University: I think [the Quapaw] have made more progress, I think in the last five years, than we have seen since the designation of Superfund. I think from a political perspective, obviously there's a lot of positives with those dollars, those funds, those resources going to the Tribe to support this kind of work, but from an environmental perspective they've been credibly efficient. The work that they've done, they've moved quickly, they've done great work. From what I know the costs that are, are very reasonable. Those dollars are staying in northern Ottawa County.

CATHY SLOAN, environmental specialist, Quapaw Tribe: Now, I believe on the waterside we have 23 water connections and that's people that have water over there [Picher], and that's including our marshals. So, we have a few businesses still there. That many years they went from 60,000 people down to maybe 25 people over there. There are still a few houses over there.

TAMMY ARNOLD, environmental grants manager, Quapaw Tribe: We have 10 grants at the moment that we are working on. Well, 11, counting climate change. We are working on getting two more to clean up. We have our basics. Our air grant, we have our water grant, we have our Superfund management assistance, which basically lets us start, that's where we basically started, with our management and systems grant, the cleanup. We get our grants through EPA, except for climate change, we get through BIA. I kind of make sure everything gets done with all of them. We stay within our money limits and we don't go over those and that all of our deliverables will be met.

Then I help with fieldwork when somebody is gone, or if they just need extra help I kind of fill in. Like yesterday with the Tar Creek conference. That's our baby. We go to the schools and try to get in the kids' heads that recycling is one of our big things too. We recycle. We try to teach the kids how important that is and try to get them up to speed on what is going on in Picher. A lot of kids don't even know that that's over there.

CATHY SLOAN: We have a casino and there are some other buildings. Our convenience store. There are some other businesses that the Tribe has over there.

TAMMY ARNOLD: Processing plant.

CATHY SLOAN: We have an air monitoring station over there and it runs continuously. They talk about how the wind blows. It's not that far from Picher. They run continuous because they are all in different directions depending on which way the wind blows. It's lead in the air so we test for that. Especially while we are doing these cleanups. We want to know if we are releasing anything into the air as far as lead goes. We have two of them that run every six days and then we have one that runs every 12 days. So, those are sent off to a lab in Wyoming. They read them and then they give us the results to see if there is any lead collected as the cleanup goes and we are monitoring the air over there. Then we have around the industrial park.

We test the water for different things. To see what metals are in there. We do sulfides, sulfates, nitrates. Of course, we do pH, phosphorus, just different things in the water. We do that on our river that is in our tribal jurisdiction and then we do four different creeks. We do that once a month, unless we have high levels, then we will go back, and we will do it more frequently to check and see if it's just something that has been applied on the land that maybe had gone into the creek or if somebody has dumped something that we may not know about.

WALLACE KENNEDY: I think the Tribe is really working to do the best they can because I've met the environmental people associated with the Tribe and these are credible people. And I really think they really are concerned about the land that they're getting and if the cleanup of Picher is very slow and methodical and takes a long time, it's okay because there's nobody there now, there's nobody being exposed.

EARL HATLEY, Cherokee, environmental activist, co-founder of LEAD Agency, Grand Riverkeeper: OU5 is a new Operable Unit that is in scope period right now, the investigation phase, and LEAD Agency is working with the two EPA regions and three states and all Tribes on this one.

OU5 addresses sediment and surface water. Under OU5, efforts to characterize sediment and surface water throughout the lower Spring and Neosho River basins, as well as understand the potential risks associated with exposures to surface water and sediment through a Human Health Risk Assessment

(HHRA), are being conducted. This effort is being coordinated with Region 7, three states (Oklahoma, Missouri, Kansas), eight Tribes (Quapaw Tribe, Peoria Tribe, Ottawa Tribe, Miami Nation, Eastern Shawnee Tribe, Wyandotte Nation, Seneca-Cayuga Nation, and Cherokee Nation), and the community. OU5 includes seven watersheds covering approximately 437 square miles and 119 river miles within Oklahoma, Kansas, Missouri, and eight tribal areas.[48]

REBECCA JIM, Cherokee, educator, environmental activist, co-founder of LEAD Agency: OU5, we're still in the paper stage of it. They sent out the latest update and so there will be a meeting on it this month to see what we are going to do, what's going to really happen, what level are we gonna do, how much of what we will do.

OU5 we believed was going to be more or less the rest of the story. But now EPA is saying no, that's just going to be the water. The sediments in the water, not in the watershed, but in where the water flows, the sediments in there is what they're gonna talk about. When you've got Tar Creek and the Neosho and the Spring River, when they flood, they flood miles of property. But this isn't going to be like that. It's only inside the banks. Very disappointing, so there will have to be an OU6 an OU7 an OU8.

ED KEHELEY, retired nuclear engineer, expert on Tar Creek: I respect the Tribe, I respect what they are doing, but what they're doing is not that significant to the overall site. I'm not being critical of the Tribe. They got a contract for $17 million to clean up two hundred acres. We're talking about 43 square miles. Do the math, and the areas that they're cleaning up are the lesser impacted areas at the site. Now, am I pleased to see them doing something? The answer is yes.

It all comes back to a matter of scale. When I look at the fact they've been here 38 years and there has never been a comprehensive plan developed for the site, it just causes me great pause. And that's what I'm saying is I think there are parts of the site that they should just write off for now. Until the technology is there to fix it.

DR. ROBERT NAIRN: The only thing I can say—then again, you know, because I'm a scientist, I'm a university professor, I am not a politician or decision-maker—but what we have seen is that under CERCLA, EPA has to provide five-year reports, five-year updates, five-year reviews on each of their Operable Units.

48. "TAR CREEK (OTTAWA COUNTY) Site Profile." EPA, Environmental Protection Agency, 20 Oct 2017.

They haven't put any money into it. Our source of funding for the current project is the state of Oklahoma, not the EPA.

ED KEHELEY: When the EPA continues to fluctuate on what they consider are the public safety issues, you can't address a problem unless you understand the problem. I don't believe that the site is understood and I don't think there is an interest to try to understand. They treat the site from a regulatory mentality, not a scientific mentality.

WALLACE KENNEDY: Even today, the EPA is funneling money into the Picher site through the Quapaw Tribe to continue the cleanup process, which is great. They're getting $15 million over the course of two or three years. And I would feel good if a little of that money was shaved off and all the people who were adversely impacted by the buyout were made whole.

BRAD CARSON, former Congressman of the 2nd district of Oklahoma, former Undersecretary to the Army: Tar Creek is not on the news today in Oklahoma. It's a problem that is not totally solved, but the acute problems of public health have been solved.

J.D. STRONG, Director at Oklahoma Department of Wildlife Conservation, former Chief of Staff to the Secretary of Environment of Oklahoma: Well, I mean, it sounds cliché because it seems like we say it all the time, but you always need to consider what your actions today may do for generations later, and Tar Creek is a perfect example of that. I don't think the folks that started mining in the 1890s thought about the damage it was doing as a result. They certainly weren't putting up funds that it was going to take to clean up the mess at the end of the day, and I think that's why you see improvements made today where, when mining is occurring across the U.S., federal government regulations that require you to set aside surety bonds and other things to be able to clean up the mess even if the company goes bankrupt, which is what happened to most of those companies that operated at Tar Creek. I mean that's obviously the most significant thing that folks need to do.

DR. ROBERT NAIRN: One of the things I say is that the people that work there and their descendants that we got to know, they mined the lead and the zinc that won the first and second World Wars. They did. There is the fact that we all had this common benefit from what went on there and it was good for the country. We beat the Nazis.

That's a good thing that this helped us do that, but we have a shared responsibility then to make sure that these environmental and human health-related issues that are a result of that don't continue. How do we make that happen is that we've got to have stricter environmental laws, and we do today. We have obviously much more well established, much more dedicated approaches to addressing these problems than we did back in the '40s and '50s. But that requires political will and that requires an informed public that makes sure that they force those politicians to not diminish our abilities to prevent this from happening again. We've got to have good environmental laws, but they're only good if they're enforced.

I think that's a political issue. This is not a scientific issue. I would argue that we understand the science and engineering enough to know what the problem is and ways to make sure it doesn't happen again, but it takes money to make that happen and that means we need political will to make sure those funds are available.

BRIAN GRIFFIN, former Oklahoma Secretary of the Environment, Chairman of the Board at Clean Energy Systems: Well, I think we're in a better place today than certainly we were at the time the environmental impacts of Tar Creek were being created. We do have substantial environmental regulations that help deal with these issues at the beginning [that] prevents them. You know the old saying "an ounce of prevention is worth a pound of cure" is certainly true in the environmental arena.

Hopefully, if we don't denigrate too many environmental rules, the entire regulatory framework in place today would help prevent something like a Tar Creek from ever happening again. You also have to remember that the exegesis of time, looking at what was involved, we have huge environmental problems today, like the nuclear weapons program of World War II. We didn't have time to think through all the environmental impacts that now we deal with Oak Ridge, Tennessee, and Sanford, Washington, and other places that were involved in the nuclear weapons program. These things sometimes come about as a result of what was happening as a result of the bigger worldwide picture. There's an old saying that Tar Creek provided the lead to win World War I and World War II, especially World War II, so you know, at the time we were more concerned about America surviving the onslaught of the Germans and the Japanese aggression. Worrying about the environmental impacts at the time didn't seem like the most urgent thing to think about. Sufficient regulatory restrictions and approaches that will help prevent something like this happening again, I feel encouraged about that. I don't think we'll have another Tar Creek but we have to always be vigilant.

SCOTT THOMPSON, Director of the Oklahoma Department of Environmental Quality: It is a very complicated story. To me, the biggest thing that people need to understand is that we dropped the percentage of kids with elevated blood lead drastically, fairly quickly. At the end of the day, the best decisions were made about whether or not this place should continue to be a place where you raise kids.

Parts of the sites are not suitable for that. Parts of the site can be cleaned up adequately and be made safe. Picher and Cardin were in the epicenter. I'm sure you have probably seen aerial photos and stuff that—it is just almost unexplainable to people who haven't been there or haven't witnessed it how large that is. Even if you are looking at aerial photos, you don't quite get the scale of it so much as when you are there in person. It wasn't a great place for people to live.

BRAD CARSON: If this happened in some of the affluent areas, Oklahoma City, Tulsa, people would have gone insane. Every politician of both parties would have been ginned up to find solutions to it. It would have been in a major driver in the state politics for months, if not years to come.

Here you have a place that's poor, mostly Native Americans, it's kind of a bit off the beaten path and they didn't have access to the media. Politicians didn't show them much love because there were no votes or money to be made out there. They just suffered as a result of it. I think that's a lesson learned. There are lots of places that can be vulnerable for these things. That in the end is, to me, the role of their advocates, of their politicians—to represent Ottawa County, Oklahoma. This is an outrage and people need to do something about it. I think the other lesson is, bold action is going to be required to solve things that have so many competing interests. So much complexity. The responsibility for this problem, about the magnitude of the problem, about what the future might bring. The bold action is needed, and in Tar Creek's case, bold action in the end happened, and I think it has been largely successful.

FRANK KEATING, former Governor of Oklahoma, attorney, author: Hopefully, today we as a people are much more sensitive to the indispensable value of a safe environment. There's no ocean here and there's no Gulf of Mexico. So, if somebody dumps nitrates into the Grand River or other rivers that flow into our recreational lakes, guess what? How do you fix that? As far as I'm concerned we have to be very vigilant, and we have an environmental group here that I think has a very good job of vigilance to make sure that we don't soil our nest, and none of us would want to do that, but things do happen. Obviously, you're going to have a train crash or a major earthquake and create all sorts of environmental issues. I'm a practical person; as far as I'm concerned, the way you sell your state for people to live here and to recreate here and to even build a business here is that the sky is clear and the water is pure.

SCOTT THOMPSON: I think we already have a lot of rules in place so that something like Tar Creek couldn't happen again, but the genesis of a part of the big problems at Tar Creek were that the federal government kind of operated in lieu of the Tribe or Tribes in terms of the ownership and the management of the mining and the mining material and all that. It's about the property, the use of the property, and the future of the property is looked at as more valuable than it used to be, I believe personally. So, I think that will drive a lot of the land-use decisions that you just can't do this anymore. You can't look at all these properties as something you can waste and walk away from.

EARL HATLEY, Cherokee, environmental activist, co-founder of LEAD Agency, Grand Riverkeeper: It's been a great success really, and when I look back on everything, it's been very successful until right up to the past few years. The projects going on right now are so big and so hard that victories don't come like they used to—dealing with climate change and pipelines and fracking and stuff like that. There's no real solutions. I mean solutions are too vague and organizing takes a few grand. It's like Jesus!

More and more, the local issues are morphing into the big picture, because those are the local issues now. There used to be an incinerator here, or a landfill there or whatever. Now, a pipeline here takes on the whole fossil fuel thing. You can't just fight a pipeline because you are taking on the whole industry. You can't take on fracking in a particular place or a particular state because you take on the whole industry, and on top of it all is climate change. The whole thing has to be woven together and that's hard. And in Oklahoma of all places, because it's the center of it all. I'm finding myself in a quagmire deeper than Tar Creek, and Tar Creek's not gonna be cleaned up in my lifetime and so I'm now in a corner and my issues are bigger than me and I am just going, *holy shit...*

Give me an issue and I can win. Just so I'll have one under my belt for a little bit so I can brag about it. (laughs) Just once every year. Just to feel good. That's all I've got left, you know. Tar Creek, pipelines, fracking, and climate change. Wait a minute, what else is there? I've got blue-green algae in my watershed. Eighty percent of Missouri's poultry industry is shitting in my watershed.

HARPER'S WEEKLY
JOURNAL OF CIVILIZATION.

VOL. XXV.—No. 1286.
Copyright, 1881, by Harper & Brothers.

FOR THE WEEK ENDING AUGUST 13, 1881.

TEN CENTS A COPY.
$4.00 PER YEAR, IN ADVANCE.

THE GOVERNOR AND THE PEOPLE OF NEW YORK DEFIED.

SLUDGE METAL

Newtown Creek is a four-mile stretch of water in the middle of New York City that forms the natural border between northern Brooklyn and southern Queens. On the Brooklyn side of the Creek is a former industrial and manufacturing neighborhood called Greenpoint. Greenpoint was born before zoning laws existed, and popped up alongside the factories where people worked on the waterfront throughout the 19th century.

In this half of the book, we look at the shocking degree of pollution in the Newtown Creek vicinity and how it has continued to spread throughout Greenpoint. We investigate how it got there, the impact, and how the community galvanized itself around finding solutions and their continued commitment to take back their town from the legacy of industrial-strength pollution.

Throughout the industrial revolution and until somewhat recently, generations of Polish immigrants and Puerto Ricans have made Greenpoint their home while working in the local manufacturing industries. Artists were attracted to the cheap studio space available within some of the closing factories as well as its proximity to Manhattan. The rising rents in Williamsburg and Manhattan

OPPOSITE PAGE: The cover of *Harpers Weekly*, August 13, 1881.

brought an overflow of students, hipsters, and assorted young professionals into Greenpoint during the 1990s and early 2000s. Hot on the heels of these trendy in-movers were the global real estate speculators. Greenpoint was designated a Superfund site in 2010 during the peak era of its gentrification.

I lived in Greenpoint for several years and was part of that wave of young creative people in the mid-2000s. I remember where I was in 2010 hearing on National Public Radio when it was designated a Superfund site, and recall hearing anecdotal scraps about its history here and there. I did not know the profound extent of the pollution until conducting the inquiry and interviews contained in the following pages.

Hunters Point and Maspeth, Queens residents have also dealt with many of the same issues over the years. That part of Queens wasn't zoned for residential use through much of its history. They have suffered many of the same pollution problems as Greenpoint. More recently, issues of gentrification and overpopulation have emerged since the rezoning for mixed usage of residential and industrial properties. Giant towers have been built along the mouth of Newtown Creek, creating even more density.

People in Greenpoint have lived with several underground spills, fumes, cancers, raw sewage smells, waste transfer stations, truck pollution, an incinerator, and several other egregious abuses of their right to a healthy home.

This book is a snapshot. The people in this story are a part of Greenpoint's history of activism yet they don't all agree. The unchecked pollution has affected generations of Greenpointers—that's tens of thousands of people. I only met a few of them.

2002

RIVERKEEPER is a global environmental watchdog organization. Their primary purpose is to empower citizens to be the eyes on the water to report any polluting, with the goal of collecting evidence to assist in enforcement of clean water laws and regulations. They were founded in 1966 in New York by a group of local fishermen and led by Bob Boyle, an avid outdoorsman and writer for *Sports Illustrated*. Riverkeeper has done some incredible things over the years. One function of the group is patrolling the world's waterways monitoring water quality and looking for any evidence of polluters. It's proven to be a useful model for enforcing environmental law in the area. Unlike other groups who use protest and defiance to stop pollution, Riverkeeper uses lawyers. Their legal actions have successfully brought several species of aquatic life back into the Hudson River.

In 2002, while on a routine patrol along New York City's East River, Riverkeeper's boat captain John Lipscomb and chief investigator Basil Seggos were about to stumble onto an environmental disaster that would change the course of history in New York City and the fate of an entire neighborhood in America's most populous borough. Well-known by locals, Newtown Creek was the site of 150 years of industrial pollution. Politicians had ignored it for decades, and it was about to move into mainstream New York City politics.

> *But New Yorkers forget, or don't know, that a much larger oil spill sits in our own backyard: an estimated 17 million to 30 million gallons of oil, benzene, naphtha and other carcinogenic chemicals pollute Newtown Creek and a 55-acre, 25-foot-deep swath of soil in Greenpoint, Brooklyn.*[49]

BASIL SEGGOS, Commissioner of the New York State Department of Environmental Conservation (DEC), former Chief Investigator for Riverkeeper: I believe I was the first chief investigator that we had at Riverkeeper. My job was working with our team and with municipalities, and working with environmental groups up and down the Hudson to investigate allegations of pollution on the Hudson and its tributaries, look to places where perhaps people or communities are being impacted by problems, and try to merge that knowledge, as investigators, with solutions.

---

49. Alex Prud'homme. "Opinion | An Oil Spill Grows in Brooklyn." *The New York Times*, May 15, 2010.

Oil and trash in English Kills, Newtown Creek, May 5, 2003. Photo courtesy of Riverkeeper.

JUSTIN BLOOM, former attorney for Riverkeeper, Sarasota Waterkeeper: I'd have been working for Hudson Riverkeeper for probably a year. And we were based in Garrison, New York, which is kind of like mid-Hudson Valley and most of the work traditionally had been dealing with Hudson Valley environmental issues. But I and a number of my colleagues were living in the city and had an increasing interest in our backyard, environmental issues particularly in the Harlem River and the [New York] Harbor. And we started becoming involved in some of the other local environmental organizations in the city.

Basil was our investigator at the time, also living in the city. And we were all young guys that wanted to kind of strike out into new turf, where Hudson Riverkeeper, like I said, had been primarily a Hudson Valley organization or folks that were focused on Hudson Valley issues.

There are a number of different Waterkeeper programs in the New York City metropolitan, broader region. Nobody was really focusing on New York City. So Basil got with our boat captain, John Lipscomb.

BASIL SEGGOS: We were, as you probably know from talking with others, that Riverkeeper—John Lipscomb in particular, who's on the boat on the water on a regular basis—we were fielding many complaints up and down the river and helping to address all these lingering problems with legacy pollution as well as new contamination.

JOHN LIPSCOMB, Riverkeeper, Vice President of Advocacy, patrol boat operator· The only reason I'm with Riverkeeper is that the patrol boat was brought to my boatyard that I was managing in Nyack in... when was it exactly... it was '98, and we had to put a new engine in her, and through that we were working on the boat. I love the boat because she's all business. She's just work—not a yacht at all. That kind of wooden boat that is a service vessel, is very appealing to me. I'm a real sucker for that kind of boat.

[Bob] Boyle[50] enlisted me. He wanted the boat campaigned hard. He wanted the boat to live up to its potential as an ambassador, as a patrol boat, as a flagship, as a platform for research that would benefit the river. To be honest, I don't know how these things happen. He said to me, "I'd like your résumé." He had done his homework, he knew what was going on, and he knew about the film work [I did]. He knew about the lifelong relationship with vessels. And he knew that I was a homeboy from the Hudson Valley. I started in September of 2000, working for Boyle and the new president who had just been hired, Alex Matthiessen.

I had worked along its shores for years in the boatyards and stuff, but I knew nothing about it as a living river. I knew nothing about its ecology. It was a leap off of a high diving board and it's been a steep learning curve ever since. What I ended up understanding about myself is that it's easier to make sense of it when you're well down the road.

I just started having to figure out, well, what would a patrol look like? What is this job that I got? You know, there's no manual. You can't Google it. I just decided, I'm going to start running from New York Harbor to Troy. That's 155 miles of estuary.

I started patrolling. The design was based on, if you're sitting on the front steps of your home, and a police car goes zooming by down the street, in your mind, whether you are aware of it or not, you're thinking that's some business somewhere else. That cop is not interested in where you are. I thought about it, *well, if that same cop comes back tomorrow, and comes down the road at five miles an hour, and the cop is looking out the window*—if it's nighttime, he's using the spotlight; the daytime, he's looking left, looking right, looking left, looking right; windows are open and he's going five miles an hour—you start looking around. You say, what's going on here? What's happening right here? Why is there interest here? That's how I design these patrols.

I want to see what's happening, because I *do* see things that I have to deal with, but just as important, I want people on the trains, I want people in Riverdale,

50. Robert Boyle (1929–2017), founder of Riverkeeper.

I want people in Hastings and Dobbs and Tarrytown and Irvington and you name it—I want them to see Riverkeeper patrolling like that cop coming down your street at five miles an hour.

That's the game. Because deterrence is clearly a part of it. You can't measure deterrence. You can't measure what never happened because you were there. But take any community and take away law enforcement and see what happens. (laughs) It's not pretty.

BASIL SEGGOS: Our organization at the time, when I was there, had not been very present in New York City. We had enough to work on up and down the Hudson River. But John had not spent much time in the Harbor. I certainly hadn't either, so back in the fall of 2002, we decided that we would take the boat down to the Harbor and see what we could find knowing that the city had a number of environmental issues. We had major issues back then with wastewater and a few other legacy contamination issues.

JUSTIN BLOOM: Basil and John collaborate on putting together some New York City patrols with our patrol, some of which I joined. Through that process we were doing a routine patrol and ducked into Newtown Creek and discovered the terrible water quality conditions. It was pretty evident that there was a very sick creek.

BASIL SEGGOS: We go take a look at it. Neither of us knew anything about Newtown Creek, but we very quickly learned about it when we were there. I think I used to say back in the day, it was like stepping back in time, taking the boat up Newtown Creek and seeing a waterway that has been so horribly abused and neglected with communities very close to the shoreline. To me, at the time, it was shocking. It was not something you'd expect to see in the U.S. Nonetheless, especially right in the middle of a major metropolitan area, viewable from the Statue of Liberty or the Empire State Building.

JOHN LIPSCOMB: Basil was aboard for one of the patrols, and we had just stuck to the mainstem East River. We were looking at the chart together, and decided, "Let's go over and look in Newtown Creek." We ran in there, and when you get off, at the Meeker Avenue area, there was oil on the water everywhere. Not just rainbow sheen, but weathered oil that sort of looks like little panels of oil. It's almost like a sheet of material that is crinkled a little bit. It was a mess. I mean, it was so bad. I hated—I hated running the boat in it, it was so nasty.

Automobile in English Kills, Newtown Creek, May 5, 2003. Photo courtesy of Riverkeeper.

PAUL PULLO, former owner of Metro Fuels: In the 1980s I could walk the Creek, go to the dock here and on different days see things floating. Animals, cars, bodies.

BASIL SEGGOS: We took an adventure up the creek and found literally dozens of contamination sites. Then obviously this shoreline that was just bleeding oil into the creek, so much so that there were rainbow sheens on the shoreline all over the surface of the water and floating black oil product on the surface.

PAUL PULLO: Oil sheens, every time it rained there would be oil sheen for sure. Oil sheens were always a problem. Just garbage, I mean, just everything. It was like people were using the Creek as a sewer.

JUSTIN BLOOM: When the guys came back and described the conditions, we started ground-truthing it.

When we first were looking at it, we just couldn't figure out where this oil is coming from. There's sheen on water. There was a kind of oil, but it seemed to be dripping from the bulkheads and seawalls yet there were no reports of spills, but obviously it was an old heavily industrial area. We had to drill down through documents as well as follow-up investigations where we ultimately started doing

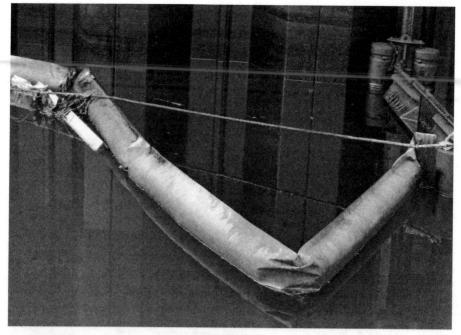

Oil boom floating in Newtown Creek, May 5, 2003. Photo courtesy of Riverkeeper.

some water sampling. For one investigation, we brought the boat into Newtown Creek, and then Basil and I launched a dinghy to paddle around because it gets really shallow up at the head of the creek.

Basil and I paddled around trying to find additional sources or whatever these sources of contamination were. It was like Joseph Conrad's *Heart of Darkness* but in a perverted way—not wilderness but urban decay. There were a few fish we saw were up right towards the surface kind of gulping for air. The water was obviously depleted in oxygen levels and a really sick creek with abandoned or old industry lining the shores.

JOHN LIPSCOMB: Basil had done his homework and we determined that there was a legacy spill. And that the property was owned by Exxon, and that the spills on the property undoubtedly dated back to the Rockefeller era of Standard Oil.

BASIL SEGGOS: It was hard to determine the source because there was so much free product floating on the surface that it didn't have a discrete source. There were a few booms that had been set up along the shoreline, these sort of floating plastic barriers and also these sort of white absorbent socks that were floating in the water. When we first saw these booms, they were badly damaged and partially submerged, so whatever they had been meant to contain, it certainly wasn't working at the time.

I don't have the exact distances along the shoreline where we had the sort of visible evidence of oil seeping out, but it was several hundred yards of shoreline that was pretty heavily contaminated and covered with this oil.

The booms are intended as a Band-Aid, as a containment measure. A properly operated boom system would be checked daily for material and would remove the product that was floating behind the boom system. Keep in mind that when oil gets in the water like that, some of the material floats, some of it sinks, some of it evaporates. A boom system is not a long-term solution. A boom system is something you put in place as an interim step to a larger solution. What we were seeing was an interim step that had been almost forgotten or at least poorly managed.

JOHN LIPSCOMB: The DEC (Department of Environmental Conservation) [was] well aware that oil was escaping the shoreline; somewhere between 17 and 30 million gallons of oil had been lost there over time. EPA were aware, the United States Coast Guard was aware, and yet there was virtually nothing being done to prevent that oil from seeping through the shoreline bulkhead for the rest of time.

BASIL SEGGOS: We ended up launching not just an investigation into the problem but also a community group, the Newtown Creek Alliance. I felt the conditions we were seeing there demanded more than just a simple approach through litigation or through calls to government or through local awareness that one could bring to the problem.

WILLIS ELKINS, activist, Executive Director, Newtown Creek Alliance (NCA): I moved to Greenpoint in 2007 and became interested in the Creek and about its inaccessibility. I got really interested in the idea of getting out on the Creek to see the water, and bought an inflatable kayak and started going out paddling. I learned about Newtown Creek Alliance and met a handful of people that were already sort of involved.

Obviously people knew about the oil and there was remediation work in place, but there were still sites where active oil coming out of the bulkheads. Riverkeeper, along with Councilmember David Yassky's office—because he was involved in the city's waterfront committee—we teamed up and got involved with a lot of the residents in Greenpoint who had already been involved in environmental issues, specifically focused on health issues. That was the birth of the Alliance. Right from the start, it was a mix of people who have been here their whole lives or a very long time.

BASIL SEGGOS: We needed a comprehensive solution that engaged all levels of stakeholders from local officials, to state officials, to the local advocates, and the businesses as well. Mind you, there were dozens of businesses on the Creek that were vital to the local economy and we wanted to get to know who they were. Certainly, we've engaged them in the decision-making because a working waterfront was, we believe, even at the time, was imperative for the future of the neighborhoods. It was a full, comprehensive plan. We put that in place and certainly part of it was investigations into the specific problems we saw that day, most notably the Newtown Creek-Greenpoint oil spill.

PAUL PARKHILL, urban planner, former director of planning and development Greenpoint Manufacturing and Design Center (GMDC): [Basil Seggos and Riverkeeper] would show up with their boat and they would visit and talk to us about what they were doing. And it was a friendly, casual relationship for a while, and then it gradually became more formalized as Katie Schmid [first director of NCA] and company, she was working with David Yassky [then New York City Councilman] at the time, started kicking around ideas with the Riverkeeper folks.

Newtown Creek Alliance became a kind of consortium—Riverkeeper, David Yassky, his office, mostly Katie [Schmid], GMDC [Greenpoint Manufacturing and Design Center]. It was an informal advisory board for a while and then they formalized later. But a lot of those early discussions also crystallized around this Brownfield Opportunity Area program, which was relatively young at the time. It's a New York State program that was designed to create planning funds for brownfield[51] areas.

KATE ZIDAR, green infrastructure research engineer, former director of Newtown Creek Alliance: The staff power—the fact that the councilperson allocated a staff member who would do things like write up an agenda, reserve a room—makes the thing go, and then the original members, individual representatives of the Alliance. Riverkeeper was just there on day one. Because of their presence on the water, they were really bringing out the eyes of the community. There wasn't a harbor watch. Nobody was out there doing kayaking or birdwatching or anything. It was Riverkeeper on their harbor patrol ending up in Newtown Creek watching pipes full of chicken blood being discharged directly into the Creek and seeing active oil spills.

JUSTIN BLOOM: The volume is really massive. You can compare gallons, but it's different because when you look at the Exxon Valdez, that was all immediately released on the surface waters. This was a massive amount of oil, but it was somewhat contained in the groundwater and was slowly leaking out. If compared in raw volume, it's up there.

---

51. Brownfield: a former industrial or commercial site where future use is affected by real or perceived environmental contamination.

JOHN LIPSCOMB: And now when I go on the Creek with people, I have a Google map that we've made, so I can narrate the history. The map is covered with pushpins—30 pushpins of cases. Some of them are little, and some of them are Exxon.

My role in the beginning was really support and also a voice for not being timid. *Let's just fight. Let's not try to weigh the chances of winning. Let's fight.* At that time it was a new generation at Riverkeeper with people like Basil and myself, and we weren't tired yet. We just went for it. Looking back, what happened on the Exxon case was really textbook.

MODERN-DAY NEW YORKERS DON'T KNOW IT'S HERE

NEWTOWN CREEK is an 11-mile long creek, reshaped by dredging, to accommodate the manufacturing businesses built during the past 150 years along its banks. For decades most of it has been obscured by heavy industry, which probably explains why most New Yorkers don't even know it's there. Until fairly recently, there was no place for the public to access the Creek. Therefore, understandably, the Creek is overlooked by busy New Yorkers, including many who have lived in the surrounding neighborhoods.

Newtown Creek passes alongside Greenpoint, Bushwick, Williamsburg on the Brooklyn side and then Hunters Point, Maspeth, Ridgewood, Sunnyside, and Long Island City on the Queens side. These names can be confusing, so I'm going to attempt to clarify a few things. Long Island City is a neighborhood in Queens, not to be confused with Long Island, which is one of New York City's five boroughs (Manhattan, Brooklyn, Queens, Long Island, and Staten Island). Hunters Point is a neighborhood within the Long Island City section of Queens. It was initially the name for the entire area surrounding the Creek until the name Greenpoint eventually stuck for the region just south of Newtown Creek in Brooklyn.

There are several famous articles in *Harper's Weekly* from 1881 that detail the pollution smell coming off of Newtown Creek that was wafting across the East River into Manhattan. The Hunter's Point in the article is referring to modern-day Greenpoint. According to historian Geoffrey Cobb, "I've gone back and about the earliest research that I've seen writing about Greenpoint is circa the Civil War. And it was already used by that time as a reference. I had been told earlier at various points it had been called Cherry Point, because of the number of cherry trees that grew there. But I'd say around the Civil War, it's already called Greenpoint."

Like much of New York City, what we know about Greenpoint's origin story dates back to the Dutch's imperialist ambitions of the 17th century.

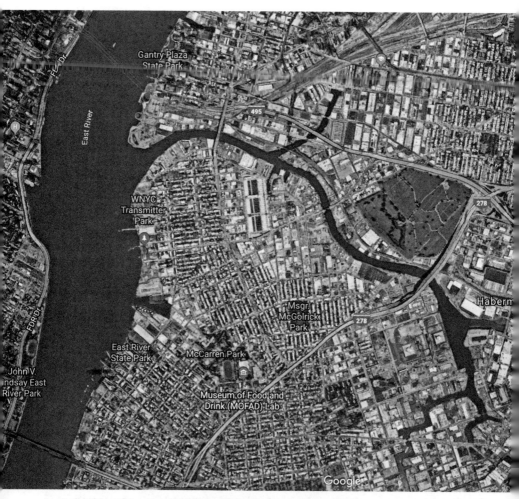

Aerial photo of Newtown Creek, New York City. Screenshot from Google Earth taken on June 11, 2019.

As by means of water-carriage a more extensive market is opened to every sort of industry than what land-carriage alone can afford it, so it is upon the sea-coast, and along the banks of the navigable rivers, that industry of every kind naturally begins to subdivide and improve itself, and it is frequently not till a long time after those improvements extend themselves to the inland parts of the country.[52]

52. "Chapter III: That Division of Labour Is Limited by the Extent of the Market." *The Wealth of Nations*, by Adam Smith and Edwin Cannan, 5th ed., Bantam Books, 1776, pp. 26–28.

MITCH WAXMAN, historian for Newtown Creek Alliance, blogger: I was working in advertising about 20 hours a day at the time and I ended up getting sick. I had a heart attack. As a part of the recovery process, the doctor told me, "I want you to start running." I come from Canarsie in Brooklyn and the only time we run is when someone or something is chasing us.

I started walking and brought the camera along to make it interesting. One day I was schlepping around from Astoria, heading south, and all of a sudden, I found this waterway that I knew nothing about.

Growing up in New York City, the notion that I knew nothing about Newtown Creek, I didn't even know it was there, just intrigued the hell out of me. I started looking into it, doing some research, and it's this proverbial puddle that you reach into, that you go to touch and you end up to your shoulder in it. It's one of the most incredible places in New York City and the notion that so many modern-day New Yorkers don't even know it's here was just astounding to me. Then I started finding out about how this is the birthplace of Mobil Oil. Great American corporations were born here and nobody outside of Greenpoint knows that.

CAROL KNUDSON, Riverkeeper, water research assistant at Lamont-Doherty Earth Observatory: I say [to people] it's a border between Queens and Brooklyn and they don't really know that either.

BASIL SEGGOS: I think if you had talked to a New Yorker 20 years ago and asked about the waterfront, they would say *what waterfront?* Today it's totally different. New Yorkers have completely rediscovered the waterfront. You look at the West Side Highway back in the 1990s when I first moved to the city, it was still under construction. It was still in that transition phase from what used to be a bunch of warehouses fenced off, no promenade, just a highway itself. Now, it's the Hudson River Park from the Battery all the way up above the George Washington Bridge—a world-class destination.

It's the same thing in Brooklyn, the Brooklyn promenade, all the housing on the East River, those massive skyscrapers. Twenty to thirty years ago, people were just not going down to the waterfront. The waterfront was a working waterfront. The waterfront was dirty, it was polluted. It's been such a change in that, over the course of the last generation, that now people have rediscovered it. The fact that they haven't necessarily rediscovered Newtown Creek may not be as surprising because it is a small working waterway that goes back into relatively inaccessible parts of the two boroughs.

What we've we found, as we began to break the story back in the early 2000s, was that people were shocked to hear not just that there was a creek called Newtown Creek, but that there was one of the largest oil spills in the country, just flowing underground into the Creek right in the middle of New York City.

GEOFFREY COBB, teacher, historian, author *Greenpoint Brooklyn's Forgotten Past*, blogger Greenpointers: Greenpoint was never inhabited by Native Americans because it was an estuary and periodically flooded. Obviously, you don't want to live on land that floods. So they lived in Maspeth, which comes from the Algonquin word for "place of bad water," *Mespeatches*, which was corrupted into *Maspeth*. The Native Americans lived in harmony with nature. And when the Europeans got there, they began a very long process of altering the landscape. One of those features that got wiped out was a bit of land that extended off of Freeman Street that was covered with grass. It was at Greenpoint that sailors could use it as they navigated the East River.

Neziah Bliss is a really interesting character. He was born in Connecticut, I believe in 1790. As a young man, he becomes a friend of Robert Fulton. Fulton teaches him how to build steam engines. He then goes out West, makes a fortune building steamboats, but then he came back to New York and set up a shipyard in the Lower East Side.

But he kept looking across to Greenpoint, which was verdant farmland. In 1834 he bought a piece of riverfront land of 31 acres. Bliss then married the only daughter of one of the original families, the Meserole family. He put together a piece of land and then he envisioned it as a shipbuilding community, because he saw was that shipbuilding was getting pushed out of Manhattan and would eventually come to the other shore. He had the land surveyed and had streets laid out. Just as his real estate venture was sort of taking off, a financial panic of 1837 hit. He was able to weather the panic and he was considered the founder of Greenpoint.

Neziah Bliss' wife, who was a very rich woman, the mother of a Congresswoman, this was her home. She had grown up here and she was very attached to the church. My summation is that she and a number of other people left because it had just started to become a fetid place to live. And then as Irish immigrants established themselves, they left. I think that's because people were aware that when it stank, it wasn't a healthy place to live.

MITCH WAXMAN: The second industrial revolution. The age of scientific manufacturing is what they called it at the time. That was the manufactured gas industry. That was the fertilizer mills. There's a whole series of industries, particularly on the Queens side, that served the carriage trade.

They were all pretty gruesome from the modern point of view. They all involved taking parts of animals, either boiling them or burning them or whatever to try and free up organic compounds which were used in the animals. Those compounds were used in the construction of those shiny old black Victorian-era carriages. These were notoriously smelly industries and they also produced a lot of organic waste. There was absolutely no law stopping these companies from

New York City views. Branch of Newtown Creek, November 12, 1952. Photo by Samuel Gottscho. Photo courtesy of Library of Congress Prints and Photographs Division, Washington, D.C.

just disposing of the waste into the marshes and swamps that would surround their properties.

By the time that the oil guys came around in the 1880s and '90s, there were parties to celebrate that these older industries were being moved out and that the oil refineries were coming in. Because the community surrounding the Creek actually thought it was going to be the end of the smell problem. There's a great series in *Harper's Weekly* that was published in 1881 that talked about the smell problem with Newtown Creek as it affected Manhattan.

July 1894: Two boys, apparently brothers, drowned after they evidently got caught in the "ooze and slime" at the bottom of the creek, which is composed of soft sediment.[53]

PAUL PULLO: This was marshes and a dump. They were just dumping everything here from dead animals to garbage and everything else. The smells back then I'm sure were much worse. They always thought that. If you look through history, you will find people complaining about the odors around Newtown Creek.

GEOFFREY COBB: Already by 1870, there was such an odor that was emanating from the creek. So that we're wafting across the East River to Murray Hill, this very affluent section of Manhattan, and people were complaining about it. But here what I noticed was that richer residents or more established residents of Greenpoint were moving out.

During the industrial boom of the 1890s, local activists calling themselves the Fifteenth Ward Smelling Committee paddled up the Creek seeking the polluters responsible for the foul stenches wafting from the once-pristine waterway. They had plenty to choose from: glue-makers and fertilizer processors produced plenty of noxious by-product. But the oil refineries were the worst offenders: Workers transferring oil and solvents from one part of the plant to

53. Sewell Chan. "Newtown Creek's Deadly History." *The New York Times*, April 7, 2008.

VOL. XXV.—No. 1287.
Copyright, 1881, by Harper & Brothers.

FOR THE WEEK ENDING AUGUST 20, 1881.

TEN CENTS A COPY.
$4.00 PER YEAR, IN ADVANCE.

LET US HAVE A CLEAN SWEEP ALL AROUND NEW YORK.
THE NEXT TASK FOR HERCULES COLEMAN.

Illustration of Hunters Point's stench wafting across the river. *Harper's Weekly* cover August 20, 1881.

another inevitably spilled; storage tanks leaked; and the process of distilling oil to make kerosene, paraffin wax, naphtha, gasoline, and fuel oil left all sorts of junk. "If roughly 5 percent of the initial crude petroleum consumed by the refineries ended up as coke residue, gas, or other loss, as the contemporary literature suggested," writes historian Andrew Hurley, "each of New York's petroleum districts would have produced the equivalent of 300,000 gallons of waste material each week during the 1880s." What couldn't be resold or burned up was simply dumped on the ground or into the water. There were more than 50 refineries in Greenpoint in 1870, and by 1892, Standard Oil owned most of them.[54]

GEOFFREY COBB: They [Fifteenth Ward Smelling Committee] actually dared one of the guys to open a vat of water from the Creek because it was that harmful.

MITCH WAXMAN: Van Iderstine's was a rendering factory. It was huge and would collect butcher's blood, meat scraps, rotten eggs, pack animals which had died on the streets of New York, poop—anything organic. They'd bring it back to the plant where they would essentially boil it down to its constituents.

The main product they were seeking was tallow, and we associate tallow with candles. But in a pre-petroleum industrial economy, tallow was the preferred lubricant oil for iron- and steel-based machinery. There was a real market for this stuff. It was recycling at a level that the modern age is not ready for, because it's the really ugly form of recycling with a lot of stink and a lot of other chemicals that came off it, but they were experts in the 19th century about finding a dollar in a penny. The material that burned off Van Iderstine's property would then be sold to somebody further up the Creek, who would use it to manufacture acid or use it to manufacture fertilizer. Don't forget this is the age of Phillip Armour's[55] "Every part of the pig but the squeal" era of American business, and waste in any form was not tolerated.

Van Iderstine had a contract with the City of New York that if a large mammal, such as a circus elephant or a giraffe or camel happened to be in the city at the time, was to die, then they can handle it for the City of New York. They brought a circus elephant in, hauled it up on a crane, they had a special set of jaws for their grinder, and they literally just fed the elephant directly into the grinder and what came out the other side just went right into rendering vats.

---

54. Daphne Eviatar. "The Ooze." Daily Intelligencer, *New York Magazine*, 3 June 2007.

55. Philip Danforth Armour (1832–1901) was an American industrial capitalist of the period following the Civil War. He helped build meatpacking into a great industry by using new technology and working out distribution methods for domestic and foreign markets.

It was something that they were left with that they couldn't find a market for, which could be something that from the modern-day point of view doesn't necessarily look like a horrible pollutant. It's organic material, but you have to remember the volume of organic material pouring into the waterway was massive. On top of that, you had all the other manufacturers, the petroleum guys and the copper people and so on, that were just literally opening pipes into the water for anything. At the beginning, Standard Oil actually released naphtha and gasoline which were by-products of the petroleum process. They had no market for it so they just let it loose into the water.

PAUL PULLO, former owner of Metro Fuels: I was actually at Van Iderstine and I smelled it personally. The smell of the neighborhood was terrible. When I was in grammar school, I started working at a local butcher shop as a delivery boy and worked as a butcher through high school and two years of college.

They would come by in a truck. We would put all the animal extra pieces, the bones and extra fat and stuff into basically garbage pails, and the truck would come and pick it up and bring it to a place like Van Iderstine where they would melt it and cook it. I don't have to tell you. In the summertime, these trucks alone, it didn't smell very well.

GEOFFREY COBB: One of the things that was evidently horrific was bone rendering plants, and they used sulfuric acid, but they would take the carcasses of dead animals and put chemicals on them so that the last vestiges of skin were removed.

There was a time when the sugar industry, which was the largest industry in Brooklyn for decades, they whitened the sugar using animal bone. There was a premium on that. The bone rendering plants also smelled to high hell. There were fertilizer plants, which I guess they used manure. There were huge barges of cow shit and animal shit that would come down Newtown Creek to be turned into fertilizer. They produced sulfuric acid.

MITCH WAXMAN: Most of the industrial activity happened in Brooklyn. Most of the business activity in Greenpoint was focused on a very narrow strip on the East River, but most of it was on Newtown Creek.

The East Side of Manhattan was super active. They would work animals to death. They would work people to death. Whatever you could make a penny off of, you would get. They would sell the dead horse to an operator who had a contract with the city of Brooklyn, the city of Manhattan, like Conrad Wissel and his night soil and offal dock, or they would sell it to Van Iderstine's or they would sell it to one of the bone breakers or they would sell it to a fertilizer mill.

The bone-blackers were part of the process. Van Iderstine would boil away the meat and then they had a bunch of essentially soggy wet bones. They would sell it to the guy who's next up on the Long Island railroad tracks, who then run them through furnaces and come out with carbon black. There were two versions of that, which came out of their furnaces. One went to the manufactured gas people to be used as activated charcoal, the other would be mixed with a kind of oil that you get from cooking horses and goats to what's called meat oil. That's what they would rub on the wooden carriages to make them that shiny black color. Nothing got wasted.

There were even straight-up acid factories, and the effluent that would come out of these plants was a material called sludge acid. They would send kids out with pails that had glass linings, and they would go right down to the shoreline and then they scooped this stuff up, bring it up to the wagon and put it in a glass tank, then it would go and be refined and then sold as a household acid. We don't have acids in our houses today but back then, having some sulfuric acid around was handy.

[Conrad Wissel] came into the historic record because he was basically a criminal. He had a contract with the city of Brooklyn and the City of New York. This is before we had modern-day sewer infrastructure. You would use an out-house, or you use a privy with a privy pod. The material that we all deposit in the modern porcelain every morning is called night soil. In parts of the world that you'll see a lot of endemic diseases, they actually use night soil to fertilize their crops. It creates a parasitic loop where people are getting infected with ascariasis and other parasitic diseases because, essentially, they're using their own poop to fertilize the food they eat.

New York City wasn't using night soil to fertilize backyard gardens. Instead, they would ship it. They would bring it to a central location on the shoreline. Wissel would show up with a barge and all this material would get loaded onto the barge. It was then supposed to be brought back to the end of Maspeth Avenue where his night soil and offal dock was. Offal are the inedible parts of an animal you would butcher for meat, which is kind of en vogue right now with the hipsters who eat the offal. It's essentially organ meat: viscera, eyes, the connective tissue and so on. You're talking about a population that ate a lot of meat, so a lot of offal and all this stuff was instantly going to start stinking if it was outside.

The idea was that Wissel was going to pick up the material from Brooklyn at a central location, and in Manhattan at a central location, and then bring it back where he would then sell it to the various secondary places. Wissel would then wait until he got out into the East River, and he had rigged up his barge with a false bottom, so he could just open a hatch and the stuff would just fall into the water. Then people noticed these huge slicks of raw sewage and animal parts which the health inspectors of New York State, another political machine, then focused on.

A lot of the stories that have persisted through the municipal journals and the Health Department documentation, when you start looking at why: Why did they take notice in this year? Why did the smelling committee form in 1883? Oh, well,

Governor Roswell P. Flower, Governor of New York State had, through agents and secondary purchasing agents, bought up a gigantic portion of what's now Long Island City. That was now his property. It was called the Sunken Meadows.

One of the best things he could do to improve the chances of him making some money was to get rid of the Van Iderstines and to get rid of all these [stink factories]. This is part of the 19th-century milieu that is alien to the 21st-century mind.

That would have been nothing back then. The mayor of New York City is accused of taking payoffs from a real estate developer. That's just the way it was.

Again, it's a whole different universe, a whole different mindset, and that's one of the difficult things from talking about Newtown Creek. It seems obvious to a modern 21st-century mind that you're not going to throw garbage in a river. It's fairly obvious, right? There's cultural taboo about it, you'll be shamed. Back then, throwing garbage in the water was just how you got rid of garbage.

Heavy industry grew along the Creek in the ensuing decades, and during the 1920s and 1930s, the Newtown Creek was dredged and widened to accommodate bigger barges. By then, all kinds of industrial businesses lined the shores. Sugar refineries, hide tanners, canneries, copper wiring producers and even soap makers joined the refineries and oil storage facilities that employed thousands of people, but at a major ecological cost that wouldn't be realized for decades.[56]

MITCH WAXMAN: Nichols Chemical, later General Chemical, had set up on the Creek as early as the 1840s and that was way back in Maspeth.

GEOFFREY COBB: Phelps Dodge the smelter was spitting out all of that stuff. The amazing thing is, it was done in such a concentrated area.

PAUL PARKHILL: Phelps Dodge is a copper and chemical conglomerate that was started in Queens and is now based in Phoenix, Arizona. It makes sense that they followed the resources. They built Laurel Hill Works.

There have been different phases over the course of time. In the process of refining copper, they also discovered other precious minerals, so, they could come up with whole processes for extracting precious minerals out of ore. It was the employer of an entire neighborhood.

56. The Old Timer. "The Dirty Yet Important History of the Newtown Creek: Our Neighborhood, The Way It Was." QNS.com, 31 Mar 2018.

Laurel Hill, which is I think among the more interesting in neighborhoods in all of New York City, is still probably the only neighborhood that is increasingly becoming more manufacturing than residential. It's the hill above the old Laurel Hill work site, which is now a Restaurant Depot. Phelps Dodge built the town. It was for the workers of Laurel Hill Works— a factory town. Everybody would just walk down the hill to the plant. It's now completely encased in highway. There's the LIE [Long Island Expressway], there's the BQE [Brooklyn Queens Expressway], there's the Kosciuszko Bridge. There's nowhere to go.

It was a case study in the company town phenomenon. They were producing all kinds of toxic stuff and that all ended up in the ground. It all ended up in the Creek. The Creek was purple and green and yellow and orange at different times of the day, back in those days.

RELY ON THE NEW LAW

FOR RELIEF FROM NEWTOWN CREEK STENCH FACTORIES.

The efforts made by the Brooklyn Health authorities to break up the various stench factories along Newtown Creek were brought to naught yesterday by the decision of Judge Van Wyck of the City Court in continuing an injunction restraining the city from interfering with the Peter Cooper Glue Company.

In this opinion Judge Van Wyck holds that if the companies agree to use properly-closed carts for transporting their stock and cease using putrescent stock in their factories, they are entitled to an injunction.

But he adds that this test case was made up and evidence submitted before the Legislature passed the Anti-Bone-Boiling act, and that he has not passed upon that law at all.

Health Commissioner Griffin was evidently expecting this determination of the old suits, for he had an entirely new procedure mapped out for the future yesterday. He instructed R. F. Strauss, counsel for the department, to call in Corporation Counsel Jenks and make up a case upon which to apply to the Supreme Court for an injunction to restrain the companies from carrying on business, basing the action on the Anti-Bone-Boiling act.

In addition, a taxpayer is to be induced to bring a test suit for damages to his property by reason of the presence of these factories. The city is to bear all expenses.

The New York Times, July 26, 1892.

PAUL PULLO: There were days it was actually neon colors. It would change colors. I remember oranges and greens. I remember total discoloration. I use the word neon. What I was told back then was the colors were from Phelps Dodge.

MITCH WAXMAN: In 1838 Peter Cooper had set up a complex of glue factories on the border of modern-day Williamsburg and Greenpoint. He was followed by Martin Kalbfleisch and Sons Chemical Company in 1842, which was established along English Kills tributary near Furman's Island, in Greenpoint/East Williamsburg, who also set up a huge complex not too far from Cooper. They were manufacturing various chemical applications. Famously, that's where Peter Cooper invented Jell-O brand gelatin, which is... if you like Jell-O, never look at what it actually is.

GEOFFREY COBB: In the 1920s the Creek was so toxic that ships used to sail into it because it would kill all the barnacles on the side by the time you sailed out. No more barnacles. No more sea urchins.

STANDARD OIL

THE SECOND HALF of the 19th century was a time of tremendous growth for the United States, and business on Newtown Creek was booming. By the mid-1800s, Newtown Creek was a world-class industrial port—serving the growing consumer needs of the country's largest metropolis. The Creek had been widened a few times during this period to accommodate the bigger barges and the new boat traffic.

In 1854, inventor Abraham Gesner opened New York Kerosene and Gas Light Company. This plant was pioneering the field of oil refining. The opening of the plant is part of the shift away from the animal rendering, hide tanning, and bone-blacking type of stink factories, but it didn't happen overnight. According to the Environmental Protection Agency, it was two years after Gesner's kerosene factory opened when, in 1856, the city began dumping raw sewage directly into the Creek. According to the *New York Times*, "the city's sewers dumped an estimated 100,000 tons of fecal matter a year into the harbor."

There was a fair amount of press on this at the time. In 1886 the Brooklyn Daily Eagle published a bombshell investigation titled "Oil Refining: How it Affects Newtown Creek and Vicinity," about the acidic sludge blocking the Creek. The city took the sludge out to Barren Island as fertilizer or just dumped it at sea, where it reportedly made its way to Coney Island. A few years later, in 1892, naturalist writer John Muir started The Sierra Club, and the nascent environmental movement was off and running.

Charles Pratt's Astral Oil opened in 1867 and was the cutting-edge industry of its day. It was widely considered the first modern oil refinery. By the 1870s, there were about 50 oil refineries along the Creek. Ten years later, it was closer to one hundred refineries. It was John D. Rockefeller's Standard Oil that was on the rise to become the world's first megacorporation. In the 1890s, he proceeded to crush competitors and consolidate power by taking over all of the oil refineries along Newtown Creek. Standard Oil had become Newtown Creek's most significant business.

The life of John D. Rockefeller has inspired countless articles and books spanning admiration to loathing. Today Rockefeller's name graces buildings and charities and was synonymous with the image of the "self-made man." His lasting mark on philanthropy is calculated to soften his legacy as a notoriously ruthless businessman who built an oil empire. At the time, Rockefeller was welcomed by the neighbors who wanted to get rid of the local *stink factories* and bring in exciting new jobs in chemical manufacturing.

John D. Rockefeller, full-length portrait, walking on street with John D. Rockefeller, Jr., circa 1915. Photo courtesy of Library of Congress Prints and Photographs Division, Washington, D.C.

The country's first kerosene refinery (1854) and first modern oil refinery (1867) brought jobs and infrastructure to the area. By the end of the 19th century, Rockefeller's Standard Oil, which began as Astral Oil Co. in 1880, had over one hundred distilleries on both sides of Newtown Creek. By the 1920s and '30s, the Creek was a major shipping hub and was widened, deepened, and bulkheads were added to accommodate bigger barges. This destroyed all its freshwater sources. Newtown Creek became home to such businesses as sugar refineries, hide tanning plants, canneries, and copper wiring plants.[57]

57. "History of Newtown Creek." *Newtown Creek Alliance.*

MITCH WAXMAN: When the petroleum refineries first came in it was seen as a bit of a boon that they were getting rid of these bone-blackers and these other stink factories—these glue factories, these fertilizer mills. The people at the time were absolutely stoked, because you had the most modern possible industry. You would be too. It would be like the perspective of having Tesla open up a factory in your town. You're not just getting a new source of jobs, you're getting jobs that are on the cutting edge of American technology and they represent the future. It was a complete sea change from what they were doing and they were looking forward instead of looking backward.

GEOFFREY COBB: You've got to bring the oil from other places and here you're situated on the East River, so it's perfect to bring barges in. You can barge the oil in and then you're sitting across from the largest metropolis in the United States at the time. It's perfectly situated to refine oil. Then in 1867 [Rockefeller] finds a large enough piece of available land. You needed large amounts of land to refine oil. Manhattan was already prohibitively expensive to do industrial-scale refining. In 1867 the shipbuilding industry is starting to die. He realizes that he's able to take over a lot of these former shipyards and set up refineries.

MITCH WAXMAN: I am certainly not a fan of John D. Rockefeller and Standard Oil. However, I have to try and remove some of my animus from the conversation when I talk about John D. Rockefeller and I talk about Standard Oil because at the time Rockefeller was not a very popular man in the United States.

You need to look at the economic effect that his companies had on the common working people of Brooklyn and Queens.

When we look at modern-day Greenpoint, particularly Milton Street, Greenpoint Avenue, where you see these beautiful old 1880s and '90s Historic District buildings, every one of them were the homes of oil executives who worked at Standard Oil.

Shortly before the Civil War, in 1854 there was a guy named Abraham Gesner, who was a chemist. He came up with a way to use high-pressure steam to free clear, hot, burning oil from otherwise garbage coal that you wouldn't buy to power a boiler or furnace. He gave that fuel the name kerosene.

Gesner created the New York Kerosene and Gas Light Company on the Queens side of the Creek, right near Cavalry Cemetery. That was the first true large-scale petroleum refinery in the entire country, where we were beginning to get the storable, high-flashpoint fuel sources that have typified the age of petrol. Gesner was the first, and his particular business ended up being acquired by Astral Oil and Charles Pratt before long, and his plant became known as the Pratt Works and we still have issues with Pratt Works today. They're actually a state DEC site now.

By the 1870s, Spotsylvania in Pennsylvania had begun to find crude and at the time, there was a cozy relationship between J.P. Morgan and a few of the other railroad barons, to begin moving this petroleum material into New York for refining. The notion of refining it elsewhere and then selling it locally hadn't evolved yet. There were a number of small family-owned refineries, particularly on the Brooklyn side. There were a few on the Queens side, but it was really a phenomenon in Brooklyn.

GEOFFREY COBB: Charles Pratt developed the first modern oil refinery in the United States. He set up the first oil refinery on the banks of Bushwick Creek in 1867.

MITCH WAXMAN: There's a great story about how Rockefeller agents approached Astral Oil. Charles Pratt and his partners pretty much controlled petroleum in Brooklyn. They were like a little Standard Oil in New York Harbor, and they became fiendishly rich. Rockefeller's agents approached them and said, *We'd like you to come be a part of Standard. If you have any hesitation about this, understand that if you don't come and be a part of Standard, we will put you out of business. We will sell petroleum at a loss. We will use every technique we have to steal away your entire customer base and we will buy your common stock until you're no longer the majority shareholders. So, there's an easy way and a hard way. One way, you become crazy rich. The other way, we destroy you.*

GEOFFREY COBB: So he ends up sitting on the board of Standard Oil and becomes the richest man in Brooklyn. But a lot of the reason why this area became a refining alley is because Pratt identified it as the perfect place to refine oil.

MITCH WAXMAN: That made Charles Pratt the vice president of Standard Oil and put him on the board. It gave Rockefeller his foothold in New York Harbor and also New York politics. By 1890, Standard Oil controlled the entirety of the Brooklyn side of the Creek from where the modern-day Pulaski bridge is, all the way back to where the modern-day Kosciuszko bridge is, which is about a mile and a half of shoreline.

GEOFFREY COBB: One of the things [Rockefeller] did was he drove people out of business. The other thing is—Did Mitch talk to you about Tidewater?

MITCH WAXMAN: There's a building directly across the Creek called Tidewater. For many years, Rockefeller enjoyed a beneficial relationship with the railroads, which would ship his oil at a significant discount as compared to what they would ship the oil of his competitors. Given that the eastern cities were the destination of a lot of the petroleum product, anything that was coming east, Rockefeller either owned shares in the railroad or he had a partnership with the railroad. Again, he had these very good prices.

Anytime the subject of a pipeline came up, however, Standard Oil would have all its political friends in Congress start talking about how dangerous pipelines were, that pipelines could explode, they could flood your fields with oil, and then your farm is going to be useless for the rest of time, that it's going to destroy the world.

Tidewater formed, and it was a cooperative of wellhead owners and refiners, and they established a pipeline that went from Pennsylvania into New York City and it came to the Queens side of Newtown Creek, right opposite the center of the Empire here on the Creek.

The Tidewater collective actually managed to get some market share against them. That's when Rockefeller invented a whole new practice in American business, which is buying 51% of the common stock on the board and replacing the entire board of directors, who then decided instantly to sell Tidewater to Standard Oil. The minute that he owned Tidewater and he owned the pipeline, that's when he flipped on his railroad guys and said railroads are the worst possible way to ship petroleum, and he started building pipelines.

When Rockefeller stopped shipping petroleum that way, it's actually what began the decline of the American railroad industry. We've held on to the pipeline model ever since. It's another one of those business things. You own the means of production, you own the means of end-customer delivery, you actually own the refinery, and now you own the connection directly between the hole in the ground and the customer's gas tank. You've got to appreciate the guy. He foresaw the modern corporate age.

GEOFFREY COBB: Are you familiar with Ida Tarbell who wrote *The History of the Standard Oil Company*?

Where did Ida Tarbell get her information from? Henry Rogers. Henry Rogers slept out many nights with a sleeping bag in the Astral Oil Refinery, because he was the head of production. And then when Rockefeller saw him, he said: *Wow, this guy is a shark; this is the person I'm going to make a corporate empire with to kind of run the United States. This is the kind of guy I want sitting on my board.* And he ended up sitting on a number of boards of Standard Oil.

"The Standard," said Mr. Blanchard, "had a force of men, real estate, houses, tanks and other facilities at Hunter's Point for receiving and coopering the oil; and they had their cooperage materials delivered over there. The arrangement prior to that time was that the Erie Company performed this service for its outside refiners at Weehawken, for which the Erie Company made specific charges and added them to their rates for freight. The Standard Company said to us: 'We do the business at low cost at Hunter's Point because we are expert oil men and know how to handle it; we pay nobody a profit, and cannot and ought not to pay you a profit for a service that is not transportation any more than inspecting flour or cotton; and the New York Central delivers our oil at

Ida Tarbell, photographer unknown, between 1910 and 1930, courtesy of Library of Congress Prints and Photographs Division, Washington, D.C.

that point. Now if you will deliver our oil at Hunter's Point and permit us to do this business, you may do so; we want to do that business, and we cannot pay to the Erie Railway Company at Weehawken a profit on all of those staves, heads, cooperage, filling, refilling and inspection, for we have our own forces of men and our own yards necessary for this work in another part of the harbor of New York; and it is not a part of your business as a carrier anyway.'

"In lieu thereof and for the profits that we could have made from the aggregate of these charges, we said to them: 'If you will pay us a fixed profit upon each one of these barrels of oil arriving here, you may take the yards and run them subject to certain limitations as to what you shall do for other people who continue to ship oil to the same yards.' They were only able to make this arrangement with us because of their controlling such a large percentage of shipment, and because of permanent facilities in Brooklyn; if the larger percentage of shipments had belonged to outside parties, and they had had no yards of their own, we would probably have retained the yards ourselves."

The History of Standard Oil by Ida Tarbell

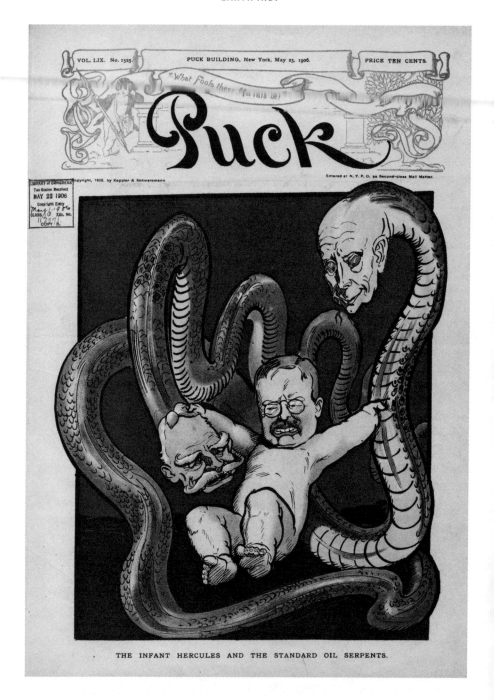

Frank A. Nankivell (1869–1959), *Puck Magazine* cartoon, "The Infant Hercules and the Standard Oil Serpents," May 23, 1906 issue, courtesy of Library of Congress Prints and Photographs Division, Washington, D.C.

GEOFFREY COBB: If memory serves, the Sherman Antitrust Act is 1890. I believe it's Theodore Roosevelt who really starts to break up Standard Oil. You have a window of 17 years where nothing is really done and he's [Rockefeller] able to consolidate. It was America's richest corporation.

MITCH WAXMAN: In many ways it had the opposite effect of what Teddy Roosevelt wanted to happen, which—it didn't encourage competition, what it did was create 34 tiny Standard Oils which then went on to hyper-dominate the local markets because it was no longer, as long as they weren't crossing state lines, Sherman Antitrust Act didn't apply.

Exxon became the de facto oil refiner and deliverer of New Jersey and Mobil of New York and there was brand loyalty. Amoco was the gas station company. They retained a lot of the Standard branding, the Pegasus with the wings, and the torch is emblematic of the torch that used to be on top of the Standard Oil building in Manhattan.

MITCH WAXMAN: You pour gasoline on your economy, it opens up. It suddenly has more energy and it can go for 80–90 years before, you know, you start discovering that there are structural problems based around that hyperactive economy.

If you pour gasoline on yourself, is the guy who's selling it to you, is it his fault? Is it your fault? Is it both your faults? Or is this just the circumstance of the area you live in? Do we look at the people who lived in the Dark Ages who would raid another castle and kill everybody inside in the name of getting to the food and the riches that they had in the castle, do we look at them and call them "asshole," you know what I mean?

Or were they just doing what they had to do?

I always try to think about explaining some of the modern political stuff to my granddad, which, in his mind, everything was great, just more and more businesses. But we've come to a crossroads in our culture where we can't get away from the fact that we need to pay our bills and keep on eating. For 99% of everybody, that's all there is.

It would appear that even a government antitrust case couldn't bring down a businessman as shrewd as Rockefeller. A few years after Ida Tarbell dropped her bombshell investigative reports of Rockefeller's malignant business practices, the government began the antitrust proceedings. It broke Standard Oil up into 34 "baby Standards," which did nothing to satiate the country's growing need for oil. Just as we saw in Tar Creek, the World Wars of the 20th century had galvanized the interests of American business.

Government contracts were pouring money into companies all along the Creek. It was not just oil; there was a great need for textiles, copper, aluminum, etc., for the war effort. Earlier we looked at Tar Creek in Oklahoma, whose main products for the war effort were oil, lead and zinc, while in Newtown Creek within New York City, the main product was oil refining. The war effort needed oil for every aspect of the military. Greenpoint grew during those years. These factories were populated by the Polish immigrant community, who had by then established an ethnic majority in Greenpoint and were willing to work in such hellish conditions.

There was so much money to be made during the gilded age that safety was an afterthought. Although no one is quite certain that the Greenpoint oil spill had its origins in the Standard Oil fires, today it's generally accepted as fact.

MITCH WAXMAN: In the early days of the oil industry they didn't use welded tanks, they used riveted tanks. The tanks didn't have bottoms; they were sitting on a pad of asphalt. They [oil companies] were making so much money per gallon that if they lost 10% of what was in the tank just to leaking or to oozing out the bottom, it wasn't even a rounding error for them on their profits. There was an 1883 fire and a 1919 fire. Between them, they lost something in the neighborhood of 20 million gallons of oil. A lot of it went up in smoke, went into the water and into the ground.

GEOFFREY COBB: That 1919 fire was a real wakeup call. There have always been fires. But the 1919 fire lasted for a week. It jumped the Creek and it really woke up a lot of people in the community. The fact that how dangerous it was, living next to these oil refineries, and despite the technology it didn't work. If memory serves me, a bolt of lightning hit one of the storage tanks. And the pumping mechanism that was supposed to pump water when there was a fire had failed. Then from one tank to the others it spread and actually burned across the bridge. They were fighting it for a week.

It was I believe the largest fire in New York ever at the time. They called in people from four boroughs to try to put it out. I think that even the oil companies realized that refining in Greenpoint was dangerous in 1919. They had begun to change from refining to just storage.

MITCH WAXMAN: Those spills, those fires, that's what contributed to and theoretically created the Greenpoint oil spill. We've got legacy spills all over the creek. It's a rhetorical thing with NCA [Newtown Creek Alliance] members where we have to remind people not to say "Newtown Creek Oil Spill" because that would indicate that it's just one. There's multiple areas around the Creek where oil is. Most of them at this stage are essentially being looked after by some regulatory agency, whether it be EPA or DEC and so on. But, there are still sites that are going to be discovered, we haven't gotten to that yet.

1978

A 1950 sewer explosion that blew manhole covers three stories high at the corner of Manhattan Avenue and Huron Street is commonly referred to as a warning shot for a neighborhood that was unaware of massive oil spills spreading out beneath it. It took another 28 years for the next major puzzle piece to emerge in 1978, when a U.S. Coast Guard helicopter discovered a rainbow sheen over black waters floating on the surface of Newtown Creek.

That discovery was one of the first big turning points in the Creek's story because it prompted city officials to acknowledge the leak and investigate. The Coast Guard followed up with a study which was released in 1979 and estimated that there was between 17 to 30 million gallons of oil spanning 55 acres in the Creek and beneath Greenpoint.

At the time there were many theories on where the oil came from, if it was coming from multiple sources or not, and for how long? But the telltale sign of provenance was the naphtha in the samples which indicated that the oil leaked from Standard Oil's descendant, Mobil Oil, around 1948, because they were the only refinery that used naphtha until they closed in 1965.

More sewer explosions followed.

MITCH WAXMAN, historian for Newtown Creek Alliance (NCA), blogger Newtown Pentacle: Prior to sometime in the 1940s Greenpoint and Williamsburg still drew their water from the reservoir system. They would pump groundwater up through a series of materials and create these cistern lakes and that would provide residential supply. Greenpoint was moved onto the New York City water system in the 1940s.

The cone of depression in the water table around the pump heads in the ground began to fill back up, and water in the ground began to move in its natural way. So instead of moving toward the pumps, it began to move in the normal hydrology that it has moved in since prehistory.

GEOFFREY COBB, teacher, historian, author *Greenpoint Brooklyn's Forgotten Past*, blogger Greenpointers: In 1950 there was this huge underground explosion. At the height of the Cold War, people thought that the Russians had dropped an atomic bomb that blew manhole covers on Huron Street, 50 feet up in the air. It was the first time that people realized that the aquifer itself was steeped with oil.

MITCH WAXMAN: The Greenpoint oil spill sits on top of the water table. When the water table was depressed and they were still pumping the groundwater out, the oil spill was far lower in terms of its strata than it would be in later years. As the water table began to rise up to its natural level, it brought the petroleum material higher up in the ground, which allowed vapors from the petroleum to begin permeating up through the streets and they began to collect in the sewers and also in the basements of people's homes.

In the sewers in particular they hit a level of combustibility where all it would take was a spark—and that's what happened several times where manhole covers in Greenpoint would just explode into the air on a pillar of flame. You'd then have fire and smoke shooting out of the sidewalk breaks and it was essentially almost like the inside of an oven or the inside of a boiler where it was perfect to maintain a fire.

BASIL SEGGOS, Commissioner of the New York State Department of Environmental Conservation (DEC), former Chief Investigator for Riverkeeper: I certainly wasn't around in 1978, it was a different world at that point. I think oil spills and waterways were just more readily impacted. I can't tell you what decision-making they may have been filtering all these facts through, but obviously it wasn't the right approach. You have a major underground oil spill with a significant amount of that getting into the waterway.

It isn't until, I believe it was 1990, that there was then a very rudimentary consent order between the state and Exxon to begin studying the problem and then ultimately putting in place with these basic controls. The communities may not have been as engaged back then. The government may have been busy worrying about other things. Maybe folks were just accustomed to pollution on waterways. I mean, there's any number of reasons why this may not have gotten the kind of attention that it did.

MITCH WAXMAN: It wasn't really until the 1970s that the water table had risen sufficiently in height and the natural hydrology had reasserted itself sufficiently for slicks of oil to be seen coming out of the bulkheads right at the waterline. That's the famous Coast Guard flyer, but that wasn't until the 1970s.

GEOFFREY COBB: And then in 1978, when the Coast Guard sees the first plume, that there's actually evidence of it. But who knows? Going back to the 1870s, there's already significant seepage from all of these refineries into the aquifer.

BASIL SEGGOS: What they started to see in 1978, in terms of oil getting into the Creek, may have been less than what we started to see in the late 1980s and '90s and up until the 2000s, when just more oil was starting to pour back into the waterway. I think that probably is at least factually what would distinguish 1978 from what we first saw in 2002.

JOE LENTOL, New York State Assembly, District 50: The Army Corps of Engineers got involved in the issue, but it never really made a big splash at the time, at least not to my recollection. Nobody in Greenpoint was up in arms. There was still a lot of civic organization in those days, more than there are today, believe it or not. And I used to go to civic meetings regularly, all the different ones that existed in Williamsburg, Greenpoint, and nobody ever brought it up as an issue.

JOHN LIPSCOMB, Riverkeeper, Vice President of Advocacy, patrol boat operator: My sense is that Exxon is a very persuasive negotiator with the state and EPA. We see that all the time. It's not that there was nothing going on, it was just ineffective.

The DEC and EPA, which, let's face it, they are both at the top, led by political appointees—they're not independent, as Riverkeeper is. The head of DEC was appointed by the Governor. The head of the EPA is appointed by the President. And there might've been some deals made, I don't know. But I do know that when it started to be daylighted by Riverkeeper and the community, the community people used to come aboard and they were so fired up because they'd been complaining about petroleum fumes in their basements and oil on the water for years.

JOE LENTOL: And unbeknownst to me, I guess I should have known that they had already dug wells to recover some of the fuel that was already underground. They had maybe one well, possibly two recovery wells, which wasn't nearly enough to clean up the mess that was under there. It would have taken one hundred years for them to do it.

SICKNESS

OVER SEVERAL DECADES, independent researchers, epidemiologists and universities have studied the health outcomes of people living on top of legacy pollution sites. The New York City Health Department hasn't explicitly stated that Greenpoint's residents have been stricken with cancer and leukemia as a direct result from the various underground oil and chemical plumes, or air pollution. But the overwhelming anecdotal evidence of mass contamination of cancer-causing agents leading to Greenpoint's cancer clusters is in need of closer inspection. Many of the neighborhood's most afflicted residents have moved on or have passed away. Some of the Polish immigrants returned to Poland to retire, which, if they got sick in Poland and not Brooklyn, left gaps in the tracking data. Yet today we still have countless examples of leukemias and lymphomas affecting long-term residents in particular.

"The Victims of Hunter's Point—How the Foul Odors Aggravate the Miseries of the Sick Room."
Illustrated by W.A. Rogers, August 20, 1881, *Harper's Weekly.*

A New York City Health Department survey has found that the residents of the Greenpoint and Williamsburg areas of Brooklyn face a greater risk of stomach cancer and some kinds of leukemia than other New Yorkers.[58]

LISA DLOODGOOD, Director of Advocacy & Education, Newtown Creek Alliance (NCA): If you want to talk about health effects, [Laura Hofmann's] family is full of crazy, crazy problems. You have to look at who lives in this neighborhood, who has lived in this neighborhood, and who no longer lives in the neighborhood and why. There was a big influx of Eastern Europeans at one point. And they're maybe not so willing to talk to anybody about their health or their property or anything. There's a lot of speculation that people may be sicker, maybe left and illness manifested and they died elsewhere.

BASIL SEGGOS: Laura and Mike [Hofmann], no doubt they were the real heroes. They were the ones living on the Creek and fighting for it for many years prior to when I got there.

LAURA HOFMANN, activist, lifelong resident, O.U.T.R.A.G.E., Newtown Creek Alliance, many other nonprofits: As a child I lived on Clifford Place and then I basically grew up on Java Street until I got married. I recall the neighborhood being very smelly. Sometimes it was to the point where it could make you gag and vomit. At that time it was the sewage treatment facility. There were a lot of smells—issues that weren't regulated. In fact, the Newtown Creek Monitoring Committee, that I belong to, we didn't see the 1972 Clean Water Act [standards] actually being met by the sewage treatment facility until a few years ago.

To give you some context on how the odors might've been, when my parents used to bring us home from vacation, I always remembered falling asleep in the car as a kid and when we passed over the Greenpoint Avenue Bridge the smell was so strong that it would wake me up. Quite a few times my father would put his hand to his chest and say things like, "Drink it in, put a tiger in your tank." In case you don't know, "Put a tiger in your tank" was an old Esso[59] Station commercial motto. As a kid, I grew up knowing that there was oil and some kind of contamination.

Years down the road it became clear that there were a lot of issues from the pollution and from those smells. A lot of aunts and uncles on my father's side of the family came from the Queens side of the Creek and my mother's side of the

58. Robert D. McFadden. "Survey Finds High Cancer Rate In 2 Neighborhoods in Brooklyn." *The New York Times*, 23 May 1992.

59. After the breakup of Standard Oil, Esso was the original name of the company that became Exxon from 1912 to 1972. Exxon merged with Mobil and became ExxonMobil in 1999.

"Esso Gasoline sign, Route 1, Cary Plantation, Maine," Photo by John Margolies, 1995.
Courtesy of Library of Congress Prints and Photographs Division, Washington, D.C.

family came from the Brooklyn side of the Creek. Based on what I now know about chemicals, diseases and stuff, I could pretty much plot out which chemicals my aunts and uncles might've died from. It's that clear to me, for instance, the aunts and uncles, and including my parents too who lived closer to the northern tip of Greenpoint, they passed away from things like the lymphomas, *the brain cancers*, and family members had autoimmune diseases and even birth defects.

The ones that lived closer to the actual oil plume, those are the ones that died from the leukemias and blood-related disorders. The people from the family who lived on the Queens side—they're the ones that passed away from the bladder cancers and the pancreatic cancers.

Like I said, years later, knowing what I know now—for instance, the tip of North Greenpoint got slammed with things like PVC, dioxin, and benzene. Dioxin would come from the old Greenpoint incinerators. Now those chemicals are all known to be cancer-causers. When you look through the material online, you see that brain diseases are a part of that picture. Now, if I know that from just breezing through Google and asking questions in the doctor's office and so forth, they could stand on their head from now until doomsday and they're not going to convince me that the people in the environmental sphere and these government agencies don't know this. They do.

I believe with all my heart that it's been a cover-up, because with all of the things that happened in the community, like rezoning and so forth, they basically got to sweep away all of the residents' environmental health histories by not doing a proper health study and doing cancer cluster studies and add it to the surveys.

They didn't collect the information that they really needed to connect the dots and figure those things out.

In fact, the Williamsburg-Greenpoint area has an overall lower cancer rate than much of the rest of New York City. Still, the neighborhood has histori-cally had among the highest incidence of certain cancers, including leukemia in children and stomach cancer in adults. (Benzene is a known cause of leu-kemia.) And there is anecdotal evidence of cancer clusters: Sebastian Pirozzi, who grew up in Greenpoint, lost his leg to bone cancer at 14. Several of his old neighbors have had the same disease. "It's not a coincidence," Pirozzi says. "It can't be. There are many cancers that can be caused by different things, but bone cancer is different. It's rare." Tom Stagg, a retired detective on the border of the contaminated zone, is also convinced. He's been tracking the number of people with cancer on the block he grew up on. So far, he's counted 36. Twenty-five, including several children, have passed away. Stagg's own father died of pancreatic cancer at 53. "It's not normal," he says. "I'm sure it's because of the oil spill."[60]

My father was a printer and my mother was a housewife. Usually what I tell people is that my family's medical health history reads like an Area 51 report. It's so thick and there's so many different things that it's just beyond being a coinci-dence. My mother, father and their dog all died from separate brain diseases. My mother died from primary brain cancer and they tagged it as CNS lymphoma: central nervous system lymphoma. My father passed away from progressive supranuclear palsy, which is a brain and brain stem type of disease and it's very rare. Their dog died from a brain disease called encephalopathy. I also have lacunar infarcts in my brain. Fortunately, the infarcts have cleared up and they've healed, but I also had a diagnosis of lupus. I began to get treatment, I think it was in the mid-1990s, and responded very well to treatment. These days I'm classified as having UCTD which is Undifferentiated Connective Tissue Disorder. My daughter is currently diagnosed with full lupus and my oldest son has an array of things, autoimmune conditions among them.

My sister also has a tumor in her bone in one of her legs. She also has a very rare pulsatile tinnitus. It's a very rare condition that involves the brain stem and the ear. Now before I get off of my family, I want to mention that my oldest son who used to... of course all my children... ate from gardens that were polluted by either the Greenpoint incinerator that was down near our previous apartment like in 1985. We lived at 155 DuPont Street where we had access to a vegetable

60. Daphne Eviatar. "The Ooze." Daily Intelligencer, *New York Magazine*, 3 June 2007.

garden, and the ash from the incinerator would fall on the tomatoes every day. Back then I didn't know it was incinerator ash and I used to just wash it off and use the tomatoes. Years later we had a community garden where Mary D. Senior Housing currently is, and of course that's right across the street from NuHart, the PVC manufacturer.

We were even affected here in our building because back then we were living up on the top floor facing the pollution control system, which wasn't always there, and getting all this green plastic kind of stuff in the air conditioner until it closed up. Me and my youngest son had developed asthma.

Now taking that into consideration, my oldest son had three children. I don't know if you're aware of this, but phthalates that were pumped out by that facility [NuHart Plastics Factory] are a known cause of birth defects. All my pregnancies of course occurred here on DuPont Street. Now his three of his children—Kate, my daughter-in-law, had one miscarriage and then she was pregnant with a set of twins. One of the twins had cystic hygroma. Later on they found out that the baby actually had Edwards syndrome, which is rare, it's trisomy 18[61], a serious birth defect. The baby died in the uterus and caused her to have the other baby earlier—my other grandson. About a year and a half later she was pregnant with yet another set of twins, and the same thing happened with the other one of the babies.

One doctor compared it to being struck by lightning twice. Another doctor wasn't happy with that classification in the medical records because he said people don't just get hit by lightning twice. In other words, it was that rare. This is just an overview of my family. I could go on and on.

Now before I was even aware of my mom having the brain cancer, I was always concerned about brain cancers because sometime in the 1990s we used to run the softball tournament, and one of the coaches' wives had died very young and she died from brain cancer. Not too long after that, my husband bumped into a coworker from a factory on Green Street who also had a brain tumor. And my daughter's classmate, who was 10 years old, passed away from glioblastoma. It was primary brain cancer.

I'm leaving out a few. In the 1990s I already knew about five or six people in the neighborhood who had brain tumors or brain cancer.

When my mother had passed away in 2007, that was a couple of years before that I found out that one of her neighbors across the street, her son, had a brain

---

61. Trisomy 18, also called Edwards syndrome, is a chromosomal condition associated with abnormalities in many parts of the body. Individuals with trisomy 18 often have slow growth before birth (intrauterine growth retardation) and a low birth weight. Affected individuals may have heart defects and abnormalities of other organs that develop before birth. Other features of trisomy 18 include a small, abnormally shaped head; a small jaw and mouth; and clenched fists with overlapping fingers. Due to the presence of several life-threatening medical problems, many individuals with trisomy 18 die before birth or within their first month. Five to 10 percent of children with this condition live past their first year, and these children often have severe intellectual disability.

tumor. Then a couple of years after that and another neighbor from that block passed away from the same kind of brain cancer. I don't know where you're from but how many people do you know that have brain cancer or brain tumors?

As a matter of fact, I'm on the same block and it wasn't just my parents. It was that other family across the street. One of my childhood best friends passed away from MS. In the 1980s, there was a woman who had a child with a birth defect, but also with a brain tumor. He was kind of a popular kid because he had Down syndrome. Yeah, he was a very happy person, but he actually died from brain cancer.

Another kid that we knew, his name was Ryan, he passed away from leukemia. Leukemia is kind of a common story with the old-school Greenpointers that don't live here anymore. We encountered them on Facebook and other places. That's part of what I consider to be a cover-up, because this rezoning resulted in kind of sweeping medical health histories aside because people got displaced out of the neighborhood. The diseases that they developed here in Greenpoint aren't going to get reported in Greenpoint. They're going to get reported [as being from] elsewhere.

My mother's neighbors, the one who passed away from brain cancer whose son had brain tumors, they were lifelong Greenpoint residents. Towards the end of her life she had to move out to Long Island to live out the last couple of months of her life before she succumbed to the brain cancer. Her records will not show up on both [sets of] New York City statistics.

ACACIA THOMPSON, archivist for Brooklyn Public Library's Greenpoint Environmental History Project: One of Laura Hofmann's big issues is she felt super resentful that there's all this data that could and should be collected but it's not. People felt resentful of her for trying to draw attention to these issues, because *we don't need people coming into Greenpoint and telling us our property isn't worth what it's worth.*

Now with the Polish community, their whole thing is not as much about them moving out of the city, or to Maspeth or Ridgewood. It's about them returning to Poland. A lot of people are going back to Poland and possibly not doing well health-wise, because of living here, or all these transient people living here for a while and then leaving. You've got all these communities that will never be tracked, because the city has never made it important to find out how the industrialized pollution has affected the health of the community.

MITCH WAXMAN: We're still waiting for EPA to come back with the human health risk assessment. I can tell you there's a lot of apocryphal stories, but I'm not going to repeat them because there is actual science going on using very complicated mathematical formulas which I don't fully understand. The one thing that they've said is that it's difficult to say that somebody who got cancer who lives on Huron

Street got it because of Newtown Creek. They live in New York City, in which you have a higher risk for several diseases just because of the general state of the environment.

MIKE SCHADE, activist, environmental health campaigner, Mind The Store Campaign Director with Safer Chemicals, Healthy Families: The State Health Department did put out a report a few years ago which looked at the health outcomes for people that live within a certain mileage of Newtown Creek. That wasn't just people that live in North Brooklyn, but other neighborhoods up and down Newtown Creek. If I recall correctly, I believe that they did find some increased evidence of some health outcomes. But the Department of Health, as they often do, also said, *Well, it could be from smoking. It could be from all these other issues.*

DOROTHY SWICK, former resident, co-plaintiff in Exxon suit: Yeah, there was a cluster on one block in Greenpoint that had a lot of cancer cases for one area. But you couldn't pinpoint it to the spills.

MITCH WAXMAN: Unless you're seeing clusters of certain unique cancers or certain unique autoimmune diseases that are clustered around a particular contaminant source, this is again why I'm going to say we really have to wait for the EPA to release that document. It's science, and not introducing my own bias into the story. You got the BQE [Brooklyn Queens Expressway] which is moving 28 million cars. You've got the LIE [Long Island Expressway], which is something like 15.5 million. Then you've got this endemic waste transfer station, you've got the largest sewer plant. There's so many co-factors here.

LISA BLOODGOOD: You cannot put your finger on one thing. You can't say, "Oh, it's because I lived next to the NuHart facility and their production of PVC pipes, hoses and shower curtains gave my family lupus."

MIKE SCHADE: If you take a step back over the past 40 years, the State Health Department sadly has often been in the business of casting doubt about the connection between chemical release exposure and health problems. Going back to Love Canal, the State Health Department was oftentimes raising doubt about whether or not the families that lived at Love Canal were developing breast cancer or reproductive problems. Meanwhile, you had women that were experiencing miscarriages.

For 40 years the State Health Department has done a very poor job of characterizing elevated instances of cancer, other diseases in communities near hazardous waste sites and other forms of industrial pollution. There have been some sites where they have said *yes, there is a cluster of health problems.*

In Tonawanda, near Kenmore, the site that I worked when I was in Buffalo, they found elevated instances in certain places in Tonawanda. Here in Brooklyn, it's been more of a mixed bag. The challenge is that—I think there's a number of challenges. There's a large immigrant community that is not well documented, from Hispanic families to Polish families. That's a big challenge. There's not a lot of good data on those populations.

The state doesn't have a lot of data for certain time periods, I think between 1870s to late 1970s, when pollution in North Brooklyn was at its worst, when there were oil refineries, sewage treatment plants doing God knows what, when you had chemical plants like the NuHart plant, the Greenpoint incinerator that was pumping out significant quantities of pollution in the air. It's really hard. There's poor data. There's populations that may not be reporting information.

Science is also still developing. So, there's a variety of reasons why it's challenging to say that the next health problem was caused by exposure to these chemicals, especially in a community like Brooklyn where there are many different sources of pollution, from the sewage treatment plant to the waste transfer stations, to the toxic sites, to pollution from the air, pollution from cars and trucks going to waste transfer stations along the BQE.

While I think there's a lot of anecdotal evidence—there are people that have said that they see incidences of cancer, other health problems—I don't think any scientists have conclusively said, *Yes, we definitely have a problem.* But I definitely think there's enough anecdotal evidence for there to be cause for concern, especially given that we know that there had been historically many major polluters that were releasing significant levels of toxic chemicals that we know can pose/cause serious diseases. Can we say there's definitely a problem? No. Should we be concerned? One hundred percent.

GEOFFREY COBB: In the early 1990s, a lot of Polish people who came here that didn't speak English, they were listed for jobs where they could make cash and then go back to Poland. If you were thrifty, the amount of money you could bring back was huge. One of the things that people worked in was asbestos, which is very, very cancer-causing.

A lot of the people who lived in Greenpoint maybe lived here for short periods of time or 10 years and then they went back to Poland. Either from working in asbestos or where they lived in the neighborhood, I know anecdotally of many cases of people developing cancer. But that's never been factored into the overall cancer rate because those statistics weren't available.

JUSTIN BLOOM, former attorney for Riverkeeper, Sarasota Waterkeeper: All these cancers are in the community, and it was frustrating to not be able to really leverage that issue in the courts because the science isn't really there to make the connection between the oil spill and the cancer cluster that we believe occurred there.

ACACIA THOMPSON: It just never ceases to amaze me that it is always the onus of the community to protect themselves. Even though we are in the middle of New York City and we have all these entities that are here.

We have really wonderful people working for a lot of these agencies, but part of it is that they're only going to do as much as they can do. They're often not doing enough. It's not the legality of things. They're just not enough. They're not pushing properly. It's always on the community. If you don't have an activated community, then you don't have anything. You don't have anybody advocating for you, then you have to pester your electeds. You have to fight for everything. That's why Greenpoint is so amazing, because such atrocities happened here and they couldn't do anything but fight. You've got parts of the city that have really similar issues. They don't have that community that has the time to do it and that's something that's unique about Greenpoint too.

CONCERNED CITIZENS OF GREENPOINT: IRENE AND THE ANGRY MOMS

ONE COULD argue that Greenpoint's first activists weren't actually from Greenpoint. I'm not sure they were even activists. The aforementioned 15th Ward Smelling Committee of the 1890s sailed across the East River into Newtown Creek to patrol the sewage, rotting animal carcasses, and toxic waste chemicals to figure out where these smells were coming from and what they were.

It was many years later when the real activism got started. In 1958 Irene Klementowicz moved to Brooklyn from the Bronx. She's a native New Yorker with Polish roots who moved into a Polish enclave to run a funeral home with her husband in Greenpoint. To the best of my knowledge it wasn't until the 1980s when she began to organize other affected women and address Greenpoint's environmental problems.

Up to this point, we've only looked at the Greenpoint oil spill, but it was far from the neighborhood's only environmental problem. The same year Ms. Klementowicz moved to Greenpoint, the city plopped a garbage incinerator into the community, burning everything from medical waste to trash. It rained toxic waste onto the town every day.

From 1958 until recently, Greenpoint had 14 garbage transfer stations. The community was the collection point for trash from all over the city. The wastewater treatment plant was also in Greenpoint, creating a nasty sewage smell. Early on, the plant had open containers of raw sewage stinking up the neighborhood. Greenpoint's smell was notorious.

"Photo of Neighbors Against Garbage (N.A.G.) litter cleanup," sometime in the 1980s. Donated for capture by Sarah Porter through the Greenpoint Environmental History Project of Brooklyn Public Library.

Irene Klementowicz and her cohort of local women activists were dubbed in the press as the "Angry Moms," but their official name was The Concerned Citizens of Greenpoint. They were Greenpoint's first environmental activists. Tellingly, nearly every activist I spoke to talks about Irene Klementowicz as if they are her best friend. Like a true leader, she knew how to connect with people.

A few of the Concerned Citizens of Greenpoint were native New Yorkers. But for the Polish immigrant women, it was a remarkable act of solidarity for them to take leading roles as community activists. Many of them grew up under communism where they didn't have the freedom of speech and the right to assemble. Activist Christine Holowacz illustrated this for me in her interview, "...they [immigrants] couldn't vote, and they couldn't participate in anything. And because of this feeling that you can't do anything, they didn't."

Ms. Klementowicz, along with Christine Holowacz, Elizabeth Roncketti, Laura Hofmann and others, were a loose group of activists who organized around the mounting environmental problems that the city willfully dumped onto this working-class neighborhood. There isn't much information available on who the actual members of the Concerned Citizens of Greenpoint were. Ms. Klementowicz is in her 90s now and, to the best of my knowledge, is retired from activism.

GEOFFREY COBB: The earliest evidence we have of Polish people living in a community in Greenpoint is 1885. What really brought Polish people to the area is they did the work that no one else wanted to do.

The conditions that they worked in were hellacious—the horrendous temperatures and humidity that they worked under, let alone the dangerous conditions. That's really where the Polish community formed and by the eve of the First World War, the Polish community was the largest community in Greenpoint.

You have waves of Polish immigration. Then you have another wave after World War II when Poland became a communist country. A lot of them are displaced people. Lands that were formerly Poland were taken over by the Soviet Union. All of those people ended up in Greenpoint. And then you have my wife's generation who were Solidarity people. A lot of them came when martial law was declared in full in 1979.

ACACIA THOMPSON: It goes back to the history of the immigrant community in our neighborhood and about people still not being involved [in activism] because of not wanting to draw attention to themselves. Also, not having the freedom to do it because people worked so hard just to keep their families alive. With the Polish community, you're talking about generations of people who were taught not to talk about things, not to bring things up, not to draw attention to themselves.

LAURA HOFMANN: I wouldn't nail that down to just the Polish community. I think that that's overall, because I know people from the Polish community and there's two attitudes I've encountered. Take Christine Holowacz for example. I'm not sure what generation she's from, but she was very excited to be part of change in the neighborhood. She took the environment seriously and she was one of the people in the property owner lawsuits, so you've got a mix of Polish people who see their newfound ability to weigh in on political issues as exciting, and others that take the old-school type of attitude with them.

CHRISTINE HOLOWACZ, activist, longtime resident, GWAPP, Newtown Creek Alliance, many other nonprofits: I came here and I started living in Greenpoint. In Poland the situation was really very bad. People were poor. If you didn't belong to the [Communist] Party, you really had nothing. Whoever was able to get out of the country was trying to get out. And then once you got out, you needed to help your family that was back there by sending money or whatever.

The people that came here, they were really looking into two things. The first thing was to work and make sure that they have enough, but also to make sure that the families in Poland have enough. The whole mindset of being under communism was that it doesn't really matter what you say, or how you say it, things don't get changed because whatever the government says is whatever's been done.

Additionally to that, you have to be in this country at least five years in order to take the test and then become an American citizen and then vote. That also took a long time and you have to understand, I was lucky enough to come to this country with my green card, as they called it at the time—my permanent residency card. Many people just came here for vacation and stayed over. Some of them took years and years before they can finalize their status. During all of this time, they couldn't vote and they couldn't participate in anything. Because of this feeling that you can't do anything, they didn't.

Because of all of this, Greenpoint ended up with a larger sewer treatment plant, we had an incinerator, we have most of the garbage from the city that is being brought up to Greenpoint. Greenpoint became the dumping ground. In addition to all of this the banks that were here in Greenpoint weren't so willing to really help Greenpoint.

In the vicinity of two blocks you have like six or seven different banks today. They wouldn't be here if the business wasn't here. What did happen is that the Polish community got together, and they opened up a Polish and Slavic credit union. That union started to give loans to the Poles that lived here. And they could do their homes. They could basically stay here to work and buy a house or to improve the house. That's when the neighborhood started to really take off and change.

Additionally to that we had a woman whose name is Irene Klementowicz.

VICTORIA CAMBRANES: We knew that there was stuff going on. My dad worked for the DEP [Department of Environmental Protection]. He would hear a lot of things and have insider information, but he couldn't really share any of that because he worked for the city. His old landlady was this woman named Irene Klementowicz.

CHRISTINE HOLOWACZ: She was born in America, originally from the Bronx, but she speaks Polish still today. She really cared. She and her husband had opened up a funeral home.

She realized all of these problems that were over here. She set up an organization and that's how I actually started to get involved with the incinerator. I went to some kind of a meeting, and she was talking and I started to feel very passionate about it and I said, *oh my God, this is my opportunity to do something about something*. Whenever I heard these voices from other people around here saying that you can't do anything because it's government, well, I give it a shot. If I can, I can, if I can't, I can't. But if I don't do anything then I'm not even giving it a chance.

JOE LENTOL: I would think that the native Greenpointers think it's too much about nothing. Who cares if we have a creek that's a little bit polluted? I don't know if those folks are still around. Irene Klementowicz doesn't think that way, but a lot

"Our Town" Illustrated map of environmental hazards in Greenpoint and Williamsburg, Brooklyn, 1992. Donated for capture at the Central Library by Hank Linhart. Collected through the Greenpoint Environmental History Project of Brooklyn Public Library.

of other Greenpointers think that there's more important things in life than to worry about a creek. That's just the way it goes in life, though, isn't it?

CHRISTINE HOLOWACZ: It started when they closed the landfill in Staten Island. They [New York City] were looking for other transfer stations and there was some things that changed so Greenpoint ended up to be the dumping place for everyone. Businesses would bring in the garbage.

It was twofold: one was that the amount of truck traffic in and out was enormous for the people who are living like on Metropolitan Avenue, because a lot of that stuff goes down there.

When you get to some of these transfer stations, it's just unrealistic. If it's construction debris, they don't care how much dust is in the air and that it just carried into the community.

This was becoming horrific. We have garbage brought up from all over the city. At the same time it was also brought in from Queens onto Greenpoint Avenue and into that area because we had the incinerator there. It was just unbelievable.

There were a few organizations that started to talk. Every borough has to be responsible for their own garbage. We can't take all the garbage from the whole city into our backyard. It took a long time for the plan to be written and all, and it's still not 100% implemented. There were lawsuits but we still have most of the garbage of the city coming here, but it's much less than what it was before.

TRINA HAMILTON, associate professor of geography at State University of Buffalo, co-editor *Just Green Enough: Urban Development and Environmental Gentrification*: I think the first wave, with the five angry women, it was broader than just the cleanup of the oil plume, or the cleanup of Newtown Creek. It was really a constant battle against environmental entities.

KATIE BUSING NAPLATARSKI, longtime Greenpoint resident, teacher, activist, open space advocate: You had people there at meetings who were loud with big voices, and sometimes to the point of being disruptive—but in a good way.

ACACIA THOMPSON: You often find that everything starts with moms. It's always the moms. It seems in our neighborhood it started with Concerned Citizens of Greenpoint; it's hard to get the numbers yet because the ladies are a little bit inaccessible to talk to about it.

Additionally, there's not a lot written besides the *Greenpoint Gazette*. It's hard to find the origin story of Concerned Citizens. But in the 1980s, they definitely were fighting because they knew that the incinerator was not good for the neighborhood. The descriptions of the fights that these ladies had, like "You can't come in here!" I love the voices that everybody brings out when they're talking about them talking to city officials and just saying, "We do not trust you. We don't think you're doing what's right for our community." I've been trying to interview Irene for a while. She's down the street, but it's been, she's quite...

PAUL PULLO: Irene has not been coming to the meetings and I miss her terribly. I speak to her on the phone a little bit. I would pick her up and bring her to meetings if she would just come.

ACACIA THOMPSON: I met Elizabeth Roncketti once. She was with Irene on the Concerned Citizens of Greenpoint and she's known for doing the same sort of thing. I can recognize her now when I watch videos of community board meetings in the 1980s, because she was known for wearing an elaborate hat. Everywhere she went, a different hat. I met her and tried to talk to her about it, and she was seemingly not interested. As you've probably seen with activists, they go through these sorts of ups and downs of being involved.

The Frasers [Scott and Kim] talk about how there's this awesome high and there's depression because you either win or lose and then you see another fight coming. At some point people just aren't interested in talking about it anymore.

PAUL PULLO: They were heroes. They are all my friends.

THE CITY'S TOILET

THE SMELL of Greenpoint was pervasive. The smell stubbornly evicted people continuously on the wrong side of the wind. Unlike the silence of cancer-causing agents in the air, ground, and water, the smell of raw sewage is unavoidable. The original wastewater treatment plant was built in 1967, and since day one was overflowing with more product than it could handle directly deposited untreated into the Creek. By all accounts, it was an open sewer and was a depressing presence in the neighborhood. Raw sewage was not the only reason that Greenpoint's residents couldn't open a window on certain days. Many interviewees mentioned an incinerator that came to Greenpoint in 1958, which rained cancerous dioxin and toxic waste on the cars, kids, vegetable gardens, on everything. All of this pollution was foisted onto Greenpoint before the groundbreaking environmental legislation of the early 1970s such as the Clean Water Act and the Clean Air Act, which was put in place by the Richard Nixon Administration. These issues lingered for decades while the city did nothing.

By the 1980s, the people had had enough of being treated like New York City's toilet.

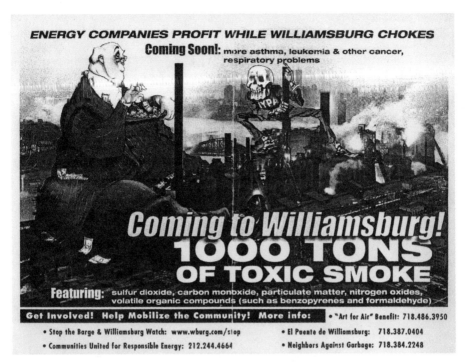

Flyer mobilizing community against proposed TransGas power plant on North 12th Street and Kent Avenue in Williamsburg, Brooklyn. Donated by Jane Pool. This project is funded through the Greenpoint Community Environmental Fund. Brooklyn Public Library, Brooklyn Collection.

KATIE BUSING NAPLATARSKI, longtime Greenpoint resident, teacher, activist, open space advocate: I moved here because of the closeness to the city and because of being able to afford it. Park Slope was a popular place; Greenpoint was not a popular place.

People didn't know the name Greenpoint. People I knew, including relatives, could not understand why I would live here. It was dirty, there was a lot of litter. There was still a lot of the remnants of industry.

TONY ARGENTO, owner Broadway Stages: I could tell you that in those days, the streets were very filthy, garbage everywhere. People would come in the middle of the night and dump right on the sidewalks with small dump trucks. Right on the sidewalks and in the streets, and pull away.

SCOTT FRASER, activist, Greenpointers Against Smell Pollution (GASP), writer and director TV and movies: We'd get this wave of smell from the sewage treatment plant that would just knock us off our feet.

G.A.S.P.

Greenpoint Against Smell and Pollution
105 KENT STREET
BROOKLYN, NEW YORK 11222

October, 1988

GASP, Greenpoint Against Smell and Pollution, is a non-profit, non-political, community-based environmental group. GASP was originally organized in the summer of 1986 when operating problems at the Newtown Creek Sewage Treatment Plant created unbearable odor problems for the community. Shortly thereafter, it became clear to the group that there were other sources of air pollution in the community which were, perhaps, less obnoxious than the Sewage Treatment Plant but more harmful to the community. Greenpoint is home to one of the three remaining, mass-burn, municipal incinerators in New York City. This plant, described separately, is a 20-year old facility which has been violating Federal air quality standards for the better part of a year.

Following is a list of the environmental issues which the members of GASP's Steering Committee try to monitor.

1. The Newtown Creek Waste Water Treatment Plant and the NYC-Dept. of Envirnmental Protection's plan to upgrade it.

2. The Greenpoint Incinerator and the on-going negotiations between the US Environmental Protection Agency and the NYC Dept. of Sanitation regarding the plant's upgrading.

3. The proposed Brooklyn Navy Yard Incinerator and the controversy surrounding the plant.

4. The Mobil Oil Co. gasoline spill and its continuing clean-up.

5. The proliferation of solid waste transfer stations in the neighborhood and the dramatic increase in truck traffic through our community.

GASP meetings are held on an irregular basis, as the issue and situation warrant. All meetings are publicized in the "Greenpoint Gazette" and "Greenline" and are held at the Greenpoint Savings Bank.

G.A.S.P. explains mission and directives with list of issues. Collected through the Greenpoint Environmental History Project of Brooklyn Public Library. Brooklyn Public Library, Brooklyn Collection.

KIM FRASER, activist, founder of Greenpointers Against Smell Pollution (GASP): Only on certain days though—rainy days.

TONY ARGENTO: It was very nasty.

LAURA HOFMANN, activist, lifelong resident, O.U.T.R.A.G.E., Newtown Creek Alliance, many other nonprofits: We often referred to what was going on as being treated as the biggest toilet in the city because we literally felt shit on.

TONY ARGENTO: That's when I learned about the waste treatment plant. It made all this smell. I mean, the smell sometimes was intense.

GEOFFREY COBB, teacher, historian, author *Greenpoint Brooklyn's Forgotten Past*, blogger Greenpointers: The odors off the Creek. Because when we first moved here, which is circa 1994, there were bad days where the wind blew from that sewage treatment plant and there was just a stink that hung in the air, your eyes would water up.

SCOTT FRASER: We didn't know about the ash in the beginning. It was the smell, the stink.

ACACIA THOMPSON, archivist for Brooklyn Public Library's Greenpoint Environmental History Project: Kim and Scott Fraser live nearby here. They started a group called GASP, which was Greenpoint Against Smell and Pollution. They worked a lot with the Concerned Citizens of Greenpoint to fight the incinerator. That was the big first issue.

SCOTT FRASER: Irene Klementowicz was really the push for the close of the incinerator. We joined her group, and we got to know her. Then we got to know other people in the neighborhood when we showed up for a protest. We got active, and then started really learning about other issues. I started doing some documentary work that coincided with the issues.

And then I did a documentary for the first Earth Day, in like 1991 or 1992. It's a lot of ricocheting between what I did for work. Kim was involved. She would travel on scouts, we met people. We got educated.

KIM FRASER: I really do think we got educated. It's not like we came to the neighborhood as environmentalists. It did involve people from around the world. And that was a real eye-opener, just listening to them speak. It did speak right to our hearts, because we agreed with them that just because of where you're born, you shouldn't have to put up with environmental degradation. The society says, *oh, I'm sorry, you were born in Greenpoint. It's just a wasteland over there.*

PAUL PULLO, activist, former owner of Metro Fuels: I saw it from the oil side because there used to be an incinerator right on Kingsland Avenue and Newtown Creek that would smell. Then the pee plant had a lot of open tanks. Depending on which way the wind blew, we got different asphalt plants, rendering plants, sewage treatment plants, incinerators. We had it all.

CHRISTINE HOLOWACZ, activist, longtime resident, GWAPP, Newtown Creek Alliance, many other nonprofits: The fact that the incinerator had operated for so many years without a real permit—they were burning medical waste there, and always the permit was under consent, which means that it's really not a permit because they would have to change things. That was the worst thing because everybody doesn't know what's going on or what you're breathing.

SCOTT FRASER: We found out that when you mix plastics with all the different things in the waste stream that you incinerate, you create dioxin, the most carcinogenic substance known to mankind. We know that we had a lot of dioxin in the ash, and it was coming out of the stack. Depending on where the wind blew, if it blew in this direction, you'd wake up in the morning and you would have white ash on your car, or on your laundry.

You could actually, with your finger, kind of rub it off of your car. Then we found out that there was a very high content of heavy metals, lead, mercury, dioxin in that ash. So we started to realize, we're getting seriously polluted. This was a city incinerator.

GEOFFREY COBB: In the 1990s you could score a really, really nice apartment through the Polish newspaper for about $500. People came here and they loved it, and then they would have constant headaches.

SCOTT FRASER: The incinerator didn't shut down for a long time. That didn't get shut down until, I would say, mid-, like early/mid-'90s. That took a while to shut down. That was a victory for us. The factory just sort of died of attrition with the gentrification.

UNDERGROUND PLUMES

FVFRY SPILL in the past 150 years left a plume that had been studied and mapped by the various environmental groups and government agencies. One needs to be specific when discussing the plumes. There were several oil and chemical spills throughout Greenpoint's history. We consider a few of the major ones at length in this book.

There were so many toxic industries operating throughout Greenpoint and neighboring Williamsburg that it's impossible to know what you will find in any given spot. The Meeker Avenue Plume runs roughly between Newtown Creek and McGolrick Park. According to the Newtown Creek Alliance website, the Meeker Plume consists of tetrachloroethylene (PCE) and trichloroethylene (TCE). They are a "result of decades of dumping and irresponsible manufacturing practices by historical and contemporary dry cleaning and metalworking businesses." These are all chemicals that have proven to be highly cancerous.

The survey was prompted by concern over sewage odors, radioactive wastes and smoke-belching factories. However, the survey drew no causal connections between the higher incidence of the diseases and the extraordinary concentration of environmental hazards in the two heavily industrialized East River waterfront neighborhoods. The 150,000 residents have complained for years that their health is endangered by pollutants.[62]

DOROTHY SWICK, former resident, co-plaintiff in Exxon suit: I was born down the other end of Greenpoint, the north part. I got married and moved to Hausman Street and I was there for about 30 years.

CHRISTINE HOLOWACZ, activist, longtime resident, GWAPP, Newtown Creek Alliance, many other nonprofits: She doesn't live there anymore. She lives upstate. Dorothy doesn't know how her neighbor was able to drill all the way down, and then what happened is when he drilled through the clay area and into where the oil is, it just started to smell. And he must have realized at that point that there was no way he can get anything out of there.

---

62. Robert D. McFadden. "Survey Finds High Cancer Rate In 2 Neighborhoods in Brooklyn." *The New York Times*, 23 May 1992.

DOROTHY SWICK: I was working. My son was going to school. My husband was working and everything was fine. Things were coming along naturally. You pay your mortgage, you pay your other bills, everything was pretty good until I got the bad odor.

What happened is I went down to my cellar where my heating unit was and there was this odor. I thought that maybe the oil was leaking, but it wasn't the oil. I went out to my backyard and I smelled it even stronger. What is this? Is it something burning or what? It had an oil odor it to it, but I wasn't sure. And it happened between my property line and my neighbor to the left. I went and bent down on the ground and I got a real strong smell, and then maybe 12 inches from the property line I saw a hole there like a drill hole. And the odor was coming from there. And I said, what is this? I didn't know what it was.

My neighbor next door was at some meeting. And there was an attorney there and he was going on saying that they could get money because there was a spill under Greenpoint. He went on and on. My neighbor decided to do that [sue ExxonMobil]. This attorney hired another company to do the drilling. They drilled the hole on the other side of the yard on his premises and they broke the seal and the odor came from the gas that had seeped through.

I called the City Environmental (DEC) and I reported the odor and apparently, while I was working, a gentleman had come. He said he didn't smell anything. Well, you can't smell it from the front, you have to go in the back. He never called for an appointment. But he said, "I don't smell anything." It kept it getting worse, a couple of weeks after I notified the city. I called the State. They sent in an inspector. I took him into the cellar, I took him to the backyard and he knew right away that it was from this spill. He knew immediately. He was very knowledgeable as to what was happening.

He had another group come down. They put piping in the ground with a big filtration unit in my backyard. What they did was come down the block and every so many houses, they drilled on the sidewalk and they put readers in the air and once a month or every six weeks they come and take these readings of the air quality.

CHRISTINE HOLOWACZ: She had to move out of her house. Then finally the DEC did find that hole, and they couldn't plug it because the fumes that are coming up could have blown up half of the block.

DOROTHY SWICK: It was horrible. And at that time, my husband... They found he had liver cancer. He was going through chemotherapy when all this was going on.

The DEC were the ones that came, took samples. They drilled these little holes in my basement, tiny ones, and they covered them right up, and they checked the air quality and it was cancer-causing material in their reports. I don't remember what all the chemicals were. It was definitely cancer-causing. It just smelled. You couldn't go down.

JUSTIN BLOOM, former attorney for Riverkeeper, Sarasota Waterkeeper: There were two concerns. One is water quality and pollution of Newtown Creek and the harbor. The second was the human health component, which was a little bit out of our wheelhouse being a Waterkeeper and focusing on protecting water quality for the benefit of the community, but this was more of a direct and very present harm that had completely been ignored.

We came to realize the vast quantity of oil was sitting at the top of the aquifer. We also began to realize the threat it posed to the community through air pollution. These pollutants were volatilizing and then traveling up through the soil into the basements of homes or being dispersed into the outdoor ambient air. That was a big concern, and Riverkeeper started doing some basic testing. And then as the private lawsuits got underway, they hired experts to do a lot of testing and monitoring with the concern again that these pollutants were going to volatilize and end up in people's living spaces.

Just a few blocks away from Dorothy Swick, Charley Friedman and his family bought a house in what was a rapidly gentrifying section of Greenpoint. Located in the same part of town, Charley lived beside another toxic underground plume containing a different set of cancerous chemicals.

The vapors that were coming up through Dorothy Swick's basement in the late 1990s were presumably from the Standard Oil spill that the Coast Guard discovered in 1978 and that Riverkeeper rediscovered in 2002. We can only speculate how long Standard/ExxonMobil's oil plume had snaked its way beneath Greenpoint. For a few unlucky residents, the Greenpoint oil spill got personal as it invited itself inside of people's homes in the form of a vapor gas. Some residents knew who to call, others learned through neighborhood meetings. For everyone who owned rapidly appreciating property in the area, these carcinogenic vapors turned their lives upside down.

The plumes are overlapping in spots, so it can be confusing keeping track of what is where.

DEC, in cooperation with DOH, began investigating the Meeker Avenue Plumes in the spring of 2007 after results from two separate investigations conducted by the ExxonMobil Corporation and the New York State Department of Transportation documented that soil, soil gas, and groundwater at numerous locations throughout the area had been contaminated with chlorinated solvents. The primary contaminants of concern are tetrachloroethylene (PCE) and trichloroethylene (TCE). These compounds have historically been used for dry cleaning and removing grease from metal respectively.[63]

CHARLEY FRIEDMAN, artist, former resident Greenpoint: My wife and I were having a child and we were renting, and knew that because we were going to be priced out, we were trying to find a place to buy. At the last moment our landlord approached us about buying our place and we said, "Sure." That was kind of it, and even at the signing he raised the price because he knew that everything was going up.

MIKE SCHADE, activist, environmental health campaigner, Mind The Store Campaign Director with Safer Chemicals, Healthy Families: I moved to Greenpoint in 2008. When I moved, I was aware of the neighborhood's toxic legacy. But it took me a few years until I really got politically active, largely because I didn't want to just parachute in and be like, *hey, I'm here to save everyone.* I had this history of working in Buffalo and working with communities around local toxic issues. I wanted to really get to know the community, the neighborhoods and who the different players were and who were the leaders before I started immersing myself in organizing.

It wasn't until I moved to Greenpoint that I started getting involved. I was very interested in wanting to get involved in issues around the Newtown Creek. I started getting more politically active in the neighborhood when I realized that the apartment that I just moved into was literally on top of the Meeker Avenue plume site. It's a state Superfund site, a hodgepodge of toxic waste sites in North Brooklyn and eastern Greenpoint, largely contaminated with TCE—trichloroethylene, which is a dry-cleaning solvent.

MARC YAGGI, executive director Waterkeeper Alliance: It felt like it came out of nowhere. Then to find out that it actually goes back to the 1950s when there was an explosion that sent all this oil into the Creek and in the ground.

---

63. Staff. "Meeker Ave Plumes." *Newtown Creek Alliance*, 2008.

I remember stories of Basil going over there and drilling boreholes and finding this oil underneath the sidewalks, vapors in the air and things like that. Knowing people living all around there was crazy and that had been going on for so long. That's what started the citizen suit.

BASIL SEGGOS, Commissioner of the New York State Department of Environmental Conservation (DEC), former Chief Investigator for Riverkeeper: We wanted to know how far the spill actually extended to the south because ultimately our objective was to ensure that it was being remediated to the full extent. To understand that and to paint a more accurate picture of the spill sites, we had to use existing groundwater data from a variety of wells in the area but also the drilling some of our own wells.

We did some of that—sampling soil and soil vapor, sampling oil in the soil itself. We then built that into a more accurate picture of the full size of the spill. It slightly enlarged the size of the spill. Our research showed that it was further to the south and to the east and the other side of the BQE at the time. Then we began sharing that information with the state and feds. It became part of our litigation. There was a time when the idea of one of our consultants mentioned the risks posed by soil vapor, so we started an investigation into soil vapor and that drew the interest of, as you would imagine, law firms that wanted to explore potential private litigation.

Then we worked *with these firms* and they used some of the evidence that we've built and shared publicly as well as some of the evidence on file and filed separate cases. We, Riverkeeper, actually did not discover cancer clusters. That was a function of the private litigation that went on.

Finally, the residents point to Roux Associates' recent statement in a published report that "there have been no documented odor complaints to the NYSDEC that would be indicative of a soil vapor intrusion problem" in Greenpoint. This is in direct contradiction to what residents themselves have experienced and ignores data known to Roux Associates and ExxonMobil.

"Can you believe it?" exclaimed Greenpoint resident Robert Conlon. "On January 25, [NYSDEC] has a meeting in Greenpoint where scores of residents come out and complain about the sickening gas and oil odors in their homes, and just two weeks later they act like everything is just okay. If they will lie about something as obvious as this, what else are they hiding?"[64]

---

64. Author unknown. "Queens Residents Lawyers Cheer Anti-ExxonMobil Stance Comments," 17 May 2006, *Queens Gazette*.

MIKE SCHADE: One of the most well-known sites in that area is the Greenpoint ExxonMobil Oil Spill. As the state was investigating that site, they started identifying chlorinated solvents, chemicals like trichloroethylene (TCE), tetrachloroethylene, which is a carcinogen—cancer-causing chemical. They started identifying it in water and in soil vapor in eastern Greenpoint. When they started looking into it, they were scratching their heads, like, *that's weird*. This is not really a chemical that is traditionally associated with oil refinery contamination or sewer contaminations from oil refineries.

When they started looking into it more and tested more, they found, and eventually the State Department of Environmental Conservation realized, that they had a whole other set of issues on their hands. The more that they tested, the more that they found, and to date, they've identified about five or six facilities that either intentionally or accidentally dumped large volumes of toxic waste into the soil and groundwater in Greenpoint.

At least one of them was an old dry-cleaning facility. Some of them were other types of industrial facilities that either used or stored TCE or PERC [perchloroethylene, also known as tetrachloroethylene]. That waste eventually leaked into the ground and essentially has migrated into the community underneath people's homes. Because these chemicals, particularly TCE and PERC, are totally volatile, they can evaporate out of the groundwater and make their way into the tiny gaps that exist between soil and vapor, and eventually migrate through the tiny cracks and fissures that exist in people's basements. It's a processing known as vapor intrusion. They can pose serious health risks to people that live in these homes.

I learned about this because within a couple of months of moving into my apartment in Greenpoint, I got a notice about a community meeting that the DEC was holding about this problem. For me, it was kind of surprising because when I moved into my apartment and was living on the side of the street in Greenpoint, I purposely rented an apartment that was not above that ExxonMobil oil spill, that was a block or two away. That essentially forced me to get involved in neighborhood environmental issues. Like I said, I didn't want to parachute in and immediately get involved, but I was essentially forced to get involved because I had moved into an apartment that was on top of this toxic plume. The good news is that the DEC and the Department of Health tested our home.

HEATHER LETZKUS, artist, blogger New York Shitty: My reasons for moving here were pragmatic. First I lived on Clay Street, then I lived on Green. It was on Green, and after my now-husband moved in, who's a computer person that could plug me into something such as a blog, I just started doing documentation of all the dog shit on my street because it was insane. It started out as fun. I had a background in doing admin assist type stuff and PowerPoint presentations because, let's face facts, what are the career prospects of somebody that has an MFA in Sculpture?

I started getting a readership and it was through that, that I've met a lot of people like Laura Hofmann. Through the meetings I met Irene Klementowicz, who's also my neighbor.

MIKE SCHADE: My landlord was a progressive guy, he was an artist. He was also concerned because they had a young daughter that lived on the first floor, so they were even closer to the possible contamination than I was, because people that live on the first floor could be exposed to higher concentrations of vapors. He was actually one of the parties to the ExxonMobil litigation, and so he got the building tested and thankfully, we didn't have a problem in our building.

CHARLEY FRIEDMAN: When I decided to join the lawsuit with a number of my neighbors, the old-time Greenpointers who had been raised in their homes, whose parents had come over from the old country, Polish predominantly, they didn't want to be a part of it. They were like, "ahh, whatever." But I said "screw that."

MIKE SCHADE: There are many other people that live in northeastern Greenpoint, whose homes are now, or have been historically, contaminated with these cancer-causing chemicals.

We only found out about this because the state was investigating the ExxonMobil spill, and they discovered this whole other universe of contamination that no one even knew about.

ACACIA THOMPSON, archivist for Brooklyn Public Library's Greenpoint Environmental History Project: It's nuts that there's this plume over on Meeker Avenue which is TCE, and PCE, from dry cleaning and metalworking. People are refusing to let their homes be tested by DEC for vapor intrusion because they are concerned about their property values. Thinking about the people who live here and understanding that lots of people have come over here and worked very hard for their homes.

But, then to rent out their basements to people and not be responsible for what's in their basement is really nuts to me. It's definitely becoming a transient neighborhood where people come and live for a couple of years and leave. You have a lot of people, a lot of young people, moving over to that part of Greenpoint who don't know anything about what's going on over there in that particular spot. I think that's hugely problematic.

BASIL SEGGOS: We were working with only five or six local individuals, homeowners. There are many others that were interested in this matter. There were like several hundred homes and a few dozen businesses on top of the spill. There's only so much that Riverkeeper could do, which is file a citizen suit. We can't go after the company for private damages. That would be a function of private litigation.

If community members were interested in that, they'd have to go to a private firm, which is how Girardi & Keese came into play. They were aligned with Erin Brockovich and brought her in as well for some of the community outreach that they were doing.

VICTORIA CAMBRANES, lifelong resident, community activist, 2021 candidate for City Council District 33 in Brooklyn: In terms of the community and people who live here, I think people don't understand how bad it is and how little progress has been made. I'm not going to blame any one group or one person for that, but we should be a lot further along than we are. I honestly believe that most people who move to Greenpoint, especially in the last 10 years, that their brokers are not telling them it's a mini Chernobyl.

LISA BLOODGOOD, Director of Advocacy & Education, Newtown Creek Alliance (NCA): They're [DEC] doing the research, the door-knocking and telling people we will put this system onto your house free of charge, these are the dangers. This is what you're living on top of. And some people in Greenpoint don't want to know. There are cultural reasons. There are socioeconomic reasons. There's a whole host of reasons why somebody may slam the door on the face of the DEC state employee.

RESPONSIBILITY

THE SIGNIFICANT difference in the reaction to the Coast Guard's discovery of the oil spill in 1978 and Riverkeeper's rediscovery in 2002 was political will. It was a different time in New York City, and particularly politicians and attorneys knew that the time was right to go after the legacy polluters of Newtown Creek and Greenpoint. After decades of toothless consent decrees between the city and the PRPs (regulatory speak for "Potentially Responsible Parties"), namely ExxonMobil, several lawsuits emerged at the state and local level. Riverkeeper, along with six resident co-plaintiffs, brought the first lawsuit. The next lawsuits were from borough president Marty Markowitz, Assemblyman Joe Lentol, and other elected officials. But perhaps most important was that Attorney General Andrew Cuomo filed suit on behalf of the state. They were all then consolidated for case management purposes.

Girardi & Keese was the law firm that was defending the oil plume vapor cases. They were a reputable firm, most notably for representing Erin Brockovich's case against Public Service Enterprise Group (PSE&G). This case, of course, became the basis for the well-known movie *Erin Brockovich* starring Julia Roberts.

LAURA HOFMANN, activist, lifelong resident, O.U.T.R.A.G.E., Newtown Creek Alliance, many other nonprofits: To be clear, people knew about the oil spill in the '50s. It wasn't until Riverkeeper came into the picture and had the political muscle and the ability to sue that we even were able to get a settlement, which, by the way, my husband and I were the original co-plaintiffs in that case.

BASIL SEGGOS, Commissioner of the New York State Department of Environmental Conservation (DEC), former Chief Investigator for Riverkeeper: I wanted to find who in the state government knew about the problem, who in the city government knew about the problem. Freedom of Information law enabled me to get into the agency where I work now, DEC, and see what files they had on the problem. We worked extensively with the City of New York as well to see what they knew about the problems there. The first day we were on the Creek, the first week we're on the Creek, we spoke to the Coast Guard and have the Coast Guard come up and observe. The Coast Guard has response jurisdiction over some of these problems. Clearly, they had been aware of this issue when they arrived at the Creek. I do recall they had some institutional awareness of that problem. It felt like everyone was aware of something and they were content to leave it at that or perhaps do the bare minimum to address the problem, the assumption being that the waterway was so badly impacted that nobody would care about the problem and no one would think about how expensive it was as long as there was a simple check-the-box approach to fixing it.

JUSTIN BLOOM, former attorney for Riverkeeper, Sarasota Waterkeeper: We started researching more and more, and through Basil's investigation and myself and our other lawyers that were working with Hudson Riverkeeper we were able to develop a case. First you see it as pollution and you're like, *wow, that's bad. It shouldn't be there. There's got to be a law broken.* Typically citizens have very limited options in enforcing environmental laws, and we were limited in that case to the Clean Water Act. And so we were able to make a case that was a violation of the Clean Water Act.

BASIL SEGGOS: We wanted to understand what was happening in the water, what was happening on the land side, use the evidence to inform whether or not to bring a citizen suit under the federal Clean Water Act and if so, whether there could be a remedy that can be put in place to stop the problem.

It took, I don't recall how many months, to put the Notice of Intent to sue together, but ultimately we did file that in conjunction with several members of the community, including Mike and Laura Hofmann, Deborah Masters, Bill Schuck, Rolf Carle, and Teresa Toro. These are names I haven't mentioned in years and they come right off the tongue because I recall many days working very closely with them on this.

LAURA HOFMANN: There were two lawsuits. The lawsuit I was involved with was actually an environmental lawsuit. That's the one that later on the Attorney General and all the higher-ups took on. But it started with Riverkeeper and six community co-plaintiffs.

JUSTIN BLOOM: We apparently had an ally in the Attorney General's office.

CHRISTINE HOLOWACZ, activist, longtime resident, GWAPP, Newtown Creek Alliance, many other nonprofits: We sued ExxonMobil and we worked with then-Attorney General Andrew Cuomo. He even called me because the first settlement they had wasn't such a great settlement. We needed him to keep on going, and that we needed some more money. As a matter of fact, when he won this lawsuit, I was one of the speakers. It was in November of 2010. We won the $19.5 million.

BASIL SEGGOS: We were joined by David Yassky, Councilmember Gioia, as well as borough president Marty Markowitz. It ended up becoming a multifaceted citizen suit under the federal Clean Water Act and the Resources Conservation Recovery Act.

JOHN LIPSCOMB, Riverkeeper, Vice President of Advocacy, patrol boat operator: This is gonna sound harsher than it is. I don't believe they got interested in Newtown Creek because of the pollution in Newtown Creek. No one could see that oil. You can't—there's no public access there. It's one of those places that is truly out of sight, out of mind. The Attorney General of the City of New York is a busy job, and you've got to go where you're going to get public support for going. And the only reason those cases, that case, got picked up by first Spitzer and then Cuomo, is because Basil and Riverkeeper and all those patrols and all that press made Newtown Creek a story that a lot of people knew about, and suddenly there was a chance for these AGs to do something that the public was interested in, where they would get attention for doing a good thing.

BASIL SEGGOS: They were all combined. It was the same suit, effectively, that a number of interveners joined and became part of. But the state's case never really took off until Cuomo took office. That's when he took a particular interest in this problem and was integral to its handling.

JOHN LIPSCOMB: That's like David and a hundred Goliaths, you know, went after a cement plant—and we went after a number of places. It was a flurry of activity. The Clean Water Act has a citizen supervision, and so goddammit, we're gonna sue 'em.

JOE LENTOL, New York State Assembly, District 50: I think it's really a question of a big corporation being able to negotiate better with all of these government agencies that don't have the same resources that they do, to paper people to death. It's easier for the DEC and the Attorney General to go after little guys than big guys like ExxonMobil and the big oil companies. That's what I really think was the problem was. Somebody who was brave enough to get into the fight and bring down an ExxonMobil and bring them to their knees.

LAURA HOFMANN: I was so thrilled when Riverkeeper came into the picture and a lawsuit started. Because it put pressure on the property owners to be part of a lawsuit and to get the information out there and to start doing things about cleaning it up, because it was still in the news. It was all over the place. There was no avoiding it.

JOE LENTOL: There was a time I said to myself that I wasn't going to be part of a lawsuit, because whenever I would try to engage the political figures who were in charge of the DEC or the DEP, they would say, *we can't talk to you because you're suing us. We can't really have a conversation with you.* I decided to back off from the lawsuits so that I could put political pressure on these people. I thought that was a wiser strategy than becoming part of a lawsuit.

But I went to battle early on with the DEC and the Attorney General's office for consistently entering into consent decrees with all of these polluters. I put in legislation that never got past the Senate to require disclosure and full openness with consent decrees, so that the community could participate in it. By its very nature, they would sign agreements and remain secret, and then they would have a private settlement, which also means some sort of monetary compensation to those who were affected. I think we only got a legitimate one when Cuomo became the Attorney General.

DOROTHY SWICK: I met with one of the attorneys that [Newtown Creek Monitoring Committee] recommended. I had pictures at the time that showed the filtration system in the wall and they knew [what it was] right away.

JUSTIN BLOOM: It was like a mass action where Girardi & Keese started just signing up and representing individual homeowners and families all with very similar claims and similar types of damages, but not so similarly situated that it would drive to class action. There were hundreds of plaintiffs all having similar claims.

JOHN LIPSCOMB: My daughter, who's now 26, I took her to a meeting of Girardi & Keese, in the basement of a senior center, I think it was in Greenpoint in the winter. There was crepe paper still wrapped around the pipes up above your head, folding chairs. That law firm was presenting to the public the possibility of joining a lawsuit. They flew in from California. All of these young attorneys had their ties, jackets, gelled hair and tans. They sat there and all the people from Greenpoint are sitting there, and you could feel it: *Here we go again.* I'm sitting there with my daughter and her little girlfriend, they were 10 or something, and in walks Erin Brockovich—she's so much more impressive than any movie depiction of her. She got up there and said, "I know what you're thinking. You're thinking that these guys are just more talking heads, but they work for me. They won for me. And if you want them to win for you, you've got to sign up as a plaintiff." And the whole room changed.

CHARLEY FRIEDMAN: We joined that one. That's when I asked my neighbor if she wanted to do it and she was like, "Screw that," and I was like "Why?" It was a lack of faith in the system, and hearing that they haven't done much to clean up even though there's all this money floating around does make me understand why she didn't have faith in the system.

DOROTHY SWICK: There was meetings and at first people didn't want to go. They felt that they're not having troubles, so why should they go to the meetings? Eventually, when these attorneys got involved, all of a sudden everybody wanted to get in on this.

JUSTIN BLOOM: We really doubted the numbers provided by Exxon—the defendants. I really doubted and I still doubt the veracity and the integrity of the reporting that they had. Especially the volume of oil that they had recovered and their estimates of the oil that remained. I think it was probably less oil recovered and more oil remaining than what they were saying.

DOROTHY SWICK: The state made them pay for this cleanup, which was good for me because I said eventually if I wanted to sell this house, how am I going to sell it? I need a letter of clearance that everything's fine.

JOE LENTOL: We got action by the DEC to allay their fears, because a lot of people, that's all they have is their property, and they were really scared that if they ever wanted to sell and move somewhere else, they couldn't get the money for their property. Little did they know that there was going to be people who would buy the property now for three million dollars, oil spill or not.

JUSTIN BLOOM: They [ExxonMobil's legal defense] were basically saying there's been oil refinery production here since the beginning of the industrial revolution. There've been so many spills by so many different companies that how can you determine who is responsible for what?

DOROTHY SWICK: I never thought in my lifetime I would go through something like that. When I went for the deposition, their [the Exxon lawyers] thing was, *well, why didn't you move? Well,* I tell them, *how could I move if my husband is getting chemotherapy? His doctors are here!* I'm supposed to uproot him and get all his doctors. He was comfortable with the doctors he had, and I said that's why I always stayed. They were really adamant on it, when they told me, *well, you should've moved.* Well, how could I pick up and move with this case? With the cancer case? Come on. They were just pushing me and pushing me, but I tell them, *you can push me so far.* And then my sister lived here. She had the second-floor apartment and they asked, *well, we know what rent you charged. Well, did she move out?* And I said since she didn't move out—my sister was killed in the World Trade Center. I had to tell them that she was killed at Tower One at the World Trade Center and my niece was young at the time. She had one year of college to go so she kept the apartment and I helped her out. They were a little pushy about that.

I just turned around… *You're not pushing me on that subject.*

CHARLEY FRIEDMAN: When I joined on, my wife and I were both were deposed. We went to Exxon's offices in downtown Manhattan, where they just tried to squash me. I remember that vividly. They tried to put holes in everything that I had with their counterarguments. But they were really trying to make me look like I was not a credible sane person.

A number of Potentially Responsible Parties (PRPs) have been named for the site. The first group, called the Performing PRP Respondents, have all signed a 2011 Administrative Order on Consent to conduct the Remedial Investigation and Feasibility Study for the Site. These Respondents include The City of New York, BP America, Inc., The Brooklyn Union Gas Company (d/b/a National Grid), ExxonMobil Oil Corporation, Phelps Dodge Refining Corporation (now part of Freeport McMoRan, Inc.) and Texaco, Inc. (now part of Chevron Corporation).

Another group of PRPs has been recently named. These include the Consolidated Edison Company of New York, National Railroad Passenger Corporation (AMTRAK), American Premier Underwriters, Inc., Connell Limited Partnership, The Long Island Railroad Company, Motiva Enterprises, LLC, Shell Oil Company and Simsmetal East LLC (a subsidiary of Sims Metal Management, Inc.).[65]

BASIL SEGGOS: It took a number of years to work its way through ultimately towards settlement. I had gone to the private sector and then several months thereafter, the Attorney General got a settlement in conjunction with Riverkeeper. It was a $25 million settlement plus a directive that the companies involved, Exxon, BP and maybe a couple of others, had to put in place advanced remediation systems.

I mentioned going back to the boom system; the boom system is only in place to keep the oil from getting out to the East River. An advanced remediation system would prevent the oil from ever getting into the creek in the first place, and that's what we helped design when I was in Riverkeeper, using an underground sort of hydrologic control system where you have a series of wells pumping water and oil into the wells and then sending that water for treatment back to a big tank.

JOHN LIPSCOMB: The Newtown Creek Alliance, that sprang out of the settlement. And now you have Willis Elkins. He's out there twice a week now. He's patrolling more than Riverkeeper now. His whole world is Newtown Creek.

Citizen patrols—that started with Riverkeeper. I get to go there and I get to see a really good outcome, better-looking water, and Newtown Creek is never gonna be alone again. It's really satisfying. It doesn't mean that Newtown Creek is healed. It's still in terrible shape, but Newtown Creek will never be alone again.

65. Staff. "Superfund Site: Newtown Creek Brooklyn, Queens, NY Cleanup Activities." *Epa.gov*, Environmental Protection Agency, 2019.

THE SECOND-WAVE ACTIVISTS

NEWTOWN CREEK and the surrounding neighborhoods of Williamsburg and Greenpoint now have second- and even third-generation activist groups. The first was Concerned Citizens of Greenpoint, known to the press as the "Angry Moms," featuring Irene Klementowicz, Elizabeth Roncketti, Christine Holowacz, Laura Hofmann, and others. They spawned even more groups to address the array of seemingly intractable problems. It seems that each activist belongs to multiple organizations. I found keeping track of all the groups very difficult. Often the activists themselves can't remember all the groups in which they belong.

As each wave of people migrated into the neighborhood, a few individuals committed their time and skills to expand the coalition of activists. Some have moved away, some passed away, and many burned out from the constant struggle. Like any group of activists, this was not a single constituency. The coalition was loose. There was a dizzying array of acronyms to learn: NAG, OUTRAGE, NCA, CAG, GWAPP, OSA, et al., in addition to working relationships with the government's initial-laden organizations such as EPA, DEC, and DEP. They often argued with each other over their goals and one another's suspected motivations. (There is a glossary on page 278 to help navigate the many agency acronyms.)

TRINA HAMILTON, associate professor of geography at State University of Buffalo, co-editor *Just Green Enough: Urban Development and Environmental Gentrification*: I think they [first-wave activists] were frustrated. They'd been doing this for decades. They [residents] weren't all willing to get on board with the activism because—well, they were just living their lives and trying to survive. But also, those who were homeowners were concerned about their property values if this became a Superfund designation, or new reports came out. That's why, for a long time, it was this strong group of long-term activists, mostly who were women, that didn't have a coalition.

JUSTIN BLOOM, former attorney for Riverkeeper, Sarasota Waterkeeper: It was just kind of a loose and broad coalition of folks that have lived in Greenpoint for a long time. And then some hipsters that were moving in and then some of the pioneering new businesses.

ACACIA THOMPSON, archivist for Brooklyn Public Library's Greenpoint Environmental History Project: Somebody gave me a flow tree for Williamsburg For Open Process, which was an organization trying to better understand how city process worked,

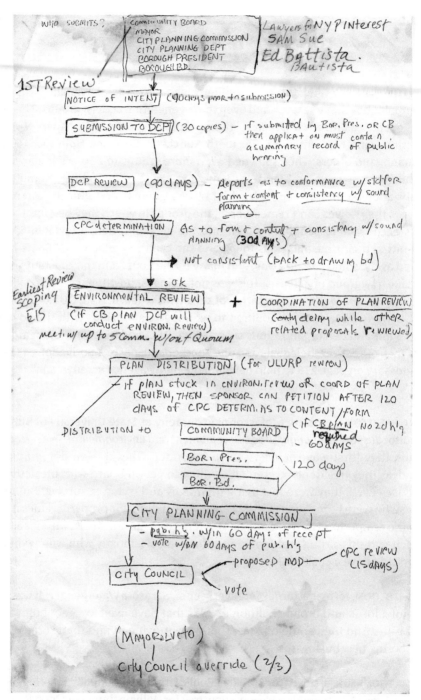

WHO SUBMITS?

COMMUNITY BOARD
MAYOR
CITY PLANNING COMMISSION
CITY PLANNING DEPT
BOROUGH PRESIDENT
BOROUGH BD.

LAWYERS fn NYP INTEREST
SAM SUE
Ed Battista.
BAUTISTA

1ST Review

NOTICE OF INTENT (90days prior to submission)

SUBMISSION TO DCP (30 copies) — if submitted by Bor. Pres. or CB then applicat on must conta n a summary record of public hearing

DCP Review (90 DAYS) — Reports as to conformance w/ stch for form + content + consistency w/ sound planning

CPC determination as to form + content + consistency w/ sound planning (30 days)

Not consistent (back to drawing bd)

s ok

Earliest Review Scoping EIS

ENVIRONMONTAL REVIEW (If CB plan DCP will conduct environ. review) meeting w/ up to 5 comm. w/ out Quorum

+ COORDINATION OF PLAN REVIEW Conly delay while other related proposals re viewed,

PLAN DISTRIBUTION (for ULURP review)
— if plan stuck in environ. review or coord of plan review, then sponsor can petition after 120 days of CPC determ. as to content /form

DISTRIBUTION to

COMMUNITY BOARD

BOR. Pres.

BOR. Bd.

(If CB plan No 2d h'g required — 60 days
120 days

CITY PLANNING COMMISSION
— pub. h'g. w/in 60 days of receipt
— vote w/in 60 days of pub. h'g

CITY COUNCIL

proposed MOD—
CPC review (15 days)

vote

(Mayoral veto)

City Council override (2/3)

Williamsburg Organized for an Open Process, city planning review process flow chart.
Donated by Hank Linhart. Collected through the Greenpoint Environmental History Project of
Brooklyn Public Library. Brooklyn Public Library, Brooklyn Collection.

and it was predevelopment. It was right in front of the rezoning. People would be like, "There's a meeting. You have to come."

VICTORIA CAMBRANES, lifelong resident, community activist, 2021 candidate for City Council District 33 in Brooklyn: Things started coming to a head around 2000. People started to move in, a lot of artists started to move in, and there was like the first kind of wave of people starting to ask questions. It had a lot to do with Irene's work with the incinerator and the treatment plants. She was very, very vocal, and around that time you started to have groups form like GWAPP (Greenpoint Waterfront Association for Parks and Planning) and NAG (Neighbors Against Garbage) and things like that, and OSA (Open Space Alliance), and they started to get really involved with Newtown Creek and their main thing was about the oil.

TRINA HAMILTON: I think the first wave was really fighting against being continually dumped on. People talked about the black mayonnaise oozing up in their gardens and that type of thing, but there wasn't a strong push, say, for a Superfund designation. So, it wasn't distinct entities over time; it was a continual broadening of the alliance.

CHRISTINE HOLOWACZ: What else? Newtown Creek Alliance, of course, I'm there since the beginning. And GWAPP (Greenpoint Waterfront Association for Parks and Planning)—well, GWAPP has recently merged together with NAG. It's in the process of merging, so they're going to be one organization. I am part of that board too. And of course, Newtown Creek Monitoring Committee. Over the years it's been a lot, a lot of different organizations.

What else? I did work for Greenpoint Property Owners, I'm part of OUTRAGE (Organization United for Trash Reduction & Garbage Equity) for the garbage, and I think that's it. It's more than enough.

WINIFRED CURRAN, associate professor of geography at DePaul University, co-editor *Just Green Enough: Urban Development and Environmental Gentrification*: I think the old-school activism goes back to the 1970s. I think those early years were very much just about raising awareness within the community. And also this idea that it's almost like a game of whack-a-mole, fighting, or putting out fires, in terms of *now they're proposing another waste station, now they're proposing a new power plant, now they're proposing a dumping site.* Laura and Christine especially were really at the forefront of educating the gentrifiers. The gentrifiers come in not knowing anything about the neighborhood, not knowing anything about the history of pollution, and then learning that they live on an oil spill, and slowly coming to the awareness of, like, *Hey, this might not be good for me*, and starting to form their own organizations, and then people like Laura started going to those meetings.

LAURA HOFMANN, activist, lifelong resident, O.U.T.R.A.G.E., Newtown Creek Alliance, many other nonprofits: It's made it very challenging because people are coming in and not knowing. They live on one of those nicely planted streets in Greenpoint that were rezoned and have all these nice buildings on it? They don't know that a few blocks down is a sewage treatment facility.

The [real estate agents and brokers] certainly are not going to tell you that there's 14 waste transfer stations. You'll see traffic, and they'll know that it's dusty, but a lot of people say, *oh well, it's traffic.* That's when the wake-up happens and they realize that they're in that situation. It was difficult getting people organized even when there was a bunch of old-school people here. But when you slash that population and now you're working with newcomers, it's that much more challenging because you need the resources and you need the actual volunteers and all of that stuff to make it happen.

WINIFRED CURRAN: I think Laura was, as another person said of her, "I think she's all the groups." She didn't let anyone have a conversation about these issues without her being in the room. That was useful in at least two ways.

One, she helped to educate people, like, *Hey, this is not just your fight that you came into when you moved into this neighborhood three months ago. We've been working on this for 30 years. Also, you don't get to claim this as yours. This is what people have had to go through. However scary this feels to you, imagine if you're the third generation dealing with these issues.* I think that really helps to create a much deeper sense of how important and serious this was to a lot of long-term residents, and make it not just about them and their property values.

I think that was really humanizing and was incredibly important. And then to realize once they are on board emotionally, that they have a lot of political and social capital that they can use in this cause.

The in-movers had the knowledge of, *how do you do a good television interview? How do you make sure that the soundbite that you want to be included is included? How do we get this message out to the press in the best way?* The merging of those two skill sets is what made it as effective as it was.

KATE ZIDAR, green infrastructure research engineer, former director of Newtown Creek Alliance (NCA): The Newtown Creek Monitoring Committee was really early on and hyper-focused. They came out of the actual expansion of the sewage treatment plant. They were real sentinel, in the sense that they were born out of a regulatory process where they had these regular meetings, there had to be a community benefit. They participated—they put their bodies into that and showed up to these meetings, took meeting minutes.

DOROTHY SWICK, former resident, co-plaintiff in Exxon suit: I was on the Newtown Creek [Monitoring Committee], the Water Treatment Plant. That's how I really got involved.

KATIE BUCINO NAPLAIARSKI, longtime Greenpoint resident, teacher, activist, open space advocate: Because it's a small community, you get to know people and you see the same faces, different places. It's really that bond and that network is very useful because when there comes an issue, you're then able to reach out to those different people and call the rest and become a force.

I'm in touch with Laura Hofmann all the time, sometimes with Willis as he has worked on the waterfront also.

WILLIS ELKINS, activist, Executive Director, Newtown Creek Alliance (NCA): Obviously, it wasn't like we want this whole thing to be covered in oil, but it's a working area and there were certain businesses that have always been sort of involved in that process too, which I think makes it [NCA] a unique organization. Katie Schmid was the first director. She worked for [City Councilman David] Yassky and then came on to help with NCA.

Kate Zidar was, at the time she was a grad student at Pratt, and had been doing a lot of research about sewer infrastructure and lived in Greenpoint. She got heavily involved so she was like the next generation. She was brought on and worked for a couple years as the executive director, and then I started.

KATE ZIDAR: My first involvement with the Newtown Creek Alliance was as a member. I was a resident. I moved to North Brooklyn in the late '90s, I became involved in environmental issues that were going on there. This is kind of the tail end of the era of shutting down the waste incineration plants for the Brooklyn waterfront, and a lot of those issues really dovetailed with the Brooklyn waterfront on Newtown Creek, and I became involved in that area, the kind of confluence of working waterfront and the broader environmental issues that were being worked on at that time.

LISA BLOODGOOD: I think NAG has the biggest footprint as far as what they'd done in the neighborhood, but NCA owned the creek [issue] and NAG began as Neighbors Against Garbage.

ANTHONY BUISSERETH, Executive Director North Brooklyn Neighbors (NBN), formerly Neighbors Allied for Growth (NAG): In August of 1994 several residents got together because they were concerned about the dumping that was happening over in the River. They created Neighbors Against Garbage and it actually was part of a video collective. They filmed what they believed to be illegal dumping by a carting company. They started filming and that got them into a lot of trouble with the owners because they didn't want to be filmed. Eventually some of the footage made NY1[66] and the organization kind of grew organically from there, from being a kind of a ragtag group of maybe the residents concerned about what they thought was illegal dumping and actually should not be illegal dumping.

The organization already started to spread its wings, and one of the issues was economic empowerment zones and ensuring that there were jobs in the neighborhood in the transformed manufacturing districts. Around 2009 or 2010 the name changed to "Neighbors Allied for Good Growth." For several years the organization worked on those sorts of issues. They also started working on things like tenants' rights issues as well. The name change came to align with the kind of broader vision of the organization.

CHRISTINE HOLOWACZ: I have been on OUTRAGE (Organization United for Trash Reduction & Garbage Equity) for the garbage fight, I have been in NAG. At the time I had an organization called Greenpoint Property Owners. That organization was for all homeowners, usually for older folks. There were a lot of rent-stabilized buildings here, and there were a lot of changes that were made in the '70s and '80s and people really didn't know how to do it, and there was an older woman who had that organization.

I spoke to everybody, I told them and that's how the first fight began. We started to meet and I went to Pierre Gillespie who was from Williamsburg. He was, at the time, the director for NAG (Neighbors Against Garbage). I talked to him and we got it together and we basically started to fight this power plant. It didn't take us long because the community got together. Because Con Edison was a big corporation and had a board of directors, all the people went to the board of directors. We found out when they had the meeting—basically people stood outside and talked to them and told them how horrible they are, and how can they do this to our community and all of this.

After that, maybe a couple of weeks, they said they were stepping aside. The deal is not going through. We fought that power plant and we had a lot of energy. Then not soon after, maybe a month or two, we heard that there was another plant.

We had this energy. We included more people. [TGE] wanted to build the power plant right in the Bushwick Inlet where the Bayside site was.

That took us years to fight. But we did win it. GWAPP was Greenpoint, Williamsburg Against the Power Plant. That's how we formed the organization, because we needed a nonprofit to fight it and to represent us. And that's how GWAPP was founded.

---

66. Local New York City television station

LAURA HOFMANN: One of the biggest battles was actually several battles against the power plants coming into the neighborhood. It was a Con Ed proposal that one day they came in and left, because they were met with such overwhelming fury in the neighborhood, (laughs) They didn't even waste their time. But then later on there was this Transgas Energy Systems. I was part of the task force and it was a lot of work. We had to do a lot of research. We had to read a lot of legal materials and work with attorneys and stuff, but the community, Greenpoint and Williamsburg, joined together and we were able to fight them off and we won that battle.

We helped with the creation of the environmental justice program with DEC. We were able to support legislation to stop any more waste transfer stations from entering the community and we fought until [NYC Mayor Bill] de Blasio signed some capacity reduction legislation. There's been a lot of wins.

KATE ZIDAR: If you look at this story, I would value the lifers, the people who really have maintained relationships, who are continuing to collaborate with one another, after being contentious, after disagreeing, after collaborating, and after even coming back, and bringing in resources from all along their careers.

I'm back in the city now, and I go back to Newtown Creek and I talk to three people, and I'm fully caught up. That water body has a unique set of people, who are telling its story. I learned that from the people who were there on day one.

2010 SUPERFUND AND A NOTE ON THE GOWANUS CANAL

IN 2010 the EPA finally designated Superfund status to both Newtown Creek and the equally polluted Gowanus Canal. Throughout these interviews there have been frequent comparisons to the Gowanus. Also in Brooklyn, the Gowanus Canal is only a few miles away and has a very similar history. It has its own activist communities and issues with the state agencies and gentrification. Where it differs is that there's less of a push to keep Gowanus industrial.

There had been a lengthy battle between (many) of the property owners concerned about property values and the rest of the community who wanted their neighborhoods and waterways cleaned up. Once a site acquires CERCLA status, EPA is mandated to remove the people or the ecological threat. This was largely a victory for the activists who beat the drum on remediation since the spills were discovered.

August 13, 2008

The Honorable Stephen L. Johnson
Administrator
United States Environmental Protection Agency
Ariel Rios Building – 1101A
1200 Pennsylvania Avenue, NW
Washington, DC 20460

Dear Administrator Johnson:

I am writing to request that the United States Environmental Protection Agency (EPA), use its Superfund authority to conduct preliminary tests at four known hotspots along Newtown Creek, in New York City (Attachment A).

Newtown Creek, which borders Brooklyn and Queens, is well known as one of the most polluted industrial waterways in North America, where chemicals from factories along the bed of the Creek have seeped into the soil, sediment and water. The New York State Department of Environmental Conservation and the New York State Office of the Attorney General have found evidence that certain hazardous substances regulated under CERCLA have been released at the Newtown Creek site (Attachment B). It is time the federal Superfund program conduct the testing that is necessary to determine whether Newtown Creek should be placed on the NPL list. As the Chair of the Superfund and Environmental Health Subcommittee and a member of the Senate's Environmental and Public Works Committee, it is of particular interest to me.

For years, the residents in the vicinity of Newtown Creek have been forced to live, work and play with toxic fumes in the air and contaminated water, soil and sediment on the ground. This exposure has led to community concern about potential pockets of serious illness. Superfund was established to address abandoned hazardous waste sites. The factories responsible for much of the chemical contamination have long since closed and as the cleanup authority of last resort, I see the federal Superfund program as the most effective way to solve this longstanding problem once and for all. The people of Newtown Creek have suffered long enough.

I appreciate your prompt attention and response to this matter.

Sincerely,
Hillary Rodham Clinton

MITCH WAXMAN, historian for Newtown Creek Alliance (NCA), blogger Newtown Pentacle: The [Army Corps of Engineers] widened it. They actually removed an island and connected another island to Queens. The Corps has been messing around with the navigational channel going back to about the Civil War. This is their function—to improve shorelines for commercial, and in the modern sense, for environmental purposes. At the time, the idea was to create a fully bulkheaded Newtown Creek, which would serve the needs of industry.

That's when we saw the modern shape of Newtown Creek emerge, which unfortunately wasn't designed with environmental hydraulics in mind. There was a terrific amount of pollution in the 19th and early 20th, but it used to flush in and out on the East River tide.

After the Corps of Engineers created the modern shape, that caused material to stay in the canal and to begin building a bed of sediments—which are the very bed of sediments that the federal EPA are so concerned about that they created the Superfund designation in 2010.

ANGELA LICATA, Deputy Commissioner of Sustainability NYC Department of Environmental Protection: The EPA does a scoring to determine whether a site is eligible for oversight under the CERCLA program. That's what they did with Newtown Creek, is they alerted us to the fact that they were about to do a score rating to determine whether or not Newtown Creek was eligible for regulatory oversight under CERCLA. That's when we got involved and commented.

MITCH WAXMAN: Exxon is maintaining a whole series of wells here in Greenpoint. They've actually showed us when we visited the location that they're fully in control of the groundwater of Greenpoint. They can basically turn the pumps on and off and the water starts flowing in different directions. You know, it's pretty interesting, but they're not doing this by choice or out of goodwill.

They had Andrew Cuomo force them to do it. You never want Andrew Cuomo to force you to do anything. He's not a nice man. But saying that, despite a lot of things that are in the negative column about the current Governor, I voted for him because there hasn't been a better friend in high politics to Newtown Creek than Andy Cuomo in the last maybe hundred years, maybe even longer. Rebuilding the Kosciuszko Bridge is going to have some major effects in terms of creating new parkland. The new highway is going to be a lot more efficient, which is going to reduce air pollution.

His role as Attorney General and forcing ExxonMobil to the table really is the predicate for EPA stepping into doing Superfund. I don't know if we'd have Superfund if it wasn't for the ExxonMobil side of it, because the political machines of New York City itself, the last thing they wanted was Superfund.

ANGELA LICATA: I don't think we, the City, contested the Superfund labeling for Newtown Creek.

JOE LENTOL, New York State Assembly, District 50: I think the Superfund was really a godsend, because it not only dealt with the Creek itself, it dealt with the sedi ment and the ground underneath. I have to give Congresswoman [Nydia] Velazquez a lot of credit, to have this declared a Superfund. Without political action in Washington, it never would have happened. That was an important step, because I think that was required in order for there to be a really good cleanup of Newtown Creek.

MIKE SCHADE, activist, environmental health campaigner, Mind The Store Campaign Director with Safer Chemicals, Healthy Families: As far as I've seen, I don't think it's impacted the federal approach. I think that it wasn't a question of if, but when Newtown Creek would be addressed under the federal Superfund program. I'm quite frankly shocked that it took this long for Newtown Creek to be added to the federal program.

The question is, will the eventual cleanup benefit the people that suffered from contamination the most? Will this cleanup benefit those that live with pollution problems for decades? Sadly, I'm not sure that it will, because so many people are being priced out and forced out of that neighborhood because the rents are too high. Even myself, a generally fairly privileged, white, middle-class guy, I can't even afford to live in that neighborhood anymore.

TRINA HAMILTON, associate professor of geography at State University of Buffalo, co-editor *Just Green Enough: Urban Development and Environmental Gentrification*: I think the concerns were that Superfund would prevent development. It hasn't necessarily harmed the Gowanus. It hasn't stopped hotels from locating right near it. When we talked to people early on, they were kind of incredulous that these high-end hotels were popping up near a Superfund site. But it doesn't seem to bother people. There was concern about them getting financing and loans and how that might have been impacted by a Superfund, and concerns about the possibility of additional responsibility being put on their shoulders for cleanup.

WINIFRED CURRAN, associate professor of geography at DePaul University, co-editor *Just Green Enough: Urban Development and Environmental Gentrification*: The other concern is that, because it is such a political process—it was all "rah-rah go Team Superfund" under the Obama Administration—but there is this recognition that if at the federal level, the Superfund project is just basically frozen because of a lack of funds, then that just leaves the neighborhood in limbo for an even longer period of time. Already, this is a massive environmental disaster that all but the best estimates are that it takes at least 20 to 25 years to clean up. Well, how much longer does it take to clean up if there's no money? What's the time horizon here? After all this fighting and all these meetings and all this division, and then nothing happens, I think that that could be the most destructive thing of all. It's just all this work that's been put into this, and then to not actually see a whole lot of things change.

NUHART PLASTICS

NUHART PLASTICS Factory is located on the northwest side of Greenpoint. It was once a busy plastic factory that had been in industrial use since 1887. The address had a number of previous lives before becoming the NuHart Plastics Factory. According to the website habitatmap.org, "Prior to the late 1940s, the site and the surrounding lots were used as a boiler shop for Logan Ironworks, two stables, a gas and light fixture factory, a sheet metal works, a soap factory, a waterproofing factory, and a scrap metal facility." The facility became a plastics factory in the 1940s, where it made vinyl siding, sheet metal, foam rubber and asbestos sheeting. Owner Sol Graf brought a lot of jobs to the neighborhood and sold the business in 2004 when it became storage.

NuHart was designated a Superfund site in 2010, the same year as Newtown Creek and Gowanus Canal.

LAURA HOFMANN: I don't recall the exact year that the incinerator closed, but it closed I think it was in the late 1990s, maybe even later. But that was running for quite a while. The PVC manufacturer was running until sometime in the 2000s. It's basically one big brownfield Superfund site because it was all industrial uses over the years. Everywhere a developer might be digging up, there's that possibility that they're running into contamination, and it's been many contaminated sites that needed remediation over the years since the rezoning occurred.

Every time those sites are unearthed, people are re-exposed. Newcomers are getting maybe not the same type of exposure we had, but they are indeed getting some kind of exposure. This is why it's so important to a lot of the old people, who've been here so long and saw all of this go down, demand that they improve things, because people that are moving into this neighborhood are moving in thinking that everything's hunky-dory. That's because it looks better, looks cleaner than it is, and it's simply not true. It's one thing if you know that you're moving to a contaminated area and it's another if you don't.

MIKE SCHADE: When the plant was in existence, many neighbors complained about air emissions and pollution from the plant. In fact, Irene, from Concerned Citizens of Greenpoint, was one of the first activists that were sounding the alarm around emissions from that plant. Irene still lives near it. The plant closed down in the early 2000s, I think by 2005 it was closed, and the facility had a number of underground storage tanks underneath it that stored waste oil and particularly phthalates—chemicals that are hormonal, endocrine-disrupting chemicals that make bioplastics soft and flexible.

Over time, either the facility intentionally dumped waste, or probably more likely, these underground storage tanks, as they often do, especially older ones, leaked. It probably leaked very slowly over time. We don't know precisely when, but probably decades ago. Over time this released a massive amount of poisonous phthalates into the soil, into the groundwater underneath the plant, which has spread to the community.

SCOTT FRASER, activist, Greenpointers Against Smell Pollution (GASP), writer and director TV and movies: We used to get headaches.

KIM FRASER: Well, I used to feel lightheaded there. But I always thought, *oh, I'm just tired. It's hard being a mother, sitting at this park for hours.*

SCOTT FRASER: No, I thought I was dying from the freakin' plastic bags.

ANTHONY BUISSERETH: At NuHart there's a bunch of residents, the building owners who don't want their areas tested. That's become the obstacle. They don't want to give you access, so you don't get access—done.

LAURA HOFMANN: I think it's a combination of our elected officials and the agencies, because it's their duty to start thinking out of the box and to really put their heads together and figure something out to get that done.

VICTORIA CAMBRANES, lifelong resident, community activist, 2021 candidate for City Council District 33 in Brooklyn: We used to hear stories about the NuHart Park, maybe in the early '80s, late '70s when NuHart was still operating, they would open up their chimneys in the summertime and the kids would all run out of the park and catch the snow on their tongues and stuff. That's the legacy that we grew up with. That's why I find it so appalling that people would even consider putting a school there now—it's like we've not learned anything.

ANTHONY BUISSERETH: We [NBN] are the state technical assistance grantee for that site. What the state does for a Superfund site is they build community trust. They partner with community organizations who apply to fund an independent consultant that works with the community organization. The consultant that reviews all the documents that come through from the DEC is like a translator for the school resident. We also submit comments on various aspects of things around the site. And then relatedly, we've done work around the site of the school that was planned for being that close to [the contamination] across the street.

We don't know how long the construction and the cleanup is going to take and the exposures that will happen to young children while the school opens. It's also a problem.

CHRISTINE HOLOWACZ: NuHart had then operated at the time and they were doing plastics. It wasn't until a few years ago, I was working at the time with the DEP as community liaison for the Newtown Creek Monitoring Committee, and so we had a sludge storage tank right there next to NuHart. And, there was a lot of complaints of all different kinds of smells. We've done a lot of studies and it is true that some of the smells came from that tank.

DEP had gone over there and put all different kinds of instruments and things, and filters so that smells would not come through, because at one point, way back, that tank was just open. I mean, think about it. Then they covered it and then they did additional work. I've gotten, again, complaints as the community liaison in that area from one of the residents that it smelled really badly. The guy from air resources then realized that this is part of the Sewer Treatment Plant. He came and he found me in the office and he says, *What's going on here? You're making a smell, I have to come in.*

The plant superintendent, whose name is James Pynn, he was an amazing person. He was really a community person. He did not live in Greenpoint, but he wanted to make sure that the plant works and it's the best that it could. I got Jimmy and I said "Jimmy, this guy from air resources is coming here. I don't know, can you go with him?" So he went with him to the tank, which was about five to seven minutes away. They went to check it. He calls me back in a little while and he says, "Christine, it's not the tank." I remembered that some people had before complained about NuHart. I said to him, "Can that guy from Air Resources go anywhere?" He asks him, he says, "Yeah, I can go anywhere I want. I can just walk in. People have to open up their stores." I said, "Could you go to NuHart? Because I think the smell might be coming from there because a lot of people are saying it to themselves, but nobody really does anything."

When the guy from Air Resources and Jimmy walked in, Jim came back and he said "Christine, it's like a third-world country. These people are working on their workstations. You couldn't see them." He says the guy shut them down right there and then. He said he's never seen anything like that, these kinds of conditions.

And that's how the next problems started with the NuHart Company, because then the DEP and other agencies went in there, because of the guy from Air Resources and Jimmy. They have gone in there and they've realized that they don't have all these permits and they asked them to do all of this. They at first shut down the plants and they said they were going to get all these permits, but then they really didn't. They said that they moved the operation somewhere else to another state and this building became vacant and I guess ready for sale.

Now when the building is ready for sale, this is where all the other problems started that Mike Schade is talking about. There was a developer who wants to take down the building, who wants to build residential, but in the meantime, because of this company, the way they have worked, there is all of this plume underneath the street and the city wants to build a school next to it and people are afraid of what's going to happen. This is how the story goes for NuHart.

ACACIA THOMPSON: I've heard from two people at NuHart, about how in the 1950s when NuHart was a functioning plastic factory, there would appear this foamy substance that came out of one of the sides of the wall at points. This is across the street from Greenpoint playground. Children would play in this. They would play with this wacky, horrible plastic factory funk. To think about what happened, and nobody said that's a bad idea—it's shocking to me.

Also in that area—the playground has been there at least since the 1940s, because I have a picture from Parks Department of Greenpoint playground—right across the street, Commercial Street, is the Greenpoint coal docks. You have these mounds of coal and then you've got the playground right there. I mean, hindsight and everything, but you would just think, *why wouldn't anybody maybe correlate all breathing problems and childhood asthma to the fact that there are mounds of coal across the street from Greenpoint playground?*

VICTORIA CAMBRANES: I grew up right on the corner of Java and Franklin. My mom is Polish, my dad is Guatemalan. I went to grammar school on DuPont Street. We would play in DuPont Park every day, like during the week, every weekend as well.

LAURA HOFMANN: The park that fronts on Franklin Street across the street from the NuHart site, that's called the Greenpoint Playground at the portion of the playground closest to Clay Street and Franklin Street. There's always been a lot of water that collected in that corner of the park and it's always been a chemical type of smell. I personally don't believe that the plume does not extend to the park. I don't believe it. If it's true that it doesn't, then something is clearly happening there, because we've always smelled some kind of chemical odor in that portion of the park. I have no reason to trust the agencies, because as I said, there was an incident and there was a plume when they said that there wasn't. There's been lies and deceit all through these years. There was no reason for me to trust the agencies. What I think is going on there with the NuHart site is that it's a contaminated site that has more contamination than's being told to the community. I just don't believe the involved agencies.

MIKE SCHADE: The DEC has estimated that there's between 40–60 thousand gallons of phthalates underneath the plant that have migrated into the community. If you look at a map, you'll see that the plume has migrated right up to the edge of the park that is directly across the street from the plant, and right at the edge of a proposed school that the city is proposing to build, or they've approved to build. It's an interesting situation where there's a connection between the overdevelopment and the gentrification and the community and the need for more facilities for children.

Because of the rezoning in North Brooklyn, there are all these high towers being built, and because the towers are being built, the city's requiring a school to be built in the community. The city reached a deal with the developer to build the school directly across the street and directly next to as much as 60,000 gallons of toxic waste chemicals that pose serious risks to children's health, chemicals that are linked to infertility, birth defects in baby boys, asthma and other serious health problems. In addition to the plume of phthalates, there's also other petrochemicals that are present underneath the facility and then there's also a plume of another chemical, TCE, trichloroethylene, the same chemical that was at the Meeker Avenue plume that I lived on top of. In some respects, that's almost a greater concern because TCE has also migrated offsite and that's underneath buildings where people today still work. There's a very strong likelihood that people that work in those buildings are likely being exposed to potentially harmful levels of TCE over the long term.

ANTHONY BUISSERETH: The school has not been constructed yet, but suppose the cleanup takes 10 years at NuHart. You would assume that a school can be built within 10 years and have students going there. They're still planning to build the school there. We are in a holding pattern. We haven't even discussed what you do while the cleanup is happening in the school? Will school be closed? That conversation hasn't even been broached because we don't want the school to be there in the first place.

MIKE SCHADE: Right before the school is approved, councilmembers had by then reached an agreement with one of the developers which essentially said that unless the offsite and onsite contamination of the Superfund site are fully cleaned up, they will not build a school there, and they will find another location. That was a written agreement that the developer made with councilmember [Stephen] Levin's office. That agreement was made because it was only a couple of days before they were voting on whether or not to approve that development, just only a few days before the councilmember's office learned that the contamination at NuHart was right up against the edge of the school property.

We've been organizing and working with community members, other neighborhood organizations; citizens concerned about this have called community meetings. We've organized online petitions. We've generated press attention, to say we will find a better, safer, smarter site for this school. This is now one of the wealthiest neighborhoods in New York City that historically was decimated by the petrochemical and waste industry. The community has suffered for far too long and if we are going to be building a new school for this neighborhood, the least we can do is build it not across the street from a toxic waste site.

I think it's an interesting confluence between environmental remediation and developing. What does it mean to redevelop a neighborhood? Where does it make sense for us to build schools? Does it make sense for us to repeat the mistakes of the past and build schools on top of or near polluted land? Or does it make sense for us to take a more precautionary approach in order to safeguard children's health? Also, for us, it's not just about the health concern, but it's also very much about the psychological concerns that we often see in impacted communities where sometimes the psychological stress can be worse than the pollution itself.

IT'S ALL A BROWNFIELD

THERE'S ALSO the non-CERCLA sites and issues that created an all-over toxic landscape throughout Greenpoint. Greenpoint's real estate success will always be haunted by the ghosts of its environmental legacy—the old incinerator that rained dioxin onto the neighborhood, the open sewer winds of the old waste treatment plant, the garbage transfer stations, the cancerous vapors coming out of the chemical plumes, and nonstop truck traffic. In doing this research I learned that there's so much more. For example, the soil in west Greenpoint is actually a man-made landfill full of lead and the neighborhood is the home of Radiac: a radiation waystation. There was so much buried industry spanning over a century that these egregious environmental disasters keep being discovered and rediscovered.

LAURA HOFMANN, activist, lifelong resident, O.U.T.R.A.G.E., Newtown Creek Alliance, **many other nonprofits:** This whole neighborhood, this whole community has been one big brownfield Superfund site.

GEOFFREY COBB, teacher, historian, author *Greenpoint Brooklyn's Forgotten Past*, **blogger Greenpointers:** Greenpoint was a swamp. It was a flood zone—it was an estuary. The first real industry that comes to Greenpoint in the 1850s is shipbuilding. What they do is they leveled a large hill called Pottery Hill. They use that landfill on to extend the coast, the shoreline out.

But there's an interesting side to it. Recently they did a test in McCarren Park and they found that there was a huge lead content. And the funny part was, again, it was a swamp, it was filled in, but it's expensive to use dirt. You want to mix the dirt in with any other substitute that you can find. So Greenpoint is an industrial center. One of the things it is producing is slag, the remnants after you burn coal. And this was the largest place in the world for sugar refining. Sugar refining was all about boiling and they imported massive amounts of coal.

When I started to dig in my garden, I found pieces of coal, that slag, even the landfill itself has a huge lead content. It's toxic because it's not pure ground, it's industrial waste.

We have a fictitious shoreline. What's interesting is during Hurricane Sandy, nature remembers these ancient waterways.

ANTHONY BUISSERETH, Executive Director North Brooklyn Neighbors (NBN), formerly Neighbors Allied for Growth (NAG): One of the lesser discussed issues is the impact of lead in soil. You might have heard recently on WNYC, they did a story about lead in the soil in the city's parks, and McCarren Park has the highest level of the three parks that they looked at. We've been working for the last several years on the project, informing residents about lead in soil in their yard and ways they can be safe and figure out adding compost and offering access to free soil tests.

LISA BLOODGOOD, Director of Advocacy & Education, Newtown Creek Alliance (NCA): There's a lot more in it than what I had the capabilities to look for. If you're using an XRF scanner, you can program it to see certain things. We were looking for heavy metals or poor metals, but it doesn't see Volatile Organic Compounds (VOCs), it doesn't see Polycyclic Aromatic Hydrocarbons (PAHs) or PCBs. It doesn't see benzene or anything volatile. No gas, it's just metal.

We have absolutely found it in Greenpoint backyards. In private spaces lead levels are 3,000 parts per million, which is an enormous amount of lead and well beyond any threshold for what's considered acceptable for industrial uses. The threshold for remediation for residential uses is 300 parts per million and some 3,000 is exponentially higher than that. And I would argue that 300 is not a safe level for, for contact, especially for vulnerable populations like kids.

SCOTT FRASER, activist, Greenpointers Against Smell Pollution (GASP), writer and director TV and movies: We also have learned about the lead in our soil. Our lead, I tested about 1,000 parts per million. The neighbors recently told me they had a test in their backyard of 2,000 parts per million. I think the safe amount, I think, is 100 parts per million, something like that. If you see over there in the corner, there's six, eight bags of organic compost. The last couple years I've learned how toxic the soil is. I have a grandson now; obviously you're not supposed to let kids play in that soil.

My son played in that soil and that's how he grew up. But I'm now capping the soil every year with a layer of organic compost, because I want that it be organic compost. That corner pot is organic compost. I make sure that his only soil that he plays in is organic.

ACACIA THOMPSON, archivist for Brooklyn Public Library's Greenpoint Environmental History Project: Something interesting [Kim and Scott Fraser] said was that they were new to the neighborhood and what the neighborhood was like then. They said, "We just don't understand why people keep putting up with this." They understood their neighborhood. They knew it was a neighborhood with people who are working to keep their families going and it wasn't necessarily something that they thought about. They just thought, *this is New York, and this is what you deal with.* They, as outsiders coming in from outside of the city, they're like, *why do we have to put up with this? This is nonsense.* But they worked with the community to change those things.

KIM FRASER: We just really were young enough, thank God, to take it to heart and to think—my big expression that I always say was, "We're going to walk the talk." We're not going to run away from this. This is wrong. We can write, we can read, we can talk, and we can speak. Let's just start going and doing that stuff. And just walking the talk.

ACACIA THOMPSON: There's a couple of interesting studies that were done in the 1980s through Hunter College, that were definitely like, *there's stuff wrong here.* A lot of the correlations were—they couldn't really get more with asthma and things like that. It was just bad citywide. But I think people on the ground here like, *no, it's way worse.*

KIM FRASER: I always bring up the big Hunter College study that happened during this time.

SCOTT FRASER: *Right to Know, Right to Ask.*

KIM FRASER: *Right to Know, Right to Ask.* There was two big parts of the study. At least at the time, it was part of Hunter College's master's degree to [encourage] young people to go into communities and be the leaders, to enable community people to be the leaders themselves. They picked this neighborhood, because after the accident in Bhopal, India—this is what we heard in one of our meetings—they were sitting around a conference table, and they were open to going anywhere where they could replicate what happened in Bhopal, India.

SCOTT FRASER: They [Union Carbide India Limited] emitted this gas that blinded people.

KIM FRASER: It happened at night, people were asleep. Their windows were open, because it was hot there. There's no air conditioning. They were just asleep. The stuff came in through their windows, and in the morning, 2,500 people were dead[67].

They [researchers] were sitting around the table saying, where could that happen in the U.S.? Is that possible? And somebody said, *Yeah, it could happen. I think it could happen right over in Greenpoint and Williamsburg.* Then they started to research that themselves to see if this is true. And they realized it is true, because the factories here were all like 20-person factories, they were all one or two stories, the smokestack was allowed to be right next to residential, small buildings. They could have an accident there and all these little companies weren't being regulated the way you would regulate a big company.

There's no place to go, no way to get out, no way to mobilize people fast enough. And so they said, *yeah, let's just do Greenpoint for our study.* They came here. First they gave seminars, under the Greenpoint Savings Bank, and we went to a lot of different rooms. They had slideshows. They had presentations, it was educational. The first front was, let's educate the people.

In 1989, the community Environmental Health Center at Hunter College published its first report on the Brooklyn communities of Greenpoint and Williamsburg: Hazardous Neighbors? Living Next Door to Industry in Greenpoint-Williamsburg. The report was prepared in response to a 1984 chemical accident in Bhopal, India, which left 2,500 nearby residents dead and as many as 200,000 others suffering from lingering health effects. Hazardous Neighbors addressed the question of "whether or not an industrial accident affecting area residents as well as plant employees could occur in New York City." The communities of Greenpoint and Williamsburg, which comprise Brooklyn Community District #1, were selected for the study for several reasons. The area has more land devoted to industry than any other district in the City. Many of these local industries store and use toxic, highly flammable, or explosive substances. And, because of the historic development patterns of the area and its small size (five square miles), the industries operate in close proximity to residential and commercial areas.

Excerpt from *Right to Know, Right to Ask,* Hunter College 1992

---

67. There's many different statistics for Bhopal. Approximately 600,000 people were exposed to 30 tons of a highly toxic gas, methyl isocyanate. According to an article in *The Atlantic,* "Estimates of the death toll vary from as few as 3,800 to as many as 16,000." The photos of the aftermath are horrific.

ONE TOXIC
CLOUD FROM ONE OF
RADIAC'S CHEMICALS COULD
KILL AS FAR AS MIDTOWN
MANHATTAN.
AN EXPLOSION OR FIRE WOULD
INVOLVE *HUNDREDS* OF CHEMICALS

Hydrocyanic acid
'puffs' from ex-
plosion travel
4.5 miles in 33
min. (wind 8 mph)
1,000 lbs chem.

'Plume' from release
in fire of 80 lbs/min
of highly toxic aniline
oil

'Plume' of phos-
gene gas 13 min
after fire, "Im-
mediate danger to
life and health"
at two parts per
million - 1.7
miles from Radiac

Methyl isocyanate:
'puffs' from explo-
sion of 500 lbs
could travel 3.64
miles in 27.3 min.

Graphics drawn from simulations of
Radiac accidents formulated using
NOAA/Hazardous Materials Response
Branch; EPA Cameo Computer Program
Large circles show areas jeopar-
dized in fire (dep. on wind direction.) Circles for explosions extend beyond map. Radiac permit
would allow holding 44,000 lbs of
these chemicals.

Map and graphic drawn from simulations of Radiac accident formulated using
NOAA/Hazardous Materials Response Branch, with map. Circa 1980s. Donated for
capture by Kim Fraser through the Greenpoint Environmental History Project of Brooklyn
Public Library. This project is funded through the Greenpoint Community Environmental Fund.
Brooklyn Public Library, Brooklyn Collection.

SCOTT FRASER: They also were the first people who did a door-to-door survey in the neighborhood. And actually they walked the streets. They would FOIA (Freedom of Information Act) request, and get the actual amount of chemicals that were being stored and that were being emitted. They did all kinds of point-by-point of all the different companies. They found out they were the first to actually add the amount of pollution, building by building, in the neighborhood. When they started to add the amounts it got to be hundreds of thousands of pounds of toxic chemicals. I think it even got to millions of pounds. It got up to astronomical amounts of pollution, that, when you added all the different factories together, that were in the neighborhood. It was a mind-boggling amount of pollution that no one discussed. And even today, no one discusses.

There's a building on Kent Avenue. It's still there—Radiac. It stores radioactive, low-level radioactive toxic waste and explosive chemicals in the same building. The radioactive truck came by just yesterday. I said hey, there's the radioactive truck. They collect low-level, radioactive waste from hospitals in New York City. It's on Kent Avenue!

You know, little plastic things that they gather from all the hospitals in the city? Where does it go? It goes right to Radiac and then it's stored there until it gets to reach a threshold. And then they drive it out of the neighborhood to someplace where it gets incinerated.

KIM FRASER: Because of the way the wind, because the concentric circles around Radiac. The campaign was to get the big shots in Manhattan up in arms. They had this map, which was trying to say, on any given day, if there's an explosion in this little factory, it's not just going to stay right here in Greenpoint, Williamsburg. It's coming; it could be coming in your direction, the plume, the radioactive plume.

The insidious thing about this kind of pollution is it doesn't kill you right then and there. It acts upon your body over the years of getting exposed. And you can't really see it; it's not in front of you. They just look like little, nondescript, one-story little warehouses with a garage door and a little stack.

SCOTT FRASER: One of the worst ones was right at Bedford and North 7th. It was a plating factory there that we knew from the Hunter study had the most toxic, the most emissions.

It was right there in the corner of North 7th Street. Every time we went over there you almost wanted to hold your breath as you walked by.

TONY ARGENTO, owner Broadway Stages: I got to point out to you one of the biggest crisis we have right now. I don't know if you are aware of it, but we have an ongoing major pollution problem right now from the asphalt plant in Long Island City that's spewing poison every morning right by P.S. 110.

And the community should really come together, we got to stop this. Because some mornings, when I'm down there on Kingsland, I'm up on my rooftop, if you smell that for two, three minutes you start getting nauseous. It's deadly. That's going on right here. Right under our eyes. How you could give a license for something like this? So close to all this residential.

Just go by there in the morning, you'll see this yellow soot shooting out of this chimney. And depending where the wind's blowing, this stuff is toxic.

ZONING ISSUES

GREENPOINT has a mix of heavy industry and residential zoning, which is a source of sustained tension. The pollution was there from the beginning. Greenpoint emerged before zoning even existed. 197-a is a section in the 1989 city charter revision that requires city councils to consider community input when zoning a neighborhood. In 2001 the city council voted for a Williamsburg/ Greenpoint rezoning. Years of meetings and debates ensued at community meetings regarding how to rezone Greenpoint and Williamsburg in ways that would best serve the mixed-use nature of the community while balancing the local economy's industrial, commercial and residential districting. Superfund or not, this was and is a highly desirable location. Close to Manhattan, developers were clamoring to colonize it. Those same developers who donated heavily to local political campaigns are the ones who ultimately dictated "planning" Greenpoint.

Greenpoint was following the gentrification cycle that happens in most metropolitan areas. Industries dry up and leave big, hulking industrial spaces behind. Next, artists move in and make it hip, quickly followed by commercial developers and global real estate speculators who decimate what's left of a neighborhood's original character and charm.

> The massive rezoning of Greenpoint and Williamsburg that the City Council just approved bears little resemblance to the community plans. Ever since the City Council voted for the Greenpoint and Williamsburg plans in 2001, they have failed to lift a finger to implement them. City agencies went into hiding. There were no budget requests to create public access on the waterfront, no initiatives to preserve the industry, and no new housing. Instead, the city turned the other way as developers illegally converted industrial properties to unaffordable lofts and did little to stop the legal conversions.

216

*Now the City Planning Commission and City Council have approved a sweep-
ing rezoning of the industrial waterfront that opens the way for 10,000 units
of high-rise housing, conversion of industrial properties to residential use,
and a 54-acre waterfront park. The final rezoning does have some elements
that meet plan objectives, but they are in there because community activists
fought a long, hard battle with the city from the first day the proposal was
launched to get some affordable housing, lower the towers on the waterfront,
protect industries, and guarantee public access to the waterfront.*[68]

PAUL PARKHILL, urban planner, former
director of planning and development
Greenpoint Manufacturing and Design
Center (GMDC): When I started in
1999, Greenpoint was a lot pokier
than it is now. We were at the north
end of Greenpoint, relatively close to
the sewage treatment plants, and
there were open tanks. The sewage
treatment work had not happened. It
smelled fairly bad on a regular basis.

It was pre-North Brooklyn rezoning. The waterfront and the upper
blocks had not been reassigned for a
combination of residential and
non-residential. There was a very
small pocket of mixed-use zoning that
was in Williamsburg. And then I
believe there was another pocket of it
in Greenpoint as well.

T-shirt to protest 2005 waterfront rezoning.
Donated for capture by Stephanie Thayer through
the Greenpoint Environmental History Project of
Brooklyn Public Library. Brooklyn Public Library,
Brooklyn Collection.

TOM ANGOTTI, Professor Emeritus of
Urban Policy and Planning at Hunter
College, founder and director of the Hunter College Center for Community Planning
and Development: The Greenpoint and Williamsburg so-called mixed-use zone
is a fraud. It's not really mixed-use.

We have to put it in a historical context. The zoning resolution, since the first
iteration enacted in 1916, created separate zones for residential, commercial,

68. Tom Angotti. "Zoning Instead of Planning in Williamsburg and Greenpoint." *Gotham Gazette*, 17 May 2005.

and industrial use. Large parts of the outer boroughs, most of the outer boroughs were undeveloped at that time.

In other words, there was no separation of usage, and so when Greenpoint and Williamsburg developed as industrial working-class neighborhoods, the mixed-uses evolved spontaneously. Industries wanted to locate where land costs were low, and workers could move into lower-cost housing in the surrounding area.

The first actual real mixed-use district was in Williamsburg. During the 1970s changes came about because there was small industry located right next to housing, and it was not legal. Businesses had trouble getting financing but the neighbors wanted to keep the industry and the housing together, so they created special mixed-use industrial residential districts. That remained until 2005 with the rezoning of Williamsburg, and the City Planning Department came in with a new concept of mixed-use zoning.

PAUL PULLO, former owner of Metro Fuels: Where I lived on Withers Street, the oil trucks were kept in the yard right by my house. Across the street was some kind of rags and textiles business, things like that.

TRINA HAMILTON, associate professor of geography at State University of Buffalo, co-editor *Just Green Enough: Urban Development and Environmental Gentrification*: Interestingly, amongst some of those first waves of activists, I heard from some of them who actually supported the first rezoning. They saw it as a way to prevent even more polluting activities happening in that area. They subsequently began acting against environmental gentrification—although not necessarily using that language, because they saw the impact that it had in terms of gentrification.

TOM ANGOTTI: Section 197-a of the City Charter enables the city to do planning. For years until the 1970s and '80s, beginning with the rise of the civil rights movement, people demanded community control and community engagement. It was from minority communities, environmental justice communities, and middle-class communities who were dissatisfied with the rigidity of the city's regulatory and planning process. The City used zoning as the main instrument for regulating land use and practice. Since it's a dark science that most people don't understand, the zoning game is governed and dominated by a small group of legal talent that is hired by big developers and small developers.

In 1989 when the New York City Charter was being revised, 197-a became a focus. It has been a big push of the civil rights movement. Taking the city to court in the 1980s for violation of the Voting Rights Act. Why? Because the main decision-making body in the city was the New York Board Estimate.

The Board of Estimate was a body made up of the mayor, the comptroller, two elected officials, and each one of the five borough presidents. The legal challenge under the Voting Rights Act was that it was a violation of the constitutional principle of one person, one vote. Places like Staten Island which have a very small, mostly white population, had one vote, while places like the Bronx and Brooklyn, that had large minority populations, each one had one vote.

That lawsuit was won, and the City was forced to revise the charter and the Board of Estimate was eliminated. Slightly more power was given to the city council which was elected by city council district, and a lot more power was given to the Mayor who's directly elected.

CHRISTINE HOLOWACZ, activist, longtime resident, GWAPP, Newtown Creek Alliance, many other nonprofits: I was part of the planning process for Greenpoint—the 197-a Plan [rezoning]. It's a community plan for the future. How do you want to develop it? That's what the 197-a Plan is.

As we were going through the process, it took us maybe a year or year and a half of meeting when we realized that somehow the needs of the community in Greenpoint are a little bit different from the needs of the Community Board in Williamsburg. With the help of the councilmembers at that time, we decided to have two plans.

Basically, we came up with a really comprehensive plan of what was here and what we would like to see as far as rezoning is concerned.

TOM ANGOTTI: The environmental justice groups and community groups advocating for community planning, who have been frustrated by the city, changed. They jiggled the charter language to say that community boards could present their community plans directly to the city planning committee for approval.

CHRISTINE HOLOWACZ: We've always been fighting for access to the waterfront. We never had access to the waterfront, and yet Greenpoint is surrounded by water on three sides. There were all these dilapidated, unused properties that kids used to go to at night.

That plan was supposed to serve as the beginning of the 2005 rezoning. I was on the Mayor's Advisory Committee after the rezoning, because everybody was so upset when the rezoning came out. No one wanted these tall buildings.

PAUL PARKHILL: The North Brooklyn rezoning was proposed in 2003 and ratified in 2005. I think they [the community groups] had different concerns around what the implications for the neighborhood were going to be.

LISA BLOODGOOD, Director of Advocacy & Education, Newtown Creek Alliance (NCA): The 2005 rezoning of the Greenpoint and Williamsburg waterfront exploded this area. We're seeing it now on Long Island City as well, once industry leaves and high-density residential is allowed.

The neighborhood changes almost daily. Things happen so fast. We see the rezoning in Gowanus. We see the rezoning all over our neighborhood then we look at the Creek and go, *all right, that's the last holdout for these significant industrial maritime areas.*

KATE ZIDAR, green infrastructure research engineer, former director of Newtown Creek Alliance (NCA): There was always gentrification during the period of Newtown Creek Alliance. Greenpoint was built as a residential neighborhood for industrial workers. There's always been proximity between the residential community and the working waterfront. Other neighborhoods around the Creek just weren't laid out that way. The Greenpoint-Williamsburg rezoning has, over time, added residential density along the East River waterfront, which has included the Greenpoint waterfront.

PAUL PULLO: Now you have people spending millions of dollars buying expensive condos and they don't like the idea that there are businesses next to them, but the businesses have been there for many years.

HEATHER LETZKUS, artist, blogger New York Shitty: As far as I can tell, the plan here is that they're going to keep building and building and leave this boondoggle for future generations to figure out. You've already built all these condos on the waterfront, which we're already paying for because we've given them tax abatements, and when they flood, we're going to be paying for that too. I mean, it may not be me, but it's going to be we. There is no plan.

KIM FRASER, activist, founder of Greenpointers Against Smell Pollution (GASP): The 197-a was what brought us to our knees.

SCOTT FRASER, activist, Greenpointers Against Smell Pollution (GASP), writer and director: We got depressed. We have these ebbs and flows.

KIM FRASER: There were these young masters students, taking notes and writing down what we said. I really believed... I guess I was naïve. I thought, *this is good. They really have come to us. They want us to take control. They want us to tell them what we want in this neighborhood.* They told us, bring your kids—Chris was already nine years old—"Let him draw a picture of—does he want a basketball court on the waterfront? What does he want?"

They had two leaders sit there with the little kids. They're not that little, I mean, they're elementary-age kids, and they understood exactly what was being asked of them. And they complied. They sat there and drew their basketball court. I sat there and listened wholeheartedly. We were told, "Look, don't be too realistic, shoot for the sky, the sky's the limit, don't hold yourself back. Think of—if you can, because if you don't step up and say what you want on your waterfront, somebody else is going to come and tell you and give you what you're going to get. Right now, in these seminars, we just want everyone to shout out, from your point of view, what would it be? How green would it be? How wide would it be from the water? What would go along the edge? How do people get from Williamsburg Bridge to Newtown Creek? Go ahead, spin, spin."

TOM ANGOTTI: New York is undoubtedly an extreme case, it's one of the largest municipalities in the country, and it's the only major city in the country that has never had a comprehensive [development] plan.

CHRISTINE HOLOWACZ: When we were writing this plan, we did seek to have some tall buildings about 20–25 stories towards the mouth of the Creek, because we thought that it would be an area that is a little bit empty, and it could be enjoyed by others. But we did not foresee all of these enormous buildings all along the Creek and on the East River.

I really feel that the development would have happened anyway. It would have happened for two reasons. Manhattan became totally overpriced, so people started to move to Williamsburg, and then to Greenpoint. That made the need for more housing, and the closeness to Manhattan is really why Williamsburg had developed first.

TOM ANGOTTI: Seventeen 197-a plans have been approved but nobody is submitting them anymore because the city planning department creates enormous hoops that people have to jump through in order to even submit a plan, and then to get it through the approval process—after which they throw it away, they ignore it, which is exactly what happened with the Greenpoint and Williamsburg 197-a plan.

SCOTT FRASER: We were optimistic. We really thought, by our activism, we were getting at real results.

ENVIRONMENTAL GENTRIFICATION

PRIOR TO the 2005 rezoning, Greenpoint was well on its way toward gentrification. It's the old familiar story to most city dwellers when immigrant communities and artists are displaced by real estate interests. As we discussed in the chapter on the original activists, most of the incoming residents didn't know the history and therefore unwittingly acted as agents of gentrification. Despite the oil spills, epic industrial toxic waste dumping, waste transfer stations, the history of the incinerator, phthalates, naphtha, benzene, lead, etc., the developers couldn't wait to turn the waterfront into profits.

Unlike what we saw in Tar Creek, Oklahoma, where the people were hung out to dry on their polluted land for decades, Newtown Creek's front yard was more desirable than ever.

SCOTT FRASER, activist, Greenpointers Against Smell Pollution (GASP), writer and director TV and movies: [In 1980] it was truly a neighborhood in crisis. Desolate is the word I would use, depressing, abandoned. You felt the last throes of what obviously had been the Industrial Revolution. This was a bustling, brawny community, we had the black arts, we had the oil refineries; we had one of the busiest seaports in the world.

We built America, so to speak. This is the workroom. This is the back room, this is where they sweat, and this is where you put your life on the line. This is where people were making maritime rope for pennies an hour, immigrants sweating in unsafe, unhealthy conditions. That's where this neighborhood flourished. As the 21st century came in, there was a sort of this downward arc, where the city was hurting, there was the white flight. Instead of things coming in by water and train they came in by freight—by big 16-wheelers.

All the trains that came out of this neighborhood started to die off. We were on that end of that bell curve where factories were closing, hookers were hawking their wares down on Kent Avenue. The factories were still toxic, belching and scary. We could smell them. We knew they were there. People were moving out. They would just almost give you their keys and say, *here's a house, I'll give it to you for a good price*, and they were gone. Honestly, that's kind of what it was like. We were the newcomers, we were the gentrifiers.

It was even worse on this block over here. We had a little son and we were sort of shunned by the residents in the block because we were the newcomers. We were not accepted for I would say a long time. We were the outliers, because there was nobody like us.

KIM FRASER, activist, founder of Greenpointers Against Smell Pollution (GASP): Honestly, I never even knew what gentrification meant. Back then [if] you had asked me, "Kim, are you a gentrifier?" I would say, "No, I'm not, what is that?" And I don't really want to say I was shunned by all the mothers of Chris' little friends.

They were there as nice as they could be to me. It was just more the old-timers that were angry that we were going to change their rent level. People like us, us and other people like us, yeah, that was hard. As far as Chris, as children do, he just rode through all of that with all those little buddies.

WILLIS ELKINS, activist, Executive Director, Newtown Creek Alliance (NCA): I think the argument is that when property values increase and there's a wave of gentrification, there's more pressure to deal with environmental catastrophes. Because there's money there. We kind of saw it.

I think Gowanus [Canal] is one case where it's kind of interesting to compare. The city really fought against a Superfund designation in Gowanus because they were afraid of what it would do to property values. Obviously that has not been the case, but there was severe concern that it was going to be an economic impact for the city.

As far as I'm aware, in Newtown Creek the city did not push back against it. There was certainly a handful of homeowners that it was less about Superfund but more about Exxon, and not wanting it to be known, with a fear that it would decrease property values and stuff like that. I think that's part of it. In some instances, a newer demographic moving into a neighborhood might be more concerned about environmental hazards, or more connected to resources to get those addressed—a new family moving to the neighborhood and maybe being more vocal about environmental conditions than other folks who've lived there for three generations.

WINIFRED CURRAN, associate professor of geography at DePaul University, co-editor *Just Green Enough: Urban Development and Environmental Gentrification*: Environmental gentrification is the cleaning up of existing and environmental harms for the provision of new environmental amenities with the goal to increase surrounding property values. Which basically then accomplishes the displacement of longtime residents, and uses the patina of greening to improve a neighborhood to the benefit of higher-income in-movers.

TRINA HAMILTON, associate professor of geography at State University of Buffalo, co-editor *Just Green Enough: Urban Development and Environmental Gentrification*: It's important to say, it happens by design, where the goal is coming from developers, or it can happen by simply not thinking about the displacement effect of a greening initiative.

TRINA HAMILTON: Right, and a by-product of just not thinking through the implications.

WINIFRED CURRAN: Having said that, I would say that that was true maybe 10 years ago. Now that we know that environmental gentrification exists and we see what these kinds of projects do, to say that you don't know that it can have displacement effects at this point in time is nonsensical. To not think through it is therefore an active, malign neglect when it comes to policymakers.

WILLIS ELKINS: Obviously Greenpoint is changing dramatically, not necessarily the areas that are closest to the more damaged parts of the Creek. The [Wastewater Treatment Plant] Nature Walk was a model to improve access and to have green space that complements and mixes in with industrial uses. Part of our mission too is that we're not advocating for rezoning the whole area.

Whereas in Gowanus, frankly a lot of people that we would consider similar organizations that are focused on the environment, they're very much like, *Yeah, if a rezoning means that we're not going to have a brownfield next to the creek then let's bring it in. Why are we even debating this?*

BASIL SEGGOS, Commissioner of the New York State Department of Environmental Conservation (DEC), former Chief Investigator for Riverkeeper: Back in 2002, Greenpoint was a much different Greenpoint. Yes, there were people moving in from Manhattan or college kids coming in, but it was at a very almost indiscernible rate.

We had aligned ourselves with the so-called Polish ladies in Greenpoint, Irene Klementowicz chief among them. At that point, there wasn't a local environmental movement. There wasn't a sort of a huge movement on environmental issues. It was just something that the local Polish community had been fighting for years and very quietly. Folks like Joe Lentol in the Assembly representing them.

JOE LENTOL, New York State Assembly, District 50: People need to live someplace, and the vacancy rate is so low, they'll live anywhere. And especially in a hot neighborhood like Greenpoint or Williamsburg, where everybody wants to live, the vacancy rate is even lower.

BASIL SEGGOS: I don't think gentrification at that point was as real as it became later in the decade and certainly now it's a totally different place. When we filed the case itself, I viewed it as an environmental justice case that you had largely working-class community on both sides, Queens and Brooklyn. That's how we proceeded, and then over time, obviously the area began to change. Of course, that's all she wrote in terms of history. Now it's a totally different place. Small buildings are worth millions, and landlords who have been sitting on waterfront property for many years and obviously seen the entire waterfront change in that time frame.

MIKE SCHADE, activist, environmental health campaigner, Mind The Store Campaign Director with Safer Chemicals, Healthy Families: If I can't afford to live there, think about all the elderly people that have lived in the community for decades, immigrants, Polish families. The Polish community is definitely being pushed out of the neighborhood. Elderly people are being pushed out of the neighborhood. So, while it's good that we're seeing more cleanup and site investigations taking place in the community, I think the fundamental question is *who benefits?* People that suffered the most historically, sadly, are not benefiting because gentrification is in some cases driving those that were most directly affected out of the neighborhood, and that's a tragedy. When we talk about environmental injustice, that's a major environmental injustice that needs to be rectified.

WINIFRED CURRAN: One of the reasons that I think Greenpoint has been more attractive for investment than it might otherwise have been is the fact that it's a white neighborhood. There's not the same kind of racial dynamics as there are in other polluted, industrialized neighborhoods, because, while it is overwhelmingly an immigrant community, those immigrants are Polish.

I think that made it seem less scary to a lot of outsiders than, for example, the South Bronx. Because of that racial dynamic, it didn't have the same reputation, in terms of the popular imagination. That lack of racial animus between long-term residents and the gentrifiers helped lead to a more cohesive movement around a lot of these environmental justice issues. That hasn't been the case in neighborhoods that are of color in which the gentrifiers are overwhelmingly white and there's not that same common cause, necessarily, where there's a much deeper level of suspicion between the in-movers and the longtime residents.

TRINA HAMILTON: In neighborhoods where you don't get that cohesion amongst incoming activists and long-term activists, you get gentrifiers advocating for new green spaces that long-term residents, including communities of color, don't necessarily end up benefiting from because they don't use them. Either they feel they weren't designed for them, they don't necessarily provide the kinds of recreational or other uses that they are looking for.

There's lots of interesting research showing some of them—not just the Highline in New York City, but other examples of those types of greening projects that the people who use them are often the white groups that have advocated for them, and there hasn't been sensitivity for understanding how they'll be used and perceived by long-term residents.

GEOFFREY COBB, teacher, historian, author *Greenpoint Brooklyn's Forgotten Past*, **blogger Greenpointers:** One of the big industries here was rope making. We men have clumsy hands. Women's hands are much more dexterous and you could also pay them less. I believe the American hemp rope manufacturing company was the fourth largest employer in New York, which had 16 buildings on the waterfront. Originally their workforce was Polish women and then later Italian women. But by the 1920s, the pay was so bad and the conditions were so horrific, they couldn't find workers.

And all of a sudden, industrial concerns were hard up for workers. They found out that the Puerto Rican women in traditional handicrafts get something similar; they were quite adept at sewing and making ropes. They actually sailed a ship to Puerto Rico and brought back 110 women. That's sort of the origin of the Puerto Rican community here. Then once there was a group on the ground, other people came to do the industrial jobs, especially during the Second World War when a lot of men left. Puerto Ricans came in throughout the 1950s. Certainly by the 1970s, everything north of Greenpoint Avenue was largely Puerto Rican.

HEATHER LETZKUS, artist, blogger New York Shitty: They've [Puerto Ricans] taken a hit. Around the time that I came here (1990s) I think the population was around 14%, and now after the rezoning, it's knocked down to 10%. And frankly I find that infuriating.

VICTORIA CAMBRANES, lifelong resident, community activist, 2021 candidate for City Council District 33 in Brooklyn: I hear about it. My cousin and I took a walk. My cousin is eight years older than I am. She grew up on Eagle Street. Last summer she ran into all her old school friends who were there and I ran into all of my old school friends, but we're kind of eight years apart or so.

Every single one of them, they were chatting to us in Spanish and they're like, "Yeah, they're offering me 10K. They're offering me 20K. They're offering 30K." My main advice was like, "Hold out for a 100K. That's all you can do. Hold out for a hundred. If they're not offering you a hundred, don't move."

HEATHER LETZKUS: It was almost an island up here and it still is an island up here. You get into the racial thing. I mean it is a lot about race and class. This is the Latino end of the neighborhood. This is where everything's put out to pasture. You can still see the effects of redlining up here. Look at all the vacant storefronts. We have no banking services here now. None. Not even a check-cashing place anymore. You've got a few grocery stores, you don't have any produce stands, and the latest is the Lorvan Pharmacy, they're actually transitioning into a very—I hate to call it a boutique form of pharmaceutical services, but basically they're going to transition into doing some oncology-type stuff, building these cocktails of specialized medications for people. We're losing a pharmacy now.

You go to the health food store at Greenpoint or on Manhattan Avenue, and right above the cash register is this nice big flashy ad for CBD oil, with this aging hipster wearing this nice little fedora. They've nailed the stereotype.

WINIFRED CURRAN: That's the long-term residents and activists who have done the work, who have laid the groundwork for the environmental improvements, are then themselves the most vulnerable when those improvements happen, especially if they're renters. They can't afford to stay. Any sort of improvement that is significant enough to lead to an increase in property values threatens long-term renters. Especially in a neighborhood that had been an enclave of affordable housing, the people who have been there the longest are most likely the people paying the lowest rents, and therefore are most vulnerable to displacement when those rents go up. Even homeowners are vulnerable when their property values go up and therefore their property taxes go through the roof.

WILLIS ELKINS: We've had people say we shouldn't be cleaning up street ends because we're doing the work of developers, by making the place more attractive. One person who said that, I was like, "Screw you, tell that to Laura Hofmann who's been here her whole life." Please tell her that we're doing the work of developers by trying to ensure that an abandoned street end doesn't remain a toxic dumping ground.

That's an extreme. But on the other side, how do we promote access and green space and these sort of things that are more enticing to a new demographic? Canoeing and kayaking—I get it. That's not the same thing as a working waterfront and that's certainly appealing to certain types of people. I don't know...

KATE ZIDAR, green infrastructure research engineer, former director of Newtown Creek Alliance (NCA): You can't put investment into an area and then be bewildered because later it gentrifies. There's a way of understanding land-use changes. That's what zoning is for, that's what good governance and participatory budgeting is for. There's so many tools that we can't pretend that we don't know, and it's really bad practice when people do so.

VICTORIA CAMBRANES: It started to get a bit more like insidious when the developers started coming in and more economically affluent people started coming in. You then started to get this sense that, *we are here to clean up after you.* It was a very pretentious kind of attitude of, like, *God, this place is a shithole. There was nothing here before we arrived.*

When I talk about the erasing of the true history of the environmental activists in Greenpoint, that's what I'm touching upon. It's this idea that, *We have come here, we have cleaned it up, there was nothing here before and we are going to write the history now and the history starts with us.*

Having been born and raised here, it's so far from the truth. You can't even call it a misrepresentation. It's just a flat-out lie. I come from the Greenpoint of immigrant communities and people speaking all different languages, community activists, political activist heroes, musicians, rappers, graffiti artists, professors, members of the intelligentsia. We have really famous people who were born and raised here. We have so much rich history here—the docklands and the manufacturing history, the farming history that happened here. There are just so many layers to that history and no one really knows about that anymore.

With Manhattan property prices skyrocketing, a luxury waterfront community called Greenpoint Landing will start rising this summer near the East River mouth of Newtown Creek, 10 residential towers with 5,000 apartments, a marina, a retail complex and a prime view of the city.

A short walk away is a hulking brick building where rope was once braided for ships. It's been turned into space for entrepreneurs and artists who are among a new breed of locals.

Newtown Creek is the story of New York's rich and poor—and the changing times, says Karl LaRocca, a 39-year-old printmaker.

When the oil refineries were booming, "The rich people were all living farther away and using this for their industry," he says. "Now we've had this reversal where the waterfront is this desirable property, and that's why they're cleaning up."[69]

WINIFRED CURRAN: This is a global process. The amounts of money we're talking about are extraordinary. Rather than just being, "Oh, I want to buy this house," it's some consortium of mortgage-backed securities, being like, "I want to target this neighborhood." The scale of it is so much broader than it was before. I think that's what makes it difficult to fight. The gentrification part isn't necessarily the people buying the apartments, or renting the apartments. In Greenpoint Landing, it's the developers who can afford to build at that scale in the first place. Once that starts happening, it almost doesn't matter—you already fundamentally changed the nature of the market. That *in and of itself* is what accomplishes gentrification.

What we see in developments like this is that they will not allow their units to go for affordable rates. Even if they can't fill it, they still won't lower the prices because what they're selling is a brand, not an actual apartment.

69. Associated Press reporter. "NYC's Newtown Creek Awaits Long-Overdue Cleanup." *USA Today*, Gannett Satellite Information Network, 2 Mar 2013.

VICTORIA CAMBRANES: So there's two patterns that you need to be aware of. There's something called the FAR limits (floor area ratio). And after the rezoning they raised the FAR limit. But it was not enough. In order to build a higher FAR, what the developers can do is buy air rights of adjacent properties. If they promise a park, which is zero FAR, they get to add on that FAR on the top of their building.

What they do is they'll say, *we'll give you a park.* And they're doing one in Greenpoint Landing right now. They opened up a space of park right on the corner of that tip right before you enter Newtown Creek. But then the space behind it is also owned by them. They're going to get perfect views as well—not crowded by their own towers, like tower in front of tower, right. So there's insidiousness on that front, and this is a very well documented thing along the river—air rights and FAR limits. That's why the parks are gone.

The other thing I want to highlight as a pattern is this kind of Machiavellian idea of using progressives to push development. The way that they do this is through parks.

I kept running into this term called the Williamsburg Blueprint and what the developer was doing, who was best friends with Brookfield which is Greenpoint Landing. The same developers are doing things here. They're all over the East Coast.

Put some shrubs around it and call it a park. This is the pattern. They're using the Williamsburg rezoning as a blueprint for how to use environmental groups as fronts for developers to get higher FAR limits. That's the fucking shtick. That's what it comes down.

HEATHER LETZKUS: It's environmentalism with the social justice taken out, which makes absolutely no sense. What are you left with? You're left with HGTV and Martha Stewart shit once you take that out.

VICTORIA CAMBRANES: There's actually very good academic studies on this as well, which proved that an area that receives more park space also undergoes something that I've coined architectural intimidation. All of these visual corridors between the towers that lead to waterfronts, tennis courts and things like that—these are all meant for a different class and it's supposed to tell a small black child *you're not welcome in this place.*

A WORKING BODY OF WATER

ONE SURPRISE that emerged throughout these interviews was the pro-business stance that many of the activists have staked out. Historically, the environmental movement has always had such an adversarial attitude toward industry that it struck me as unusual to hear activist groups sticking up for manufacturing and trade maintaining a permanent presence on the waterfront. It's a core principle for many of these groups, and many of the citizens that I've spoken to support keeping Greenpoint industrial. That certainly means different things for different people.

Besides being an open dumping ground throughout much of the previous two centuries, Newtown Creek has been an active industrial corridor since its earliest days and remains so today. Because of the rezoning, much of the waterfront is still industrial.

PAUL PULLO, activist, former owner of Metro Fuels: When we bought this property in 1986, this was a dead-end street with no fire hydrants, no sidewalks. There was nothing. This building you are in was a two-story abandoned building. The oil terminal was not maintained. Half of it was closed down. It was just kind of derelict. To be very honest everything here was derelict. Just abandoned. When we bought this building it was not a part of the oil terminal. This was a separate building that I bought from the owner of the building on the corner, which used to be a glue factory.

Across the street was the ExxonMobil plant. It was all tanks.

WINIFRED CURRAN, associate professor of geography at DePaul University, co-editor *Just Green Enough: Urban Development and Environmental Gentrification*: The important thing about Greenpoint was that it is zoned for manufacturing, and therefore is still used for manufacturing. Much of where environmental gentrification is happening these days is in industrial areas of the city, where there's been declining industry or abandoned industry.

What we've seen since is the way in which developers have been very creative about what they can do even within the manufacturing zoning designation. That's especially true of two particular land uses. One is hotels: That's an anomaly of New York's zoning code, is that hotels are allowed in areas zoned for manufacturing, so we've seen a rise in that kind of activity. And the second is storage units, self-storage. Which is a great way for developers to scoop up a lot of industrial property and then just sit on it for a while, until the market demand is there and they can realize that there was a profit for them. We're seeing both of those things

Construction supply company, Newtown Creek, May 5, 2003. Photo courtesy of Riverkeeper.

as an active threat to what is happening in Greenpoint, as well as spaces considered manufacturing that really aren't.

One of my favorite quotes from one of our informants was, "Two architects and a 3-D printer count as manufacturers." That kind of luxury office space in manufacturing areas is the other mode of threat. That fluidity of what the zoning can mean, even within what's supposed to be a protected zoning designation, that's been a really interesting thing to watch in terms of how this has evolved in Greenpoint.

ACACIA THOMPSON, archivist for Brooklyn Public Library's Greenpoint Environmental History Project: Some things that NAG did and GWAPP has done is to try to make sure to keep industry here, but to try to get them to do things that make their industries safer for the community. That was an important lesson to learn about that. Then talking to Paul [Pullo] about how he's done his best to make sure that his family business operates as safely as possible in the community.

PAUL PULLO: Both of my grandmothers were born in the neighborhood, so the family goes back a long time. On my father's side, my grandmother was a midwife who basically delivered half of Greenpoint at the time. Her brothers were in the coal business. Her two sons, my father and my uncle, started a heating oil business in 1942 because they felt it was more modern than their uncles in the coal business. That's how that started.

It wasn't a very large business. They were basically driving delivery trucks. They would pick up the oil in a place like United Metro here with tanks and deliver it to homes. They would also install heating oil systems because a lot of the houses back then didn't have central heat.

ACACIA THOMPSON: One thing that I was naïve about was how the Creek and sort of the plume spill area is still a huge economic engine. The Creek is an economic engine still. It's not as if it's just being cleaned up passively and nothing is going on. Everybody sees something going on, but do they really understand that there is still a lot of refineries going on, there's still waste transfer stations out there?

I didn't understand until quite late about how organizations like Newtown Creek Alliance's mission is partly to help keep industry on the Creek. I was sort of dumbfounded. At first, that was sort of bizarre to me. But then I understood that so much of what's happened in the neighborhood, as far as when redevelopment was happening or the waterfront rezoning was happening, it was always about making sure to keep industry here and not to let it go, to make it work more with residential and commercial, but also to make it safer.

LISA BLOODGOOD, Director of Advocacy & Education, Newtown Creek Alliance (NCA): I remember when I first looked at a map of Newtown Creek. If you look down at it and you look all around, you see the residential blocks and they're all really small blocks. But you look and it's all industrial and it's these big, massive areas. In my mind I was like, *oh, well, that's just all of the areas that need to be reclaimed and made into wetlands and it'll be this beautiful restored wetland area.* That was before I knew anything about the Creek, just looking at the map.

There are industrial waterways all around the world and that's not going to change. But what we have an opportunity to do is to find these creative solutions. How do you have this hard-flat edge and still create habitat? How can you redesign a bulkhead to serve industry and serve mussel populations?

KATE ZIDAR, green infrastructure research engineer, former director of Newtown Creek Alliance (NCA): What can we learn from the East River waterfront? If you're an environmentalist, and you understand that this began with incineration, the garbage portion of this story is just a great narrative through-line, because if you understand why we needed to fight incinerators, you understand why we needed to fight the marine transfer of waste and you understand the toxic effects, intergenerational effects of gentrification in New York City. You can stack all this together and see that you must not gentrify, you must not rezone Newtown Creek. A city needs an industrial area. It needs to move things. A city of islands needs to move massive amounts of material by water. And that has to do with climate change, it has to do with air quality, and it has to do with equity in the land. All of that plays out on Newtown Creek, all of that plays out in Gowanus. All of that plays out on Staten Island, all of that plays out in New Jersey. There's a unifying thing, too, it's not just Newtown Creek, and it's just that Newtown Creek is a big, old one right in the geographic center of the city. If not there, then where?

LISA BLOODGOOD: It's funny, sometimes you'll meet the industrialist, who's like, *wait, you're sure you're supporting me? You sure you're not just out to, like, you're not going to trick me?* And then it's really interesting to the ecologists or the other activists, environmentalists will come up to you and go, *wait, you're saying ecology and industry can get along? What are you saying?*

WINIFRED CURRAN: What activists have been very explicit about is wanting to envision and enact the 21st-century industrial corridor. Rather than just continue old-school industry, and holding on to old industry no matter what, but rather to be very much a part of reimagining what an industrial corridor can look like, and what that means. It doesn't have to be just dirty, oil-spewing things. That's because the history of the industrialization that had happened in New York, and Greenpoint in particular, most of the worst, dirtiest industries had left the neighborhood. It had become too expensive for them or whatever. What was left is a much more diverse and smaller scale.

I think no one is that sad when an oil refiner leaves the neighborhood, or animal rendering. But much of what is driving the manufacturing sector in Greenpoint now is smaller-scale, artisanal work. We have a lot of craft manufacturing businesses that are, for example, in the Greenpoint Manufacturing and Design Center are a lot of very small-scale, artisanal, woodworking, design-oriented kind of jobs. In the industrial parks, you see a lot of food manufacturing—stuff that is really kind of core to what we imagine New York City to be. Your muffin company is right next to your wonton company. Manufacturing does not have to mean pollution.

It can mean good jobs. It means local entrepreneurship. It means walking to work and supporting diverse local economies. I think that's what people really want to get on board with, with industrial corridors that we don't have to have this 19th-century image of what industry is. That industry is, in fact, much cleaner than people think it is, and much more of a driver—has a much higher multiplier effect on the local economy than retail and the construction jobs that will come from condos and that kind of thing.

PAUL PARKHILL, urban planner, former director of planning and development Greenpoint Manufacturing and Design Center (GMDC): These emerging small industrial businesses that were often creative businesses, sometimes immigrant-based businesses, they were different from the old massive factories—the

Domino Sugars and the Navy Yard—everybody brings their lunch pails to work kind of places. GMDC was created to help foster those kinds of businesses, by creating stable below market [rents]—not deeply subsidized, because it wasn't. There aren't a huge number of deep subsidies for economic development projects like that.

TRINA HAMILTON: The definition of a sustainable business is tricky. On the one hand, some people would consider all of the scrap-metal recyclers who are in the neighborhood sustainable business, because it's part of a broader reuse of materials, even though it can also create toxins and negative environmental impacts. That has been one core set of businesses in the neighborhood.

One thing we heard following Riverkeeper's intervention is that they trained the community members and others to be able to constantly monitor what was going on. Then no matter what the manufacturing activity or industrial activity is, there's now much more vigilance to make sure that they're not dumping into the Creek.

WINIFRED CURRAN: One of the business owners [Paul Pullo], who was most in the forefront until recently because he sold the business, is called Metro Fuel. It's not often that you think of a fuel company being at the forefront of the greening of an area. But he was. He was absolutely one of the most active business owners in the area in terms of advocating for this stuff.

That's what the focus should be, rather than on the shiny new thing. The BOA [Brownfield Opportunity Area] was supposed to be this opportunity to maybe think these big thoughts, and sort of have a systematic vision for how these things could happen. But what seems to have happened, thus far anyway, is that there have been a lot of studies and reports, and then not a whole lot of money put towards actually accomplishing any of those projects. That's the other thing, too. The vision on the ground was there, in terms of activists and even individual business owners. But even in what technically should be a friendlier policy environment, with a Democratic mayor and governor, has not necessarily been as friendly as we would like to see.

TONY ARGENTO, owner Broadway Stages: I came here in the 1990s. I wished I came here in the '80s. My uncles told me all you had back here was the asphalt plants. My uncles worked here on the asphalt plants and stuff. This is where they were, but even to this day, we have a lot of the leftover stuff. We have four scrap metal yards right here in Greenpoint in our backyard. We have one of the most expensive dirt recycling facilities in this city. Right here at 520 Kingsland.

We have Metro Fuel Oil which is a major oil distribution facility. We have three oil distribution facilities. What gets me is that this is heavy industry. This is not just industry, this a M3-1 Zone, it's the heaviest industry you can have.

One of my complaints to City Zoning, now they're looking to rezone all this, the Northside industrial corridors, which is one of the biggest industrial corridors in the city

It just boggles my mind that we haven't gotten the city of New York, under Bloomberg, under de Blasio, rezoned all these residential sites! Our zoning laws, industrial zoning laws, the "M" zones were established in 1961 and created in the '50s.

PAUL PARKHILL: I think that you can make a case that the M3 zoning in some of those areas is probably out of date, although, do they all need to be soundstages? I think that the counterargument is, there need to be varied uses. There need to be places even within the city limits that can accommodate heavier kinds of uses or dirtier uses.

MARC YAGGI: We've always felt like good environmental policy and good economic policies go hand in hand. You can have business and people and nature co-exist if it's sustainably done well and done right.

THE SETTLEMENT MONEY

A LITTLE OVER a decade had passed since Riverkeeper rediscovered the oil spill on Newtown Creek; the ExxonMobil settlement money came in 2013. It became the responsibility of the community to figure out how to best spend it. What projects would most benefit the community? The competition for funds created bitter rifts within the activist community. Everyone involved had a project that they wanted to see funded.

I chose not to dive too deeply into the weeds of these battles because I frankly don't find the local infighting very interesting. What I do find interesting is the overall outcome. Did the people most affected by the contamination feel that they were treated fairly throughout the process? Did the moneyed in-movers hijack the process and get their children suburban-like soccer fields? As you'd imagine, there's a lot of different takes on whether or not the Greenpoint Community Environmental Fund (GCEF) spent the money properly.

The Greenpoint of 2013 was a very different place than it was in 1998 or 2002 when the spill was rediscovered. Throughout the 2000s, the neighborhood transformed from a working-class Polish group of blocks to a hip majority of upwardly mobile, young creative professionals. Many of them had no idea about the cancerous pollution right under their feet.

To date, GCEF has awarded 61 grants totaling almost $17 million to 47
projects and leveraged an additional $50.4 million in matching contributions
from grantees, bringing GCEF's total investment in improving Greenpoint's
environment to over $67 million.[70]

WILLIS ELKINS, activist, Executive Director, Newtown Creek Alliance (NCA):
Greenpoint Community Environmental Fund (GCEF) was the result of the settlement between New York State and Exxon about the oil spill. It was under
[Governor Andrew] Cuomo when he was Attorney General. There was a better
cleanup plan in place, but then there was also a penalty paid out to make up for
what the community of Greenpoint has suffered.

It was a $20 million fund and overseen by the state. DEC [Department of
Environmental Conservation] is in charge of the money. They selected National
Fish and Wildlife Foundation as the administrator of the money. They ran a
granting process. That started in 2013, and there's been three rounds or something
like that. I lost track of how many. They've done different size grants, there's been
some major projects funded for the Greenpoint Library. The biggest is the
[Kingsland Wildflowers] Green Roof up here. That was another one of the bigger
projects, about a million dollars. There's a lot.

We're still working on two of them right now, I guess six different projects.
One was actually a continuation of water quality sampling. We've managed six
and then we've partnered on—I kind of lost track of how many we've partnered
on, because some of the partnerships are very minimal, and some like Kingsland
Wildflowers are more substantial. We've been pretty involved.

JUSTIN BLOOM, former attorney for Riverkeeper, Sarasota Waterkeeper: I moved
on and started my own practice and as a solo practitioner represented a number
of the plaintiffs and worked with Girardi & Keese on those claims. They were
co-counsel. At that point I was working on the private claims. I ended up representing a good number of the homeowners and working with Girardi & Keese in
pursuing their claims. I was still involved in the case, but not representing
Riverkeeper, when it finally settled.

**VICTORIA CAMBRANES, lifelong resident, community activist, 2021 candidate for
City Council District 33 in Brooklyn:** Attorney General Andrew Cuomo sued
ExxonMobil in 2006—he signaled intent to sue four other oil companies but
ultimately declined to do so. That's important because Exxon is not directly
responsible for cleaning up adjacent BP or Texaco sites unless they were

70. Greenpoint Community Environmental Fund (GCEF) website.

found to be affected by Exxon. How you find out which oil came from who is beyond me.

The DEC was put in charge of the "Environmental Benefits Projects," which became the GCEF. They are a state agency, while the Parks Department is a city agency. The conflict lies in the fact that the state matched the funds paid to the plaintiffs, but then also had a hand through the DEC in where and how the money was being used. They claimed to hire an independent outreach coordinator, but I've never been able to find out who that was. If you find out, I'd like to know.

The approximately $25 million that ExxonMobil will pay under the settlement will be distributed as follows:

- *$19.5 million will fund "Environmental Benefit Projects" that will benefit the environment in Greenpoint.*
- *$1.5 million will go to New York State to compensate for past cleanup costs related to the spill.*
- *$3.5 million will be available for future oversight costs.*
- *$250,000 in penalties will be deposited in New York's Oil Spill Cleanup Fund and Marine Resources Account.*
- *$250,000 in damages will be used to fund projects to compensate for the damaged natural resources in Greenpoint.[71]*

WILLIS ELKINS: It was an interesting time because 2013 was when the Greenpoint Community Environmental Fund, the Exxon settlement was coming online. That was the first rounds of grants. The first grant deadline was like two months right after I first started. That's been a lot of our work over the past five years. It has been heavily focused or heavily funded by GCEF, which has been good. I mean, there's been some downsides to it too, because it's Greenpoint-focused and we're trying to cover both sides of the Creek.

CHARLEY FRIEDMAN, artist, former resident Greenpoint: At some point they settled and we got some money out of it. What I really wanted was this unbelievably gigantic football-field-size vacuum cleaner that's gonna suck all this out! I don't need trees planted there. I want those fumes to come out. I want them to put in some kind of crazy enzyme, some kind of microbe which can eat it all up, and it doesn't sound like it's happening. Like the old-timers there, I became a little bit disgusted with the system.

---

71. ExxonMobil settlement breakdown from the website of New York State Attorney General Letitia James.

CHRISTINE HOLOWACZ, activist, longtime resident, GWAPP, Newtown Creek Alliance, many other nonprofits: It [the settlement] was for $19.5 million. I went to the Attorney General. I was already talking to Cuomo because he called me during the lawsuit. I said, "Hey, something else has to be done here. We need to figure this out." There was a meeting and they invited a couple of people to the meeting from the community.

I remember telling them what I feel and how I feel. I believed the community is the one who has to receive the money, and the community has to be the one who has to be able to divide it and have some kind of projects. The projects have to be decent projects and there has to be a very open process, not just a couple of people deciding, *okay, you get it, you get it and that's it, that's stamped.*

We're very cognizant about the fact that, not to make it so that one group could just bring in like busloads of people so only one project will be accepted then.

JOE LENTOL, New York State Assembly, District 50: I don't even know all the projects, but some of them, I think, were very good. Greening Greenpoint, planting trees.

KATIE BUSING NAPLATARSKI, longtime Greenpoint resident, activist, open space advocate: From what I know of it, it's well-handled. I worked with the tree project—Greening Greenpoint. The last tree was just planted in the park on Friday—635 trees.

JOE LENTOL: It was really good for the neighborhood; it was a lot of work. The eco-schools, for example, where these people went into the schools and are training people to be environmental stewards of the future.

The library project is fabulous. It's going to be a new, beautiful library, I hope.

ACACIA THOMPSON, archivist for Brooklyn Public Library's Greenpoint Environmental History Project: [The Greenpoint Library] were doing oral histories in the area. Parts of us have a larger program called Our Streets, Our Stories, which is an oral history component of the public library. They knew that this had to be about the environment, and creating an Environmental Center was absolutely necessary.

They also knew that it was a unique opportunity to have a partnership between the library, the GCEF Fund and the community. Unlike a lot of GCEF projects, this is a legacy project that people can see in years, which is unique, because a lot of the GCEF things that have happened, we don't see through day to day. The library is going to be amazing. It's also going to be a place where community groups can come together, because we have a huge hole in our life at Greenpoint right now about where we meet, and our community groups are always looking for space.

VICTORIA CAMBRANES: The problem with the Greenpoint Library getting GCEF funding is that the fundamental purpose of city budgets is to fund public works, operations and assets. Public libraries are public assets. DPL should not be selling public assets or dipping into public community settlement funds to subsidize budget deficits. It is another way that this administration is selling off every public asset it can, and it has systematically been doing so.

I would definitely bar public agencies from receiving this fund. I would have put it to the community, identified victims and survivors.

CHRISTINE HOLOWACZ: In the community there is $25 million, the whole settlement. $19.5 million went to the community. The rest—some of it went to DEC and some of it is still ready if we need to sue them for any other reasons. You see, the original consent order that they were under didn't require them to clean the soil. This one does and that's one of the things that we're pushing, not just to take out the free product [oil], but also to clean the soil, because there are methods that you can do this right now. That's what they have to do. They still have another 20 years or so of doing it. I don't know all of the details, what year it has to be done by, but that's the gist of the decision.

CHARLEY FRIEDMAN: From my own perspective, I think that there is this idea that through the litigation there will be an ethical fulfillment of the promise of what that litigation meant. In the end I realize it meant kind of a continuation of a certain kind of cosmetic capitalism. Which means that there's a lot of money that went from hand to hand and its politics—money transferred to the coffers of the city.

At the end of the day there was no accountability. There's legal accountability but there wasn't ethical accountability. Ethical accountability would have meant cleaning up the area and making it safe so any ExxonMobil executive who has a child or a grandchild could say, "Hey—you wanna live here, because I want that to happen." I can't imagine them saying that. Until offspring and the leaders of ExxonMobil want to have their children here, I think it's a sham.

COMBINED SEWER OVERFLOW
AND THE DEPARTMENT OF
ENVIRONMENTAL PROTECTION

Hypothetically, even if all the historic contamination were removed from Newtown Creek, New York City is, according to 2018 statistics, dumping nearly 1.2 billion gallons of raw sewage into it per year. After fighting oil spills and industrial dumping, human waste is the number one pollutant of Newtown Creek today. In 1998, the Greenpoint Wastewater Treatment Plant underwent a multi-billion-dollar upgrade. Decades after that construction, the city is still in violation of the Clean Water Act and will continue to be for the foreseeable future. New York City has an old combined sewer system, which means that when it rains, the stormwater gets mixed in with the usual sewage from sinks, toilets, etc. During storms, the Treatment Plant gets overwhelmed with the additional volume and has to dump the overflow into Newtown Creek untreated. At this point in the story, you may be getting confused between these two very similar-sounding government acronyms: DEP and DEC. Early on in my research, I certainly was. The Department of Environmental Protection (DEP) is New York City's local organization responsible for all of the city drinking water and water pollution.

The Department of Environmental Conservation (DEC) is the state agency that is in charge of all environmental matters on land, air, and water. When I asked the Deputy Commissioner of the DEP what the difference is between the two similarly named agencies, she responded, "I guess the way you would look at us is we are operators, and the safety you see, they're regulators. When I say that we're operators, we are the ones who are overseeing the protection of our drinking water supply."

A combined sewer system (CSS) collects rainwater runoff, domestic sewage, and industrial wastewater into one pipe. Under normal conditions, it transports all of the wastewater it collects to a sewage treatment plant for treatment, then discharges to a water body. The volume of wastewater can sometimes exceed the capacity of the CSS or treatment plant (e.g., during heavy rainfall events or snowmelt). When this occurs, untreated stormwater and wastewater discharges directly to nearby streams, rivers, and other water bodies.

Combined sewer overflows (CSOs) contain untreated or partially treated human and industrial waste, toxic materials, and debris as well as stormwater. They are a priority water pollution concern for the nearly 860 municipalities across the U.S. that have CSSs.[12]

ANGELA LICATA, Deputy Commissioner of Sustainability NYC Department of Environmental Protection: I have a portfolio that includes the Superfund program, specifically the Gowanus Canal, Newtown Creek, Wolff-Alport, and other sites. I'm also involved in citywide hazardous materials assessment and remedial strategies. I oversee a Bureau of Environmental Planning and Analysis that is engaged in many planning activities involving the rate structures, studies for the department, the demand management or conservation programs, water reuse, stormwater management, including CSO, which is combined sewer overflow program. Separate sewer programs, which is what is normally referred to as an MS4 permitting program. And then I'm also supervising the enforcement of the air noise and asbestos.

MITCH WAXMAN, historian for Newtown Creek Alliance (NCA), blogger Newtown Pentacle: They [the DEP] are the inheritors of three separate municipal entities worth of sewer systems: Long Island City, Newtown, and the sewer system of the City of Brooklyn. After city consolidation in 1898, all the pipes began to be hooked up, and Manhattan became connected to the sewer systems of these other three municipal entities, which are all combined into the modern city. The Bureau of Sewers Brooklyn and Queens, and the Bureau of Sewers borough of Manhattan, operated as separate entities with separate commissioners right up until about 1983 when the city charter revision created the DEP [Department of Environmental Protection].

WILLIS ELKINS, activist, Executive Director, Newtown Creek Alliance (NCA): They've inherited this very broken system and now we're all dealing with the ramifications. And because the city is so paved over, we generate so much stormwater during rain events that goes into the sewer.

ANGELA LICATA: We're using on average about a billion gallons of water a day by New York City residents, and then another million used by people to the north or within our watershed.

72. "Combined Sewer Overflows (CSOs)." *EPA*, Environmental Protection Agency, 30 Aug 2018.

MITCH WAXMAN: But under current conditions, DEP is releasing anywhere from 1.4 to 1.8 billion gallons of untreated wastewater into Newtown Creek alone. Harbor-wide, they have four hundred outfalls, which essentially means the raw sewage runs directly into the water. At Newtown Creek, you've got four of the largest outfalls in the entire city.

ANGELA LICATA: On the wastewater side, we have an intense job of treating that very large volume of water, which is about one million gallons of drinking water per day. And then, of course when it rains, we are trying to get to two times dry weather flow at the wastewater treatment to maximize the amount of wastewater treatment that we can do so that it's not just the sanitary flow, but also the storm-water flow. Anything in excess of that is combined sewer overflow.

WILLIS ELKINS: Wastewater is a huge issue. Rainwater from the streets goes down to the storm drain and those pipes are combined with our sanitary system, where we flush our toilets, and that all goes into one giant pipe which goes to the treatment plant. They can only clean so much water at the treatment plant.

Most newer cities are built with totally separated sewers where stormwater does not go to a treatment plant. There's a long history, why it happened—people were trying to get their sewage out of their house.

JOHN LIPSCOMB, Riverkeeper, Vice President of Advocacy, patrol boat operator: We are the polluter through our sewer discharges. We are the ones that are preventing Newtown Creek from living again.

LISA BLOODGOOD, Director of Advocacy & Education, Newtown Creek Alliance (NCA): The worst thing would be if the combined stormwater and sewage were to back up into the streets or into people's homes and businesses. The safety valve, that was built into the system a hundred years ago, is all of this just goes straight into the waterways.

ANGELA LICATA: That was the conventional way in which people developed sewers at that time. The idea was *let's get this flow off the street. Let's move it to our surrounding water bodies as quickly as possible.* But they were concerned about cholera and those types of diseases and all of the waste that had landed on the street. The first thing they did was develop sewers even before they built wastewater treatment plants. That came much later. And in New York City, with over seven hundred miles of coastline, they took advantage of the shortest runs to those water bodies.

MITCH WAXMAN: There's one [CSO] that's all the way back on Metropolitan Avenue, that's the size of a tractor-trailer truck. It's a seven-vaulted sewer.

JOHN LIPSCOMB: I take people in there and they imagine a pipe, they say, "Well, is it a pipe?" I say, "Nah, it's really big." They say, "Well, is it a big pipe?" They're imagining four-feet diameter, six-feet diameter. The CSOs in Maspeth Creek are the size of a double garage door. They're tunnels, they look like garages more than they look like pipes.

As long as we keep dumping a high volume of sewage and contamination that's in street water, we're going to perpetuate the contamination of creeks and water bodies like Newtown Creek. The city sewage problem makes Exxon look like a light job.

ANGELA LICATA: The DEP has been engaged for over 10 years now with programs to reduce CSOs. While we were doing maybe 30% with our treatment plants, we have now developed water body watershed plans that have now brought that figure probably up to about a 65% capture.

The idea behind these holding tanks is to store the water until the wet weather event is over and then pump that stormwater and wastewater back to the treatment plant. Since we've built those facilities, we've gone around the block again to say, *okay, what other cost-effective strategies are there to do more CSO volume control?* We've moved the dial from about 65% to approximately 83% capture with additional storage concepts, which now utilize tunnels. Tunnels are a more modern way in handling the CSO problem because you get storage and you get conveyance all in one shop.

In New York City, just to give you a sense of scale, we have spent approximately $4 billion on CSO control. And in our 10-year plan we have approximately another $4 billion. And when all is said and done with our Long-term Control Planning process, we are probably looking at somewhere close to spending $10 billion in total CSO program costs.

CAROL KNUDSON, Riverkeeper, water research assistant at Lamont-Doherty Earth Observatory: The threshold for acceptable water quality for the EPA standard using enterococcus is 60 cells per hundred-milliliter sample. That's the baseline. Anything below 60 is considered acceptable. Above 60 is a beach advisory. The levels at Newtown Creek have been close to zero. We've also had an excess of 24,000 after a few rainstorms. What we're noticing is that after rain, the numbers of fecal bacteria go higher because of all the combined sewer overflows.

ANGELA LICATA: We had a CSO reduction of about 5.6 billion gallons a year, and that was for a price of $4.2 billion. And then we're showing that after that reduction, we can reduce by another 3.2 billion gallons a year of CSO reduction and treatment. That will cost an additional $5 billion. We're on the flat side of the curve. It's diminishing returns, is what we're seeing. The financial concern about addressing CSO is certainly something that we're grappling with and we continue to make investments, and we continue to believe that reducing CSO is a very good thing, but again, it needs to be done in a measured way.

KATE ZIDAR, green infrastructure research engineer, former director of Newtown Creek Alliance (NCA): They [DEP] is the largest polluter in the Creek and some of the leading environmentalists on the Creek.

ANGELA LICATA: I think that there is a very healthy tension between the department and the stakeholders. The stakeholders are not professionals that have to take into account the balancing act between rates and impacts on customers.

WILLIS ELKINS: It's an interesting relationship with the DEP. It's definitely been historically antagonistic because people are like, "What the hell, you're dumping billions of gallons of untreated sewage into our waterways. You've built these treatment plants that smell like shit, and we have to deal with that."

There used to be a lot of butting heads and disagreements, frustrations on our part, on the community side and I think now we've seen more progress. I think the relationship with DEP has evolved in the past five to ten years, and it's in a more productive place.

ANGELA LICATA: I respect what our environmental advocates are doing and the desires that they have to improve the environment. I think on the part of the department, we have this professional obligation to balance a lot of factors. One of those is being a good steward of the resources that this department oversees and being a very cautious spender or investor when it comes to taxpayer dollars. That is why I am the deputy commissioner for sustainability. I'm very much looking at the environmental benefits, social impacts and the financial issues associated with all of the decisions we make every day.

WILLIS ELKINS: The idea of fixing it by separating the pipes is like an impossible task, because it means going and taking out all the streets, sewers, and reconfiguring them. There were sections in the city up until 1986 that were not connected to treatment plants at all. Every time you flush the toilet in one of these areas of the city, it went directly out.

ANGELA LICATA: Our treatment plants and our facilities are aging, our water supply is aging, you hear all the time about the aging infrastructure. We're trying very hard to spread funding around so that we can maintain the facilities that we have and reap the benefits of all of the investments that we've made to date.

WILLIS ELKINS: It's really about money, and the city has other issues. The DEP's budget is not like other agencies. DEP's budget is coming from the water rates. They can't, even if they wanted to, increase their budget fivefold. This treatment plant, depending on who you talk to, it's like a $4 billion project. But it's still a major issue.

MARC YAGGI, executive director Waterkeeper Alliance: Stormwater always tends to be a tough issue to get people engaged in, and everybody's part of the problem, but it's not sexy. It's always a tough one. It's also super expensive to dig up parts of Manhattan and Brooklyn and Queens and build massive holding tanks. That's where the benefit of looking back at the analysis as it can be just as cost-effective to treat it naturally.

WILLIS ELKINS: Those tunnels are great. They take a long time to build and they're really expensive, so there's that. There's green infrastructure, building green roofs and rain gardens on the streets that collect stormwater that is either stored on top of the building or slow the flow of it into the sewer system or ground. Those are two approaches the city's been using.

We've been trying to advocate for more education, because in the most extreme example, if no one flushed the toilet when it was raining, no actual sewage would be overflowing.

LISA BLOODGOOD: As an organization, we've come up with a system where we will send you a text message when it starts raining so that you can maybe save your shower for the morning or your laundry for the next day or hold off on those dishes and maybe don't flush your toilet unless necessary. It lets people know that they can be active participants in preventing some of this water pollution from happening. The city noticed and kind of implemented their own text messaging notification system.

ANGELA LICATA: We were able to measure that there was a 5% decrease in water use among the participants, which is really fantastic. We do have a phase two underway now. If changing people's behaviors can help resolve this problem that's a good thing.

IS REMEDIATION POSSIBLE?

THERE'S BEEN a lot of money floating through northern Brooklyn. Greenpoint is a trendy neighborhood and home to many in the New York power elite. The brownstones and condos are worth millions of dollars, and it's a highly competitive market.

With all this wealth and power, why have we not heard more talk about remediation? Yes, ExxonMobil has sucked a substantial amount of oil out of the ground and continues to do so, but there is also the Creek, NuHart's phthalate plume, and numerous other brownfields everywhere.

ExxonMobil takes its environmental remediation responsibilities seriously. Our goal is the same as the community's — to remediate the petroleum contamination stemming from our historical operations in Greenpoint as quickly and safely as possible. We will be in Greenpoint until the job is done and done right. Remediation projects such as the one in Greenpoint — where petroleum products are underground and not easily accessed — simply take time to complete, and remediation is expected to continue for a number of years. Throughout this time, the health, safety and welfare of those living and working in the Greenpoint community are our number one priority.[73]

VICTORIA CAMBRANES, lifelong resident, community activist, 2021 candidate for City Council District 33 in Brooklyn: They got the Superfund designation in 2010. Then in 2013, a payment was paid out to the Greenpoint Community Environmental Fund GCEF. That fund totaled $67 million and that was for all of the oil that was in the Creek, which was estimated between 17 and 30 million gallons. They said they were remediating it since the '80s, but that wasn't really so.

WILLIS ELKINS, activist, Executive Director, Newtown Creek Alliance (NCA): Even in the vaguest sense, EPA is not engaging us in those conversations [about remediation].

---

73. ExxonMobil press release. "Our Greenpoint Commitment | Our Greenpoint Commitment." *Our Greenpoint Commitment* (date unknown).

Newtown Creek Wastewater Treatment Plant. Looking west across Kingsland Avenue at three of the eight large sewage digester tanks built at the turn of the century, north of Greenpoint Avenue in Greenpoint, Brooklyn. Photo by Jim Henderson. Wikimedia Commons

JOHN LIPSCOMB, Riverkeeper, Vice President of Advocacy, patrol boat operator:
There have been a number of meetings with a group called the PRPs, the Potentially Responsible Parties. I think there are five big businesses that are assumed to be the source of the legacy contaminants that are in the sediments. It's a Superfund site, and in principle, the EPA will essentially task, charge and invoice the responsible parties for cleanup in some kind of agreed-upon percentage of responsibility. Those meetings have stopped recently, but we had a number [of meetings] with representatives from these companies. The idea is, first of all, everyone understands that Newtown Creek will never be restored the way it was.

It was an enormous marsh and we'll never get that back, obviously. But there are plans, perhaps, to turn Maspeth Creek into a marsh, because it's no longer used for water-dependent business. What's changed is we've stopped just dumping industrial contamination, mostly. The Exxon site is being remediated. They're pumping oil out of the ground, and we've busted a number of cement operations there. They're no longer discharging their cement waste.

There's a long history of reducing and eliminating the traditional pollution that everyone thinks of big, bad, dirty industry that's dumping something to save money. That's what it all amounts to.

JOE LENTOL, New York State Assembly, District 50: We probably still have companies that are polluting in that Creek now, but it's much better than it's been. There's some evidence of fish coming back now, and a cleaning of that Creek probably won't happen in my lifetime where It's pristine, but I think it's going to get a lot better in the future as a result of that action.

WILLIS ELKINS: On a whole, the Community Advisory Group (CAG) have been vocal about demanding as much remediation as possible. Mostly that means dredging. Because the idea is that full dredge, getting rid of all the contamination there, is more expensive, it takes more time, but it ensures that there's never risk of exposure to those pollutants in the future.

LISA BLOODGOOD, Director of Advocacy & Education, Newtown Creek Alliance (NCA): It's weird being an advocacy organization where you're really limited in what you can actually physically engage in. We have to talk about it a lot and you have to present what could be and help steer the narrative of what a "good" remediation looks like.

Are you just going to dredge the entire waterway and then what? You have to take into consideration all of the contamination on the land and how that's moving towards the water all the time and so, is there re-contamination that way? You don't want to just put in bulkheads and keep it out. You don't want just a bulkheaded waterway and CSOs. That is actually the one element of remediation we can address.

WILLIS ELKINS: In large part our work of taking on the Riverkeeper role of being the eyes on the waterway working with Riverkeeper to document conditions, instances and then working with the appropriate agencies, usually state DEC because they're more like an enforcement branch to investigate, prevent issues of illegal dumping—those are different categories of the remediation site.

VICTORIA CAMBRANES: When it comes to Newtown Creek it's a little bit more difficult because you have the IBZ (Industrial Business Zone). About 80% of Newtown Creek is IBZ. In order to fully remediate that and introduce public-private partnerships you would have to rezone it. The IBZ is currently undergoing a rezoning strategy.

There was actually just the big presentation about it at Community Board 1 on Tuesday. They are planning to reinforce the industrial and commercial value of that area. They are trying to raise the FAR (floor area ratio) limit, eliminate parking requirements, things like that to spur economic growth. What they are not allowing is residential. Unless they rezoned IBZ in North Brooklyn along Newtown Creek for residential, that remediation is not going to come for decades

Thompson, Kevin M /C ████████████████████████████████   Thu, Apr 25, 11:38 AM ☆ ↰ ⋮
to me ▾

Dear Mr. Nirenberg,

Thank you for your interest in the Greenpoint Petroleum Remediation Project and the Newtown Creek Superfund site. I wish you luck with your book, but respectfully decline to participate in your series of interviews. If you would like information regarding the progress being made on the Greenpoint remediation, I would direct you to the following websites:

NYS DEC Greenpoint Petroleum Remediation Project

Our Greenpoint Commitment

For information regarding the Newtown Creek Superfund investigation I would refer you to:

NEWTOWN CREEK | Superfund Site Profile | Superfund Site Information | US EPA

Newtown Creek

Thank you,

Kevin M Thompson
Public & Government Affairs Advisor
Environmental & Property Solutions (E&PS)

ExxonMobil Global Services Company
38 Varick Street
Brooklyn, NY 11222

████████████████████████

ExxonMobil has declined to be interviewed for this book.

and decades. It's only when they finally push residential that you will see significant improvements because they are relying on the private sector for that.

WILLIS ELKINS: Look at this from the standpoint of protecting human health and ecological health. That's the long-term solution. Whether or not that's more viable in certain places remains to be seen. A dredging cap is removing a certain amount of contaminated sediment and putting a cap in place to ensure that the other contamination further down below poses no risk.

Then a cap only is just saying we're just going to put some stuff on top. That is definitely certain areas of the Creek that could be conceivable. Again, it really factors in with the navigability of ships and how deep the Creek is right now. That's certainly a cheaper option and it's something that they were sort of preparing for.

CAROL KNUDSON, Riverkeeper, water research assistant at Lamont-Doherty Earth Observatory: I don't know the details of the shad and the striped bass and some of the signature seafood of the Hudson. But I'm pretty sure that most of the fisheries had been closed, but now thinking about it, I don't eat any fish anymore because I think that we've taken enough and I want them to come back. They need to come back. It's fantastic when you see that happening, especially the oysters, because the oysters are a great indicator of water quality.

TONY ARGENTO, owner Broadway Stages: We have a four-acre site on the other side of Long Island City and all these crabs underneath now. I see fish there from time to time. And every year, the water is clearer and clearer. It changes twice a day. It's when we get the overflow from the city sewage that it really, it gets contaminated.

PAUL PULLO, activist, former owner of Metro Fuels: The remediation from the 1980s to now is day and night on how much better the Creek is. If you go there, instead of seeing dead things, you see life. You see grass growing. You see birds and fish. Believe it or not, the oil well is somewhat organic and there are microbes that eat oil, but you've got the heavy metals and you've got the sludge from the gas plants. That stuff just doesn't seem to be going away. People aren't spilling oil like they used to anymore.

What's happening is some of the sludge is building up in the Creek. We all went out last year on the Fireboat (FDNY's maritime vessels) and we got stuck because charts don't show what actually the depth of the water is.

CHRISTINA WILKINSON, activist, founder Newtown Historical Society: I mean this is really, really seriously polluted. A lot of the sites around here, they dig to a certain depth and they put on a concrete slab and then they say it's done. We're talking like hundreds of years of pollution of all kinds of chemical things that you can't even imagine.

There's even typhus in the water. I know they always like to point to, *Oh well, fish are coming back.* I'm like *Yeah, would you eat them?* No, people also live in highly polluted areas, it doesn't mean they should. It doesn't mean the area is healthy.

GEOFFREY COBB, teacher, historian, author *Greenpoint Brooklyn's Forgotten Past*, **blogger Greenpointers:** There's a man who lives around the corner, he's an 83-year-old retired industrial chemist and he sees people eating [the fish]. Their crops have returned and their fish have returned. And he said, "You're crazy to do it because there's still that black mayonnaise. That is super toxic sludge sitting on the bottom of the Creek and the bottom of East River." It's somewhat out of my expertise, but this man is a trained chemist and he tells people, "Look, this stuff hasn't gone away. It hasn't been dealt with." And there's still pockets of oil that nobody knows about.

Recently near our street, people kept smelling gas. This stuff still leaches into the Creek. I think everybody's taking a risk. I lived here now for a quarter-century. How much of a risk have I taken by living here? We have friends who've developed cancer, who live on that street. It's crap living here for long-term.

ANGELA LICATA, Deputy Commissioner of Sustainability NYC Department of Environmental Protection: I don't believe that Newtown Creek will achieve these swimmable, fishable standards when you're looking at the EPA's beach standards. I don't think you're going to achieve those standards in many of our tributaries. They don't have the flushing ability to cleanse after wet weather the way the ocean-facing and larger bodies of water do. I do think that's a bar that has been set too high.

I do think however, though, we can make it safe for secondary contact. It's very important that when people think about swimmable and fishable waters that they understand that those epidemiological studies rely on a lot of assumptions about youngsters ingesting large quantities of water, at least a liter or more of water, and what that might do for gastrointestinal concerns and issues like that. I hope we don't have too many youngsters in these water bodies because I personally don't think that's the place for them.

LISA BLOODGOOD: The wildlife returning is excellent. It's helpful to be able to point to the things that are alive in the water, on the water, and around the water and say, *there's so much potential here. If it were* a completely dead waterway, like it was a couple of decades ago, it would be harder to have that vision for the future.

CAROL KNUDSON: Just when you think things are getting better... if you look at our data kind of long-term, we had a few dry years in 2014, 2015, and 2016. The whole river in general was looking much better and different communities up and down the river had done support of their infrastructure, sewage treatment plants and everything. And you think, *oh great, this is really working, everything's looking so good.* But then we were hit with 2018 last year, which was a very wet year. And many of the stations that we do, set records of high counts. It really depends on the rain, and the flow of the water in the river in general is something to be considered. Although we haven't really quantitatively figured that out yet.

Newtown Creek—you can have good years, good counts, good months and then get a bad rain or bad conditions over an extended period of time and then it's really bad again. There certainly have been a lot of things going on in Newtown Creek that have been possibly improving the water quality in different ways. As far as our data goes, you still get heavy rain and you're going to get high counts of enterococcus.

ACCESS AND RECREATION

MOST RECENTLY, there is a movement to encourage kayaking and recreating on Newtown Creek.

When I went out with John Lipscomb on *R. Ian Fletcher*, the Riverkeeper patrol boat, I got a firsthand look at all the industry that still lines the Creek. There remains a constant threat of industrial dumping all along the Creek, all the time.

JOHN LIPSCOMB: I remember when the Summer Olympics were gonna come to New York. See, they can't have Olympic rowers out on the East River. It's too rough, and there's too much current. Where in New York Harbor are you gonna go to have nice, clean—I mean—I don't mean clean. (laughs)

Where are you going to have nice, calm water, not a lot of current, no waves, where are you gonna go? And it can't be a hundred yards long. Newtown Creek was the obvious place to put the rowing events for the Olympics. Somebody asked the mayor at the time, "Are you aware of what Newtown Creek looks like? Have you seen what's in there?" And the Mayor's response was, "If we get the Olympics, we have a fast-track plan to clean up Newtown Creek." "Fast-track" are the words I remember. Then the Olympics dream vaporized, and the fast-track plan was never spoken of again. But it would be fun to look up, what was the fast-track plan to clean up Newtown Creek?

KATIE BUSING NAPLATARSKI, longtime Greenpoint resident, teacher, activist, open space advocate: You couldn't get to the waterfront. There was barely a spot where you could stand at the water. For example, when it was July 4th, if you wanted to watch the fireworks, there was literally no place to go to do that.

KATE ZIDAR, green infrastructure research engineer, former director of Newtown Creek Alliance (NCA): Maybe the philosophical thing is, if you live on an island, you should be able to touch the water surrounding your island without getting sick.

The water needs to meet specific criteria. The lowest would be fish survivorship. And then the higher level is full-body immersion; you should be able to swim in that water. Then finally, you should be able to consume fish that you find in that water. It's called "swimmable-fishable," that's the highest quality standard.

Newtown Creek was designated for basic survivor, on the low end of that scale: fish should not die. But you are not supposed to immerse yourself in that water, and you're not supposed to eat out of it.

WILLIS ELKINS: I'm always cautious in saying this: I think people overestimate some of the risk of health impacts. I think the general notion that people are like, *Oh my God, Newtown Creek, the entire thing is toxic, you shouldn't be anywhere near it,* is overestimating or exaggerating.

CHRISTINA WILKINSON: I think there's a misunderstanding that the Creek is actually healthy enough for recreation. I think it's absolutely ridiculous that anybody is putting that idea forward, and I don't think that this should be encouraged.

WILLIS ELKINS: Exaggerating the reality also discredits the big improvements that we have seen in water quality, for instance. In my opinion and based on a lot of the information I've seen, going to the Nature Walk is no less dangerous than walking underneath the BQE. Because you're not drinking the water. You are not rubbing your hands in the sediment below; the sediment is actually not that contaminated. The biggest issue would be air quality and that's no worse there than it's going to be in other parts of the city.

The reason that bugs me is because it's sending a message to stay away. And the more people that stay away and stay disengaged and treat it like it's a lost cause ensures that it's going to remain a polluted site for longer.

ANGELA LICATA, Deputy Commissioner of Sustainability NYC Department of Environmental Protection: I personally have canoed the Gowanus Canal. I have been in the dragon boats on Flushing Bay. I find both of those water bodies to be more hospitable. I've been on a boat on Newtown Creek. I think it is dangerous. There's too much maritime commerce, industrial usage, to provide safe access for a novice like myself. I know that our boat captains, the ones that are driving the DEP sludge boats and vessels, tell me that they cannot stop on a dime. They cannot maneuver very easily.

KATE ZIDAR: The people who go onto the Creek might be hobbyists. They might be just so bonkers about boats and that might be the only water they have access to. Or they could also be people who are willing or are so committed to living in a better environmental condition that they will be the canary in the coal mine, and they will put their bodies on the water and demonstrate that what they're committed to is the water.

CHRISTINA WILKINSON: There's a sign telling you that if you put anything in the water you should rinse it off and decontaminate it. This is what makes me laugh— these boathouse people, when they pull their canoes and stuff out of the water, what do they do? Like, just hose them off?

KATIE BUSING NAPLATARSKI, longtime Greenpoint resident, activist, open space advocate: I think it's incredibly important. I think the water is kind of like the feeling of the veins of Mother Earth and they feel alive to us and somehow they really do draw us, and even though the Creek is polluted, it's somehow a remnant of Mother Earth. It is a part of it. It's a whole system. When you go there, it's about the past and it's also about the future. It's a juncture between an ideology of making the most that you can regardless of what you spoil, and moving forward to how things can be and should be.

CAROL KNUDSON, Riverkeeper, water research assistant at Lamont-Doherty Earth Observatory: I think it's great. I think it's fantastic. It spreads awareness. They have to be careful because it is not the best water quality in the world, but there are days when it's good.

WILLIS ELKINS: I think that one of the things that's important for us is to try to bring people here so they can actually see it. It's not Central Park. But I think that some people do say, "I could see that's not so bad now, and I can see how it can be a little bit better and see value in it being an open interesting space."

It's also a way to see industrial uses that people don't understand and is a fenced-off operation. We think actually bringing people to the Nature Walk here and seeing how materials are moved—that giant pile of stuff over there, that's all your recycling, and it gets put onto a boat, and these are the good and bad things about how that works—maybe that will change your behavior.

MARC YAGGI, executive director Waterkeeper Alliance: People have powerful formative memories of water. You think about some of your special memories: maybe it was a great trip, you go to the beach as a kid, or the first time you learn how to swim, or like fishing with your mother or father or seeing a whale breach.

Part of that comes from studies showing how our brain reacts when we're in and out of water, and that they're showing that people tend to be happier, more at peace, it increases peace and reduces stress. They're going to vacation at the beach or at a lake or a river or something like that because of that intense connection with water.

I think that that same type of feeling can apply in an urban setting. We always try to get people because of that strong, powerful emotional connection you can feel in the waterway. We always want to encourage our Waterkeepers—we have events where they're bringing the community out to the waterway because if they establish those connections and those bonds, they're more likely to convert to being an advocate for when there is a threat facing that waterway, to make their voices heard and be part of the process.

And I think that's one of the ideas—I mean, I'm not involved in the kayaking on the creek, but I would posit that that's one of the compelling reasons to do it—is to get people out onto that waterway and say, *we own this. I mean,* that's part of the public trust. People here in New York City own Newtown Creek, they should be able to recreate on it. We've allowed Exxon to rob us for 70 years or something like that. They've stolen from the public and I think this is an opportunity to try to take back what belongs to the people.

THIS COULD BE ANYWHERE, THIS COULD BE EVERYWHERE

LOOKING AT the problems that Greenpoint faces today, it's mostly complications between the old contamination problems (Newtown Creek, NuHart, the various brownfields, etc.) and the hyper-gentrification of the neighborhood. We mentioned the massive Greenpoint Landing luxury towers, but that's not the entire picture. When you're in Greenpoint today, you can see the construction boom occurring on nearly every corner. Local politicians have historically had a hard time standing up to New York's dominant real estate donor class. To put it bluntly, most of the local politicians in Brooklyn have sold out their constituency to an interest group.

As we addressed earlier in the chapter on environmental gentrification, these Greenpoint Landing towers are going to bring in approximately 40,000 new residents. This population boom is going to put further stress on the aging water system, and the overburdened sewer problem. More volume will be spewing into the Creek. It doesn't end there. There's the single subway that services the neighborhood, the school system, a barrage of truck traffic, and the further whitewashing of local culture. It's what economists would call externalities.

Aside from the Greenpoint Landing mega-project, some great things are going on today. The activist communities are crackling with energy. They all seem to be growing and doing lots of projects that are helping to educate and revitalize the landscape.

In 2019, there are still a few polluting factories to fight and environmental initiatives to take on, but the days of the city bringing in the incinerators and waste transfer stations are foreseeably over now that Greenpoint is home to the hip, upwardly mobile, upper-middle and wealthy classes. Despite a few wins in the affordable housing market, nearly everyone I spoke to is still up to fight the growing problem of gentrification, and protects their neighborhood from a different menace.

*ExxonMobil is actively siphoning up the oil lake that sits underneath
Greenpoint, but says it has to do it slowly. They claim if they siphon too fast a
large part of Greenpoint would fall into a sinkhole.*[74]

*The Remedial Investigation (RI) commenced in July 2011 and is focused on
a study area defined in the Consent Order as the waters and sediments of
Newtown Creek. Fieldwork for the RI was conducted in two phases under
the oversight of EPA to determine the nature and extent of contamination at
the site. The Phase 1 work, which included surveys of physical and ecological
characteristics of Newtown Creek, as well as sampling of surface water,
surface sediments, subsurface sediments and air, began in February 2012 and
was completed in March 2013. The Phase 2 work began in May 2014 and has
been substantially completed. The Phase 2 RI work includes, but is not limited
to, further delineation of surface sediments, subsurface sediments and surface
water, as well as the investigation of non-aqueous phase liquid, groundwater
and other sampling in support of the human health and ecological risk
assessments, such as biota sampling. An additional phase of fieldwork for
the Feasibility Study (FS), including ebullition studies and further NAPL
delineation, began in spring 2017. The Respondents are also developing
models that will assist, during the FS phase of the RIFS, in evaluating
remedial alternatives.*[75]

**MITCH WAXMAN, historian for Newtown Creek Alliance (NCA), blogger Newtown
Pentacle:** There are one hundred different environmental conditions around the
Creek. It's everything from open sewers, which are building sediment beds that
are exposed to the air and outgassing into the air. As I tell people on tours all the
time, if you could smell it you're breathing it. That's Maspeth Creek and Ridgewood
section of the Creek. You start moving closer to the East River, it's like you have
the leave-behinds of Blissville, and you've got the leave-behinds of an oil plant.
Then you've got the leave-behinds of automotive industrial sites. There's a huge
well of crankcase oil that's along Review Avenue.

Then you've got modern usage issues. About a third of New York City's garbage
ends up on the Queens side of the Third Avenue Bridge every single day. Then
they're just pulling this huge trail of crap with it in their wake. Then they're leaving
heavy metals and whatnot, instead of recycling, they're leaving the black bags to

74. "Greenpoint Oil Spill." Atlas Obscura, 12 Sept 2010.

75. Staff. "Superfund Site: Newtown Creek Brooklyn, Queens, NY Cleanup Activities." *Epa.gov*, Environmental
Protection Agency, 2019

trusted Waste Management. There's heavy industry down there which is loading up all this stuff, which is its own carbon stream. You've got CSO issues along Dutch Kills. Then you've got the Pulaski Bridge, which like every other bridge in New York City, the sewer drain is up on the deck drain directly into Newtown Creek.

Then you've got this broken shoreline that's leading directly into the gentrified section of Long Island City where we have this new problem. A sewer system that was originally designed for a few factory buildings and a rail yard, is now handling tens, if not hundreds of thousands of residential wastewater flows. I could continue up the Queens side all the way to Astoria. Again, it's this post-industrial landscape.

KATIE BUSING NAPLATARSKI, longtime Greenpoint resident, activist, open space advocate: I live in the community and I really had the intention to stay here. Whatever I can do to make it better, because there were things which were unacceptable. When it comes to different projects, you end up knowing who the different people are who might support your vision and your feeling about things. And then, you reach out to those other people and you form a group which then could be an advocate for that.

For example, the waterfront—when we found out about a year and a half ago, about the Greenpoint Landings parcel and that they had put in a proposal to the Community Board, and we found out what the design would look like and that this was unacceptable and did not match what the Waterfront Masterplan, the vision of the Waterfront Masterplan or the subsequent text amendment components, we coalesced as a group to form a strong advocacy and actually made incredible gain on the design.

TOM ANGOTTI, Professor Emeritus of Urban Policy and Planning at Hunter College, founder and director of the Hunter College Center for Community Planning and Development: Any rezoning, but of course it's always upzoning, it's always increasing developments, because the philosophy of MIH: Mandatory Inclusionary Housing is that the city will recapture some of the value created to guarantee affordable housing. That affordable housing becomes anywhere between 20 and 30 percent of the new units.

WINFRED CURRAN, associate professor of geography at DePaul University, co-editor *Just Green Enough: Urban Development and Environmental Gentrification*: The scale at Greenpoint Landing is so massive. People are calling it Dubai on the East River. It's not compatible. Christine [Holowacz] told me, she's like, "It's like a whole separate neighborhood on its own, just like appended onto Greenpoint." I think, in the long run, it will be really interesting to see whether it really even attempts to integrate the neighborhood in the way that it exists now, or if it becomes a really vocal critic of the existing industrial uses, because obviously these things, in most people's imaginations, do not go together. Like, "Luxury condo with view of water treatment plant" is not your typical real estate listing. In the long run, I think it's a threat, even as there has definitely been distinctive community victories in how it's emerged along the way, but again, in this kind of constrained realization of *this thing is going to happen, even though we don't want it to, so we're getting the best we can within a situation which we never wanted in the first place.*

TRINA HAMILTON, associate professor of geography at State University of Buffalo, co-editor *Just Green Enough: Urban Development and Environmental Gentrification*: I think a concern for the activists is that, in contrast to some of the earlier gentrifiers who were in public service or they were in the arts and those were the people they were able to form coalitions with, the people moving into these towers, that's a whole different type of gentrification. And the concern, as Winifred said, is they will not be brought into the coalition, but instead they'll be the ones complaining about the industrial zone, and maybe they will come in to go to a party at the Kingsland Wildflower rooftop, but they are not necessarily going to be the ones joining the advocacy for a working waterfront. I think that's a real concern, that that could reshape the environmental activism that goes on in the community.

WINIFRED CURRAN: In fact, that's something long-term residents brought up, and people have been bringing it up since the early 2000s, and the city—it's largely fallen on deaf ears. Infrastructure matters. You can't just plunk tens of thousands of new people into a place and expect things to run along smoothly.

PAUL PARKHILL, urban planner, former director of planning and development Greenpoint Manufacturing and Design Center (GMDC): The infrastructure issue in the neighborhood—Greenpoint in particular because it's on the G train—but I think also just because of the way it is laid out, there's going to be a lot of growing pains for a long time. The environmental impact statement that was done for the North Brooklyn Rezoning, as with every EIS (Environmental Impact Statement), can only look for maximum development impact over the next 10 years. Because on the premise that anything beyond that is too hypothetical and you don't know what's going to change beyond a 10-year threshold. They try to be aggressive in their projections about how much will get developed over the next 10 years.

The reality is that when you rezone a neighborhood, you're rezoning it for probably the next 40 or 50 years. In 1961 it was the last time the map was seriously changed in North Brooklyn and it was 45 years later. It's crazy that you're saying *We're rezoning a neighborhood for the next 50 years, we're only really going to look at the environmental impacts of the next 10. And we're going to be aggressive about that.* Come on.

There is no real study of what it's going to mean for actual full buildout or even a heavy buildup of the waterfront of what the impacts on schools are, what the impacts on transportation are. The only mitigation that the EIS in North Brooklyn suggested on a transportation front was the widening of one staircase in the Bedford Avenue L train. That was it. It's kind of a broken system. There should be better ways to anticipate what this is going to be. And generally, what the impacts are going to be. And generally, the response when you say, *Well, what are you gonna do about schools? What are you going to do about fire department resources?* The answer is generally we have to wait until the population's in place before we can address those things.

TOM ANGOTTI: It's a phenomenon and it's been adopted by pro-growth development and especially big developers. It's very contradictory and used in favor of selling their new developments. Contradictory because in one sense they can do in new development in neighborhoods like Greenpoint, Williamsburg, Gowanus, they can build more energy-efficient buildings and they can build buildings that are relatively protected from contamination in the surrounding areas. They can build following the city's new regulations of 10, 15 [feet] above high water and the buildings will be good, but what about the surrounding areas? What's the relationship between these buildings and what's going on around them, what is going to happen in Greenpoint, Williamsburg and Gowanus 30 years from now? Nobody knows 30 years from now how many feet sea level is going to rise, but it's going to rise.

Bottom line is always the bottom line—the developers make investments that they can recover in 15, 20, 30 years maximum. They can invest in these neighborhoods, sell apartments, rent apartments, recover their original investments, and then walk away and these will be ghost towns. There's no long-term planning, it's all about making the deal today, and selling waterfront property. They're also used increasingly for investment rather than for people to live there.

It's a scam. If you think of the long-term consequences, our children and grandchildren and great-grandchildren, if they're still able to survive through all of this, are going to wind up dealing with the catastrophe that's left. We're still going to have the contaminated land and waterways and you're going to have a lot of rubble, buildings that are useless.

WILLIS ELKINS, activist, Executive Director, Newtown Creek Alliance (NCA): We do a mixture of education, planning, and restoration where it's possible. On the planning side, stuff that I've been involved with, the biggest one is we worked on was with Riverkeeper on this new vision plan. I don't know if you've seen it; it's a great resource, 150-page document. Then we put it together over the course of about a year, it was pretty quick. Basically we know we're going to have the Superfund cleanup and major sewer improvements in the next 20–25 years. What else do we want to see for the Creek beyond that? There are these four lenses that the vision plan uses, or remediation, restoration, resilience and recreation. There's like 95 projects total in the booklet and some of them are projects that are already underway or have been discussed for a very, very long time; some of them grew out of conversations during the process and meeting with stakeholders and stuff like that.

That's been a great resource. That came out just about a year ago, seems like a whole lot longer. But we're using that a lot to sort of push forward with some of these ideas. We've done some other sort of planning things about specific sites.

There's an empty lot that's owned by the city. It's part of the Treatment Plant. They've long promised it as an open space or some sort, but kind of sat on it for 15 years. We got a small grant through GCEF to do a planning process. We're having a workshop, our second community workshop is on the 5th—we're basically coming up with what we want to see happen there. Then, getting the city to hopefully build it out in a reasonable time frame.

PAUL PULLO: The Gateway to Greenpoint is this piece of property on the corner of the Creek. It's on the corner of Greenpoint in Kingsland. If you look at the fence, you will see that there is a piece of property there. Evergreen and NCA are working together on that. The trouble is it's not happening quickly enough. That's really what it comes down to. You need people to carry the torch, because things take forever. We should be able to be using these things already.

WILLIS ELKINS: In terms of planning projects, trying to get community input to really think about a lot of these physical spaces on and around the Creek that have been so neglected and overlooked for so long, and we really feel like have potential. There's that on the restoration side. It's tricky because of some of the contamination, we can't actually be out in the Creek and doing work when you're not wanting to come in contact with the sediment and stuff like that. But also, there's a lot of stuff that we advocate for, which is recreating some of the natural ecology or shoreline topography in certain areas of the Creek is also, maybe in the long term, not the smartest approach, because some of that stuff may have to get removed as part of the remediation.

LISA BLOODGOOD: It's fairly simple and straightforward. It's Newtown Creek, Urban Ecology, STEM curriculum. STEM is the science, technology, engineering and math. And it's really playspace learning. How do you learn all about a situation or an issue or a problem and then problem-solve and creatively think about that and create solutions or design things or whatever it is? That's what we did and we piloted this year and the four public Greenpoint schools and it's fourth, fifth, sixth and seventh grade. It's showing these kids.

PAUL PULLO: The depth of the Creek has silted up and charts for navigable waterways are not accurate anymore, because no one is doing the maintenance on this Creek to maintain the depth of the Creek, which is a problem for navigation. You can't bring boats in with bigger barges because there is not enough water in it.

That's why the DEP did some dredging at the Creek, but normal businesses can't do that. Especially with the Superfund sites. You have certain things that have to be moved by water. You have the Simms property which has the metals, you've got a locker. You have all the gasoline in New York City. A lot of it comes from this Creek. It gets here by pipeline, but a lot of the gasoline is distributed from Newtown Creek. All of it has to have 10% ethanol in it by law. But ethanol is not shipped by pipelines.

The ethanol has to be delivered by either truck or boat. We would much rather boats. You need the Creek just for the boats that are bringing ethanol in, besides everything else. There is definitely a need for the Creek.

I have good hopes for the Creek. I think that they can't stop it. We are going to have to keep at least an 18-foot depth of the Creek, so that's basically 18 feet down. One way of possible solution, which doesn't work, is cap it. But if you just cap it, all the stuff is going to stay down there. Basically, as boats go by and everything else is just going to blow it away and they are going to end up with the same thing. They've got to take some of the dirt away and if they want to cap it, then let's cap it.

LISA BLOODGOOD: And it'd be harder to convince the EPA, and all of the other powers that be, that it's a place worth investing in, because that would be more debt. But that's life, that's hope, and that's exciting. Last summer we had partnered with Hudsonia, which is a research nonprofit.

There at Bard College, there's a field station there that they operate out of, but we did a survey of all of the vascular plants a hundred meters from all 11 miles of shoreline. We almost did everything, but we got a lot of it covered and we found there's more native plant species than invasive plant species, and there's a real nice biodiversity in all vascular plants. Which you probably would have been hard-pressed to convince somebody of a couple of years ago, that those plants are there and, and doing fairly well. And that also opens the door to say we can have nice things here. We can have habitat and pollinator gardens, and we can support the wildlife there through additional plantings and restoration work.

They've survived, they do just fine. And if the grasses can make it in a box on the side of the bulkhead, imagine what, how well they would do if they were given an actual shoreline and those invasive species management implemented. It's the things that we're doing are really small and symbolic. But they do signal much greater things are possible and they inspire, which is the biggest thing.

JOE LENTOL: I'm going to give you an update that I think is very important. I don't know what's going to happen yet. But there was a meeting last week, I was in Albany, and my staff attended, on Freeman Street, regarding a lot of evidence of gasoline smell in the neighborhood, in homes, in the sewers and in various places.

I was very upset about that because I don't think people remember the neighborhood like I do. A lot of people were saying they think it's part of the ExxonMobil spill. I said to my staff person, Emily, "People don't realize that there was a Shell Oil and Motiva plant—I think it was Paidge Avenue," which is right near the Newtown Creek. But I'm guessing if it's not contamination of the sewers by the public utilities, who like to do that, to dump their stuff in the sewers.

I used to see Con Edison at the sewer, and I'd wonder what the hell they're doing there.

I don't know if they're doing it anymore, but the report of the meeting was that it could be dumping in the sewer that's causing the gasoline smell. I don't know who's dumping, whether it's Con Edison, National Grid that dumps, or any of the other utilities, or even somebody else, for all I know.

I called the commissioner, actually last weekend, Basil Seggos. And I told him that I'm suspicious that this is another oil spill. *I want you guys to really look into the ground; I don't care what it costs.* I'm afraid it may cost a lot to determine whether it's another oil spill coming from an old transfer facility, or a gasoline facility, that was located on Paidge Avenue—first it was owned by Shell Oil Company, and then they sold the property to Motiva.

GOING FORWARD

JUST LIKE in Tar Creek, the industries in Greenpoint helped us win the World Wars and move entire generations out of poverty. Industry put food on the table and built our communities. Despite climate change and legacy pollution, society has benefited greatly from the industrial revolution. It's easy, but simplistic, to blame the industrialists for all this pollution.

In the two cases I laid out here, you can assign some blame to the companies and their executives, but I don't think they thought the bill would come due on these sites. They didn't have the science to predict these outcomes. Even if they had, I imagine they were making too much money to care. Generally, people who run companies don't think in the long term. That's still true today.

Currently, Greenpoint is facing gentrification, overpopulation, aging infrastructure on a highly polluted multi-Superfund site. Greenpoint's economic prospects were aided by a smooth dovetailing between the activist groups' agendas and cooperation with the neighborhood's industrial and business community.

In the late 1990s, Broadway Stages owner Tony Argento saw the opportunity to expand his soundstage empire in Greenpoint. He worked with the DEP to get his soundstages up and running all over the town. This turned out to be a prescient move as the demand for TV and movie production has increased in New York with the birth of streaming services like Netflix, Hulu, and Amazon among others, all producing content as well as a city government that no longer withholds the TV and film tax credit[76] which incentivizes production companies to stay in New York City. A rival Hollywood sprouted out of the oil and chemical spills. Without Greenpoint's environmental disasters, there would be no film industry there. The land and buildings were cheap because the pollution was egregious.

Broadway Stages has been an innovator in the business by introducing solar panels, among other large-scale green projects. The Argentos have been criticized as having too much influence in the neighborhood due to their expansive political contributions and charity work. They have faced opposition from some in the community who believe that neighborhood residents aren't doing the jobs the industry provides. I haven't seen any numbers to prove that.

I have no doubt that the emergence of the film industry has contributed to Greenpoint's gentrification issues. During the industrial revolution, the distasteful business of animal rendering was replaced by the chemical plants and oil refineries, which created this massive pollution problem. With some traditional industrial companies like concrete plants continuing to operate amongst a smattering of artisanal trades on the Creek, it's really the movie and television industry that has truly captured the spirit of gentrified Greenpoint. As Winifred Curran said to me about this, "Obviously movies and television are way more attractive than Boar's Head Meat as an entity, in terms of defining what the neighborhood and an industrial corridor looks like." It's appealing and glamorous to many people to live on a movie set.

During the process of writing this book, I struggled with how much of the local Greenpoint politics to include. I hope someone with a passion for it does go ahead and write that book because a lot of shady shit has gone down alongside all this well-meaning activism. Many of the wealthy in-movers have wormed their way onto the community boards and environmental groups to push for projects that clearly promote gentrification.

What we saw at Tar Creek was an early industrial boomtown go bust in slow motion. It was psychologically difficult for the people of Picher, Cardin, etc. to admit that mining wasn't coming back. There are small towns like this everywhere that depend on a single economic source that both sustains and poisons its residents and workers. As the ground gave way and began to sink, so did the

---

76. From NYC.gov: The Film Production Tax Credit is a 30% tax credit on qualified costs incurred in New York State for eligible productions. There are no caps for potential benefit for this credit.

hope of a resurgent 21st-century Tar Creek. Greenpoint amazingly experienced the opposite where their polluted land is worth millions, if not billions of dollars of real estate. Comparing legacy pollution sites bring about all kinds of questions about race, class, and environmental justice. All sites are not equal. Sites like Greenpoint have advantages that sites like Tar Creek do not. This problem of Superfund inequality is one I've never seen addressed in the media. How do local governments respond? How does a blue state compare against a red state in measuring the adequate response to remediation efforts? CERCLA needs work, and we can start by depoliticizing the EPA. We can put a stop to making it a Presidential appointment position and consider hiring an environmentalist who cares about the mission of the agency and will fight like hell for us.

One thing I've learned throughout this process is that legacy contamination sites will be with us forever, and the best you can hope for is that they stay stabilized and don't give anyone cancer anymore. Our species will eventually have to learn to protect itself from our worst impulses or face extinction. In my lifetime, I would say that the environmental movement has has been in the mainstream of American culture for a decade or less. And yet as the environment and particularly climate change have become mainstream, we have elected the worst corporate monsters who don't even pretend to care about their children or grandchildren. The sites profiled here will be nothing compared to what happens after we climb another few degrees of global temperatures.

There are some brave people in Greenpoint. I have come to admire a few of them. They've kept true to their convictions and are continuing to stay the course today. Some of these people had the guts to stay and fight when they could have just as easily moved elsewhere. The activists and the residents who supported the activists continue to make a difference there today. You know Laura Hofmann and Christine Holowacz will be training the next generation of activists because if you understand the scale of the pollution, it's clear that it's going to take several generations to solve this thing. It will yield technological breakthroughs and a continued focus on educating the newcomers.

In some ways, the problems are getting better. Behaviors have changed, ExxonMobil is slowly sucking the oil out of the ground, fish are returning to Newtown Creek. In other ways, the remaining problems are going to be compounded, buried underneath gentrification, wealth disparity, aging infrastructure, population explosion, and the horrors of climate change.

I have hope. The people I've met along throughout this investigation make me naïvely optimistic that somehow these legacy contamination sites are going to have some future in the 21st-century. They may never get thoroughly cleaned up. I guess we'll have to wait and see.

GEOFFREY COBB, teacher, historian, author *Greenpoint Brooklyn's Forgotten Past*, blogger Greenpointers: Pete Seeger was considered a dangerous radical. He questioned the idea that corporations were beneficial to America, were part of the American fabric. For a lot of people it was unquestioned. They destroyed the Hudson River. That was just the price of progress. I think that's one thing that we forget. The other thing that we forget is that these industries provided jobs, and this has always been the first stop for immigrants. A lot of immigrants were able to make it in America, because there was a massive amount of employment here that was provided by industrialization. It's easy after the fact to tut-tut, to portray Exxon and some of these other industrial people that made their fortunes here as evil characters.

But we should view it with hindsight: industrialization made America great and it happened here. It's a mixed bag. People forget that very important aspect.

BASIL SEGGOS, Commissioner of the New York State Department of Environmental Conservation (DEC), former Chief Investigator for Riverkeeper: We've gone through several stages of environmental awareness, the 1960s with burning rivers ,and here we are today with people becoming acutely aware of climate change, but also acutely aware of drinking water impacts. You see communities like Flint, Michigan, obviously, experiencing that very, very powerfully. I don't know that there are any regulations or laws that necessarily hit the Grand Slam to fix these problems. I think ultimately we have very strong laws on the books.

The environmental movement itself was successful in getting that down on a bipartisan basis over the last 40-plus years. I think what makes this work is having engagement at all levels. I think if there's a step that the city or state or country can take to prevent these pollution events, I think it is in remaining engaged, getting out of your desk, going out meeting with ordinary people and finding out what their concerns are, what their problems are, because I guarantee you no matter what their political strategies are, they care about clean water and clean land and clean air. Ultimately, I think we can we can be effective if we remain connected.

ANTHONY BUISSERETH, Executive Director North Brooklyn Neighbors (NBN), formerly Neighbors Allied for Growth (NAG): Number one, we have to have a reckoning on what actually has happened. I don't know if we've actually discovered all the horrible things that have happened in the past, but I do think we need to be preventative. We need robust policy, but we also need technological advancement where companies and organizations are responsible for this kind of commerce that bring value and not destroying the earth.

CAROL KNUDSON, Riverkeeper, water research assistant at Lamont-Doherty Earth Observatory: We need to respect that we've taken more than our fair share. We need to respect the other things on the planet that are here, which will make it better for us in the long run.

Don't just do something, not a quick fix for today, but look into how it's going to be affected 10, 20, 50 years down the road, and plan for that.

JOE LENTOL, New York State Assembly, District 50: Eco-schools, teaching environmental science and environmental awareness in the public school system to kids who won't stand for it, like the new people of today aren't standing for it. There aren't enough of us, but there will be enough of them to stop it if we do that.

VICTORIA CAMBRANES, lifelong resident, community activist, 2021 candidate for City Council District 33 in Brooklyn: We have Newtown Creek happening every day, all around the world. You have these massive oil spills happening. You have huge amounts of contamination, defunding by our current administration to environmental issues, trying to drill in the Arctic, the DAPL pipeline. There are so many Newtown Creeks happening every day. It's very hard for people to wrap their heads around it because it seems like you are playing whack-a-mole when it comes to the environment. But there is also a changing of consciousness, I think. You have the Paris Agreement. You have all these countries around the world, even China, who are implementing climate change and sustainability policies.

It's going to take time and time is not on our side, but it is starting to kind of come to a head and I always see revolutions as paradigm shifts. That pressure is building now and it will erupt one day and then there will be a complete change of consciousness. I hope it doesn't require an apocalypse for that to happen. But it's going to require something big for people to say, *I've got to change my entire ways.*

MITCH WAXMAN, historian for Newtown Creek Alliance (NCA), blogger Newtown Pentacle: It's a living waterway. There's critters, there's birds, there's fish. It is not a wasteland. It is not a dead place. It is also not a post-industrial zone. It is still a major employer for blue-collar New York. There are facilities along the Creek that provide functions that are vital to the survival of New York City. This is the dead-bang center of the city.

The potential is enormous and the question is, what creative way can we come up with to screw up the Creek for future generations to fix, because that's what everybody before us has done. By bringing in enough voices and enough points of view, we can come up with something that's really not going to screw the pooch as badly as prior generations have.

It's our waterway. It's not theirs. It's ours. We own this by birthright. We have stock in this waterway. I personally am not going to allow somebody else to impose their ideas on something that's mine.

JOHN LIPSCOMB, Riverkeeper, Vice President of Advocacy, patrol boat operator: It's not surprising, looking back, that—that being drafted into an effort to protect a mighty river that is powerless and mute to protect itself, that that would appeal to me. And that ends up being what drives me. It's the insults to the river that are perpetrated because the river is silent, and that really just stokes the fires for me.

I'll say one thing because I don't want to forget to say it. There is a developer that has a project plan for the river, and I still hope to defeat it. The project doesn't matter, it's a large-scale project. And the developer said, "Why are you going to build this power cable in the Hudson? Why don't you bring it down by land?" You know, "Why don't you run overland with it?" He says, "Well, because fish don't vote."

Well, when you say that to me, you've just bought yourself a 'till death do us part' adversary.

CHRISTINE HOLOWACZ, activist, longtime resident, GWAPP, Newtown Creek Alliance, many other nonprofits: I am proud to have my kids here and the reason I fought it was because I wanted my kids to have a better life and there was no reason that I have to move. I decided that they had to change, not me. I wanted to make this place living and I have a beautiful yard. I'm just looking at it now and I love it.

JUSTIN BLOOM, former attorney for Riverkeeper, Sarasota Waterkeeper: In perspective now, looking back, it was certainly really exciting to be involved as a young lawyer. And it was like the case that now in retrospect, I see as having really contributed to the community kind of coming together and realizing the importance of environmental protection, and the importance of dealing with legacy contamination in a growing community—core community activists come together and then appreciate what was an abandoned and ignored Creek that now seems to be more and more of a focus of like a recreational amenity. Hopefully one day it will be a front door of the community instead of what was the back door.

KATIE BUSING NAPLATARSKI: Nature in all its forms is fundamental to our lives, to the health of our bodies, minds and spirits. If that is not known, understood, felt, appreciated, then we get industrial pollution and plastic benches. It's all the same.

CHARLEY FRIEDMAN: Greenpoint has the shittiest subway.

HEATHER LETZKUS: You have to have a sense of humor to live here.

APPENDIX

ACKNOWLEDGMENTS

I couldn't have done this without my editor, friend and consiglieri Christina Ward who midwifed this thing. She knows where the bodies are buried and had enough savvy to keep them there. I'm of course forever grateful to Jessica Parfrey and Process Media for believing in these stories. It's honor to publish it with the house that Adam built. I was a fan first.

The research for this book brought me into the orbit of Rebecca Jim and Earl Hatley, who early on were instrumental in helping me understand the complexity of Tar Creek and its human faces. A special thank you to Ed Keheley who was so generous with his time, expertise and archive, without whom this book would have suffered tremendously.

Thank you to Marc Yaggi and Waterkeeper Alliance for bouncing ideas with me early on. Fredas L. Cook for his generosity with his archive, and Jodi Ann Irons for deftly transcribing my recordings. I solicited and received a lot of helpful input regarding Newtown Creek from Laura Hofmann, Acacia Thompson, Mitch Waxman, and Victoria Cambranes, who all were patient with my pestering questions and introduction requests.

I'm eternally grateful to all of the people who have given their time to me and trusted me to tell their stories: (alphabetically) Don Ackerman, Tom Angotti, Tony Argento, Tammy Arnold, Mary Billington, Lisa Bloodgood, Justin Bloom, Anthony Buissereth, Brad Carson, Geoffrey Cobb, Winifred Curran, Virgie Curtis, Willis Elkins, Scott and Kim Fraser, Charley Friedman, James Graves, Brian Griffin, Trina Hamilton, Christine Holowacz, Dr. Howard Hu, Frank Keating, Mikalya Keller, Wally Kennedy, Carol Knudson, Larry Kropp, Joe Lentol, Angela Licata, Tom Lindley, John Lipscomb, Heather Letzkus, Matt Myers, Dr. Emily Moody, Dr. Robert Nairn, Katie Busing Naplatarski, Paul Parkhill, Paul Pullo, Mike Schade, Basil Seggos, Cathy Sloan, Daniel Stevens, J.D. Strong, Dorothy Swick, Acacia Thompson, Scott Thompson, Christina Wilkinson, Dr. Robert Wright, and Kate Zidar. Please pardon the omissions, but there wasn't enough room for everything. Sacrifices were made to serve the big picture.

Work like this takes a village to coordinate. The following people were kind enough to lend a hand at various points: Bradley Beesley, Earl Dotter, Millree Hughes, Natiba Guy-Clement and Deborah Tint at the Brooklyn Public Library, Maureen Wren, Eric Radezky, Neale Gulley, Angela Espinosa, Monica Holowacz, Nick McKinney, Flynn Hundhausen, John Torrani, William and Ana Nirenberg, Mary Hunnicutt, Scott Meier, and always Sal Calcaterra as counsel.

Thank you to all my friends on the TV show I work on. There's too many of you to name, but know that I appreciate your support while I was there working on my laptop in the dark corners between shots.

Most of all this book is dedicated to Jessie, who was pregnant throughout the first part of this process. It was not an easy time, but it was a happy one. She patiently listened while I experienced the highs and lows that accompany big projects. I can hardly remember my life before my kids Oliver and Vivian came along and filled the void. We left their generation a ton of problems that we need to get a handle on.

Most importantly this book is for the people who have suffered, got sick, died or lost loved ones through these two environmental disasters. Let's not let this happen again.

BIOGRAPHIES

(in alphabetical order)

TAR CREEK

DON ACKERMAN is currently an Environmental Health Specialist in Fayette County, Georgia. Mr. Ackerman was with the Commission Corps for 28 years and retired as Commander.

TAMMY ARNOLD is the Environmental Grants Manager for the Quapaw Tribe.

MARY BILLINGTON is the director of the Baxter Springs Heritage Center and Museum. They have an incredible treasure trove of archival materials on Picher and the local mining history. Mrs. Billington lives nearby in Galena, Kansas.

FREDAS L. COOK is an archivist, photographer. Mr. Cook grew up in Cardin, Oklahoma at the end of the mining era and has since lived throughout the area. Mr. Cook maintains the website cardinkids.com which hosts over three thousand items—photos, newspaper clippings, maps, etc., related to the local mining and town history.

VIRGIE CURTIS is the owner of Classy Brass Antiques in Miami, Oklahoma. Ms. Curtis was born in Seneca, Missouri and has lived in the area her entire life.

BRAD CARSON is a former Congressman of the 2nd district of Oklahoma. Mr. Carson went on to become Undersecretary of the Army from 2014–2016, appointed by President Barack Obama. Mr. Carson has been a Professor of Public Policy for the last two years at the University of Virginia's Frank Batten School of Leadership and Public Policy.

JAMES GRAVES is a former school board member, World War II veteran, and chairman of Governor Keating's Task Force Committee.

EARL HATLEY is a veteran environmental activist, co-founder of LEAD Agency, Grand Riverkeeper. He's worked on 18 Superfund sites throughout his career. Mr. Hatley continues to work as an environmental consultant to Indian tribes, Alaska native villages and indigenous grassroots groups around the country.

BRIAN GRIFFIN is the former Oklahoma Secretary of the Environment under Governor Frank Keating and is currently Chairman of the Board at Clean Energy Systems.

DR. HOWARD HU is an epidemiologist, physician, researcher and clinician. Currently Dr. Hu is a professor at University of Washington School of Public Health. Some of his previous posts include Founding Dean of the Dalla Lana School of Public Health at the University of Toronto from 2012 to 2018, Professor and Founding Director of the NIEHS Center for Children's Environmental Health. Dr. Hu has led research teams around the world studying an array of issues pertaining to the environment and health.

REBECCA JIM is an educator, environmental activist, Tar Creekkeeper and cofounder of LEAD Agency and their annual National Environmental Tar Creek Conference held in Miami, Oklahoma which just reached its twenty-first year. Ms. Jim is a member of the Cherokee Nation.

MIKALYA KELLER is a college student, Northeastern Oklahoma A&M College.

WALLACE KENNEDY is a retired journalist and columnist with *The Joplin Globe* and has written extensively about Tar Creek since the 1970s.

ED KEHELEY is a retired nuclear engineer from Lawrence Livermore National Laboratory and expert on all things Tar Creek. Mr. Keheley has served on numerous Oklahoma Governors' and U.S. Senator James Inhofe's task force committees. He is currently working on a cold murder case to find the remains of two missing girls thought to be in a mineshaft at Tar Creek.

FRANK KEATING is a former Governor of Oklahoma. Mr. Keating is currently the director of four financial service boards. He is the author of six children's books on historical figures. The latest, *Hamilton,* will be released in 2020.

LARRY KROPP operates a third-generation family farm in Ottawa County and has recently retired from the East Shawnee Tribal Council. Mr. Kropp is also a member of the Quapaw Tribe.

TOM LINDLEY is a former journalist with *The Oklahoman, The Flint Journal* and the *New Orleans Times-Picayune,* among others. He also is the author of three books: *Out of the Dust, Opening Doors* and *To the Max.* Lindley has written extensively about Tar Creek for more than 20 years.

MATT MYERS is a filmmaker who wrote and directed the documentary *Tar Creek.*

DR. EMILY MOODY is an internist and pediatrician and Pediatric Environmental Health Fellow in the Department of Environmental Medicine and Public Health at the Icahn School of Medicine at Mount Sinai in New York City.

DR. ROBERT NAIRN is an environmental scientist, researcher, and professor at the University of Oklahoma. Dr. Nairn is the director of ongoing research efforts in the University of Oklahoma Center for Restoration of Ecosystems and Watersheds (CREW).

CATHY SLOAN is the environmental specialist with the Quapaw Tribe.

MRS. SMITH is a pseudonym for an Arkansas Quapaw Tribal Elder who wished to remain anonymous.

DANIEL STEVENS is the executive director Campaign for Accountability, a government watchdog group in Washington, D.C.

J.D. STRONG is the director at the Oklahoma Department of Wildlife Conservation. Mr. Strong was former Chief of Staff to the Secretary of Environment of Oklahoma and subsequently Secretary of the Environment of Oklahoma.

SCOTT THOMPSON is the executive director of the Oklahoma Department of Environmental Quality.

VICTORIA WARREN is a college student at Northeastern Oklahoma A&M College.

DR. ROBERT WRIGHT is a pediatrician, medical toxicologist, and environmental epidemiologist at the Icahn School of Medicine at Mount Sinai and is the Ethel H. Wise Chair of the Department of Environmental Medicine and Public Health. Dr. Wright has participated and has headed up several studies on chemical toxicity.

NEWTOWN CREEK

TOM ANGOTTI is an urban planner and educator. Mr. Angotti is currently a Professor Emeritus of Urban Policy and Planning at Hunter College and the Graduate Center at City University of New York, as well as the founder and director of the Hunter College Center for Community Planning and Development.

TONY ARGENTO is the founder of Broadway Stages. Together with his sister Gina Argento, president and CEO, they manage more than 50 soundstages, ancillary spaces and services across three boroughs in New York City, where they are also involved in several philanthropic enterprises.

LISA BLOODGOOD is currently the Director of Advocacy & Education, Newtown Creek Alliance. Ms. Bloodgood also serves as the NY Co-Chair for the NY/NJ Harbor Estuary Program's Citizen Advisory Committee, the Steering and Technical Committees for the EPA's Newtown Creek Superfund Community Advisory Group, and Co-Chair of North Brooklyn Neighbors Board of Directors.

JUSTIN BLOOM is an environmental attorney who specializes in toxic contamination and pharmaceutical litigation. Mr. Bloom is the founder of Suncoast Waterkeeper. Mr. Bloom was formerly a staff attorney for Riverkeeper.

ANTHONY BUISSERETH is the Executive Director of North Brooklyn Neighbors.

GEOFFREY COBB is an educator, historian and author of the books *Greenpoint Brooklyn's Forgotten Past, The Rise and Fall of the Sugar King* and *The King of Greenpoint.* Mr. Cobb blogs at Greenpointers.com.

VICTORIA CAMBRANES is a community activist and 2021 candidate for City Council District 33. Ms. Cambranes works as a digital marketing consultant and is a lifelong resident of Greenpoint.

WINIFRED CURRAN is Professor and Chair of Geography at DePaul University. Dr. Curran is the author of *Gender and Gentrification* and is a co-editor, with Trina Hamilton, of *Just Green Enough: Urban Development and Environmental Gentrification.*

WILLIS ELKINS is the Executive Director of the Newtown Creek Alliance and community activist in Greenpoint, Brooklyn.

KIM FRASER is an activist and co-founder of Greenpointers Against Smell Pollution (GASP).

SCOTT FRASER is an activist and co-founder of Greenpointers Against Smell Pollution (GASP). Mr. Fraser works as a writer and director of TV and movies.

CHARLEY FRIEDMAN is an artist and former resident of Greenpoint. Today Mr. Friedman lives in Lincoln, Nebraska.

TRINA HAMILTON is an associate professor of geography at the State University of New York at Buffalo. Dr. Hamilton is a co-editor, with Winifred Curran, of *Just Green Enough: Urban Development and Environmental Gentrification.* Her research focuses on sustainability politics.

LAURA HOFMANN is an activist and lifelong resident of Greenpoint. Mrs. Hofmann is the co-founder of Barge Park Pals, a Steering Committee Member of Organizations United for Trash Reduction & Garbage Equity (OUTRAGE), board member of the Newtown Creek Alliance (NCA), Newtown Creek Monitoring Committee member, and active with other local community groups.

CHRISTINE HOLOWACZ an activist and longtime resident of Greenpoint. Ms. Holowacz is a member of Greenpoint Waterfront Association for Parks and Planning (GWAPP), Newtown Creek Alliance (NCA), and many other nonprofits.

CAROL KNUDSON is a Research Assistant at the Lamont-Doherty Earth Observatory of Columbia University. Ms. Knudson is currently working on the Hudson River Water Quality Program with Riverkeeper.

JOE LENTOL is the New York State Assemblyman of District 50 in Brooklyn. Assemblyman Lentol has served in the New York Assembly since 1973 and is a lifelong resident of the Greenpoint/Williamsburg area.

HEATHER LETZKUS is an artist who has lived in Greenpoint since 2000. Ms. Letzkus created and maintains the blog New York Shitty.

ANGELA LICATA is Deputy Commissioner of Sustainability, NYC Department of Environmental Protection.

JOHN LIPSCOMB is a Vice President of Advocacy at Riverkeeper and is the boat captain on the *R. Ian Fletcher*, Riverkeeper's patrol boat.

KATHERINE BUSING NAPLATARSKI is a teacher, activist and open space advocate. Ms. Naplatarski has lived in Greenpoint since 1982.

PAUL PARKHILL is an urban planner and the founder of Parkhill Planning and Development LLC. Mr. Parkhill was formerly the director of planning and development Greenpoint Manufacturing and Design Center (GMDC) for 12 years and later served five years as Executive Director of Spaceworks NYC.

PAUL PULLO is a community activist, entrepreneur, steering committee member of the Newtown Creek Community Advisory Group, and a member of the Newtown Creek Monitoring Committee. Mr. Pullo is also President of North Brooklyn Development Corporation and Board Chair of the Greenpoint YMCA.

MIKE SCHADE is an activist and environmental health campaigner. Mr. Schade works as the Mind the Store Campaign Director for Safer Chemicals, Healthy Families. This national campaign challenges the nation's leading retailers to transform the marketplace away from hazardous chemicals and toward safer alternatives. He also serves on the board of North Brooklyn Neighbors (NBN) and Community Advisory Group for Newtown Creek (CAG).

ACACIA THOMPSON is an archivist for Brooklyn Public Library's Greenpoint Environmental History Project. Ms. Thompson also serves on several local environmental committees.

BASIL SEGGOS is the Commissioner of the New York State Department of Environmental Conservation appointed by Governor Andrew Cuomo. Mr. Seggos is the former the Chief Investigator for Riverkeeper.

DOROTHY SWICK was a co-plaintiff in the ExxonMobil civil suit when gases infiltrated her home. Mrs. Swick served on the Newtown Creek Monitoring Committee and is a former resident of Greenpoint. Today Ms. Swick currently lives in Damascus, Pennsylvania.

MITCH WAXMAN is a photographer, and historian for Newtown Creek Alliance (NCA). Mr. Waxman's maintains the blog Newtown Pentacle and is the author of a new photo book about Newtown Creek titled *In the Shadows of Newtown Creek*.

CHRISTINA WILKINSON is an activist on the Queens side of Newtown Creek. Ms. Wilkinson is the founder of the Newtown Historical Society.

MARC YAGGI is an environmental attorney and the Executive Director at Waterkeeper Alliance.

KATE ZIDAR is a green infrastructure research engineer. Ms. Zidar was formerly the director of Newtown Creek Alliance (NCA) during its early days.

GLOSSARY OF TERMS

ACRONYMS

ATSDR	Agency for Toxic Substances and Disease Registry
BIA	Bureau of Indian Affairs
CAP	Community Advisory Panel
CDC	Center for Disease Control
CERCLA	Comprehensive Environmental Response, Compensation, and Liability Act, known also as Superfund
CfA	Campaign for Accountability
CSO	Combined Sewer Outfall (or Overflow)
DEC	Department of Environmental Conservation
DCP	Department of City Planning
DEQ	Department of Environmental Quality
EIS	Environmental Impact Statement
EPA	Environmental Protection Agency
FAR	Floor Area Ratio
FOIA	Freedom of Information Act Request
GCEF	Greenpoint Community Environmental Fund
HRS	Hazard Ranking System
IBZ	Industrial Business Zone

LICRAT	Lead Impacted Communities Relocation Assistance Trust
NICRAT	National Impacted Communities Relocation Assistance Trust
NIH	National Institute of Health
NGO	Non-governmental Organizations
OSA	Open Space Alliance
OU1–OU5	Operable Unit: During cleanup, a site can be divided into a number of distinct areas depending on the complexity of problems associated with the site. These areas called operable the units may address geographic areas of a site, specific site problems, or areas where a specific action is required. An example of a typical operable unit could include removal of drums and tanks from the surface of a site.
PRPs	Potentially Responsible Parties, essentially existing companies that can be sued today for their past environmental crimes.
RHIA	Registered Health Information Administrator
ROD	Record of Decision is a public document that explains the remediation plan for the cleanup of a Superfund site.

SOURCES FOR PART ONE
HEAVY METAL: TAR CREEK, OKLAHOMA

FILMS

Tar Creek. Directed by Matt Myers.
This Creek Runs Red. Co-directed by Bradley Beesley, Julianna Brannum and James Payne.
The Quapaw Tribe. Director unknown, Quapaw Tribe, DVD, year unknown.

PUBLICATIONS

Baird, W. David. *The Quapaw Indians: A History of the Downstream People*. University of Oklahoma Press, 1980.
Baird, W. David, and Frank W. Porter. *The Quapaws*. Chelsea House Publishers, 1989.
Cook, Fredas L. *Pictures From the Mining Era: Cardin-Picher, OK Area*. Gregarth Pub. Co., 2011.
Jim, Rebecca. *Disasters: Flood & Ice*. LEAD Agency Inc., 2008.
Jim, Rebecca and Marilyn Scott. *Making A Difference At the Tar Creek Superfund Site*, 2007.
Keheley, Ed. *Chronology of Mining in the Picher Mining Field/Mining Camps and Towns in the Picher Mining Field/Chronology of the Tar Creek Superfund Site*.
Robertson, David. "Picher." *Hard as the Rock Itself: Place and Identity in the American Mining Town*, University Press of Colorado, 2010, pp. 121–183.
Stewart, Todd, and Alison Fields. *Picher, Oklahoma: Catastrophe, Memory, and Trauma*. University of Oklahoma Press, 2016.

Eco Horror Issue, *Drive-In Asylum*, issue #6, January 2017.

PERIODICALS, WEBSITES, PRESS RELEASES, SCHOLARLY PAPERS

I used so many articles by Wallace Kennedy of the *Joplin Globe* and Tom Lindley of the *Oklahoman* that I won't list all of them here. Below is a list of materials that I found incredibly helpful in one way or another while researching Tar Creek.

Bernstein, Lenny. "Lead Poisoning and the Fall of Rome." *Washington Post,* WP Company, 30 Mar 2019, www.washingtonpost.com/news/to-your-health/wp/2016/02/17/lead-poisoning-and-the-fall-of-rome/

Burnley, Malcolm, and M. Scott Mahaskey. "The Environmental Scandal in Scott Pruitt's Backyard." *Politico Magazine,* 6 Dec 2017, www.politico.com/magazine/story/2017/12/06/scott-pruitt-tar-creek-oklahoma-investigation-215854

Gamino, Denise. "Synar Receives Documents From EPA Informer." Oklahoman.com, 17 Feb 1983, oklahoman.com/article/2014199/synar-receives-documents-from-epa-informer

Gillham, Omer. "Errors Trouble Buyout." *Tulsa World,* 20 Jan 2008, www.tulsaworld.com/archives/errors-trouble-buyout/article_8423a240-da73-5c88-9e9a-ccdeb9d5d073.html

Goforth, Dylan. "Still Life in Picher: 'Imagine a Small Country with Few People...'" *Tulsa World,* 9 Feb 2014, www.tulsaworld.com/news/state-and-regional/still-life-in-picher-imagine-a-small-country-with-few/article_e30a5796-0afb-5a26-aba5-347d7b6f1401.html

Hu, Dr. Howard, et al. "The Challenge Posed to Children's Health by Mixtures of Toxic Waste: The Tar Creek Superfund Site as a Case-Study." Pediatric Clinics of North America, 14 Feb 2007, www.sciencedirect.com/science/article/pii/S003139550600160X?via%3Dihub

Jim, Rebecca. "Tar Creekkeeper." *Local Environmental Action Demanded,* 2019, www.leadagency.org/tar-creekkeeper

Kennedy, Wally. "Business Hub of Former Mining District Center Burns." *Joplin Globe,* 15 Apr 2015, www.joplinglobe.com/news/local_news/business-hub-of-former-mining-district-center-burns/article_44dbf53c-4352-5595-82ac-ce14d41781e1.html

Logan, Layden. "A Conversation With Oklahoma's Long-Time Water Boss | StateImpact Oklahoma." NPR, 17 Nov 2016, stateimpact.npr.org/oklahoma/2016/11/17/a-conversation-with-oklahomas-long-time-water-boss/

Lindley, Tom. "Cleanup Records Seized." Oklahoman.com, 24 Feb 2000, oklahoman.com/article/2687447/cleanup-records-seized

Jack, Lewis. "Lead Poisoning: A Historical Perspective." *EPA Journal,* Environmental Protection Agency, May 1985, archive.epa.gov/epa/aboutepa/lead-poisoning-historical-perspective.html

Meyer, Richard. "Acid Water Drowns Tar Creek as Cleanup Delayed." Oklahoman. com, 6 Feb 1983, oklahoman.com/article/2012758/acid-water-drowns-tar-creek-as-cleanup-delayed

Morris, Frank. "Oklahoma Mining Town a Victim of Its Success." NPR, 11 Feb 2007, www.npr.org/templates/story/story.php?storyId=7357401

Moulden, Yolanda. "Southeast Commerce Mine Water Passive Treatment Project." AAEES Leadership and Excellence in Environmental Engineering and Science, 2018, www.aaees.org/e3scompetition/2018honor-universityresearch.php

Myers, Jim. "Inhofe Blasted for Tar Creek Comments." *Tulsa World*, 6 Dec 2003, www.tulsaworld.com/archives/inhofe-blasted-for-tar-creek-comments/article_a2ce2478-8510-5448-b77b-3c7bc660648c.html

Myers, Jim. "Keating Makes Last Push on Tar Creek." *Tulsa World*, 10 Mar 2002, www.tulsaworld.com/archives/keating-makes-last-push-on-tar-creek/article_4544949f-6817-53eb-9f29-542fce2a5233.html

Nagle, Rebecca. "Toxic Tar Creek Continues to Harm Residents, as Cleanup Stalls." *ThinkProgress*, 1 Feb 2018, thinkprogress.org/toxic-tar-creek-site-clean-up-4deb5fcba042/

O'Dell, Larry. "Ottawa County: The Encyclopedia of Oklahoma History and Culture." Oklahoma History, www.okhistory.org/publications/enc/entry.php?entry=OT003

Paynter, Ben. "Take a Tour of America's Most Toxic Town." *Wired*, Conde Nast, 30 Aug 2010, www.wired.com/2010/08/ff_madmaxtown/

Ridge, Betty. "Protesting Pollution at Tar Creek." *Tahlequah Daily Press*, 20 Apr 2009, www.tahlequahdailypress.com/news/features/protesting-pollution-at-tar-creek/article_a244003f-34ae-5939-b39b-95363451fcac.html

Roosevelt, Margot. "The Tragedy of Tar Creek." *Time Magazine*, Monday, 19 Apr 2004, content.time.com/time/magazine/article/0,9171,612395,00.html

Schafer, Shaun. "Part One In a Five-Part Series: Superfund: Damage Control." *Tulsa World*, 12 Dec 2003, www.tulsaworld.com/archives/part-one-in-a-five-part-series-superfund-damage-control/article_217b05e4-4023-5c39-9905-d45a4271fe1e.html

Schafer, Shaun. "Elusive Tar Creek Report on Horizon." *Tulsa World*, 12 Sept 2002, www.tulsaworld.com/archives/elusive-tar-creek-report-on-horizon/article_1cdd0953-4262-5042-bdb4-020f0e623103.html

Shepherd, Dan. "Last Residents of Picher, Oklahoma Won't Give Up the Ghost (Town)." NBCNews.com, NBCUniversal News Group, 25 Feb 2017, Historical Society, date unknown, www.nbcnews.com/news/investigations/last-residents-picher-oklahoma-won-t-give-ghost-town-n89611

Short, Carla. "Buyout of Tar Creek Progresses." *Joplin Globe*, 15 July 2006, www.joplinglobe.com/news/local_news/buyout-of-tar-creek-progresses/article_067d819c-960d-5533-b19f-2ceb46a8a729.html

Stevens, Daniel. "How Scott Pruitt Failed Oklahoma." *Campaign for Accountability*, 24 Apr 2018, medium.com/@Accountable_Org/how-scott-pruitt-failed-oklahoma-408ab75446b4

Stotts, Melinda. "Huge progress, long way to go." *The Miami News-Record*, 28 Sept 2018, p. A3.

Wingerter, Justin. "A War of Words Heats up Again over the Tar Creek Audit." Oklahoman.com, 13 Feb 2018, oklahoman.com/article/5583082/a-war-of-words-heats-up-again-over-the-tar-creek-audit

author unknown. Press release. "Gov. Henry Sets Tar Creek Relocation Plan in Motion." Governor Brad Henry, 14 July 2006, www.tkvw.com/bradhenry/press-5.htm

author unknown. "Governor Brad Henry Unveils a New Buyout Plan for the Tar Creek Superfund Site." News On 6, 25 Jan 2004, www.newson6.com/story/7714736/governor-brad-henry-unveils-a-new-buyout-plan-for-the-tar-creek-superfund-site

author unknown. "Congressman Brad Carson Calls Tar Creek Buyout 'Drastic' but Necessary." News On 6, 1 May 2003, www.newson6.com/story/7709557/congressman-brad-carson-calls-tar-creek-buyout-drastic-but-necessary

author unknown. "House, Senate Pass Tar Creek Buyout Bill." *The Oklahoman*, NewsOK, 27 May 2006, newsok.com/article/1855898/house-senate-pass-tar-creek-buyout-bill

author unknown. "Minerals Information: Chat." Oklahoma Department of Mines. 27 Aug 2007, web.archive.org/web/20070827093256/http://www.mines.state.ok.us/id68.htm

SOURCES FOR PART TWO
SLUDGE METAL: NEWTOWN CREEK, BROOKLYN

PUBLICATIONS

Bullard, Robert D. *The Quest for Environmental Justice: Human Rights and the Politics of Pollution*. Counterpoint, 2005.

Cobb, Geoffrey. *Greenpoint Brooklyn's Forgotten Past*. North Brooklyn Neighborhood History, 2015.

Cravens, Curtis, et al. *Copper on the Creek: Reclaiming an Industrial History*. Place in History, 2000.

Curran, Winifred, and Trina Hamilton. *Just Green Enough: Urban Development and Environmental Gentrification*. Routledge, 2018.

Hamboussi, Anthony. *Newtown Creek: A Photographic Survey of New York's Industrial Waterfront*. Princeton Architectural Press, 2010.

Lerner, Steve. "Greenpoint, New York; Giant Oil Spill Spreads beneath Brooklyn Neighborhood." *Sacrifice Zones: The Front Lines of Toxic Chemical Exposure in the United States*, MIT Press, 2012, pp. 247–264.

Parkhill, Paul Boyle, et al. *LIC in Context: An Unorthodox Guide to Long Island City*. Furnace Press, 2005.

Tarbell, Ida. *The History of the Standard Oil Company*. McClure, Phillips and Co, 1904.

Waxman, Mitch. *In the Shadows of Newtown Creek*. Newtown Pentacle, 2019.

PERIODICALS, WEBSITES, PRESS RELEASES, SCHOLARLY PAPERS

For the Newtown Creek section, I was helped tremendously by the local blogs, particularly Mitch Waxman's *Newtown Pentacle*, Geoff Cobb's *Greenpointers* column and *New York Shitty* by Heather Letzkus. I referred to these among others fairly often throughout my research.

Cobb, Geoffrey. "Sister Francis Kress, Pioneer in Greenpoint Environmental Movement, Has Passed Away." Greenpointers, 21 Jan 2019, greenpointers.com/2019/01/21/sister-francis-kress-pioneer-in-greenpoint-environmental-movement-has-passed-away

Chan, Sewell. "Newtown Creek's Deadly History." *The New York Times*, 7 Apr 2008, cityroom.blogs.nytimes.com/2008/04/07/newtown-creeks-deadly-history/

Confessore, Nicholas. "An Old Oil Spill Divides a Brooklyn Neighborhood." *The New York Times*, 1 Nov 2005, www.nytimes.com/2005/11/01/nyregion/an-old-oil-spill-divides-a-brooklyn-neighborhood.html

Corona, Jo. "A Factory That Saw 'Smoky Skies, Blazing Blasts' Awaits a New Chapter in Greenpoint." Bedford + Bowery, 20 June 2019, bedfordandbowery.com/2018/12/a-factory-that-saw-smoky-skies-blazing-blasts-awaits-a-new-chapter-in-greenpoint/

Del Signore, John. "Spotting Signs Of Life On The Poisoned Waters Of Newtown Creek." Gothamist, 2 May 2018, gothamist.com/news/spotting-signs-of-life-on-the-poisoned-waters-of-newtown-creek#photo-1

Eviatar, Daphne. "Exploring the Massive, Viscous Oil Blob That Lies Just Beneath the Streets of Greenpoint — New York Magazine - Nymag." *New York Magazine*, 1 June 2007, nymag.com/news/features/32865/"Newtown Creek Site Profile."

EPA, Environmental Protection Agency, 20 Oct 2017, cumulis.epa.gov/supercpad/SiteProfiles/index.cfm?fuseaction=second.Cleanup&id=0206282#bkground "What Are Combined Sewer Overflows (CSOs)?"

EPA, Environmental Protection Agency, 10 Apr 2017, www3.epa.gov/region1/eco/

uep/cso.htmlGreenpoint Community Environmental Fund, 22 Apr 2019, gcefund. org/

Henshaw, Victoria. "Don't Turn Up Your Nose at the City in Summer." *The New York Times*, 23 June 2014, www.nytimes.com/2014/06/24/opinion/summer-in-new-york-season-of-smell.html

Hogan, Gwynne. "Elderly Woman's Decomposed Body Found at Newtown Creek, Officials Say." DNAinfo New York, 31 Oct 2017, www.dnainfo.com/new-york/20171031/east-williamsburg/body-found-newtown-creek-alliance-nypd/

Hu, Winnie. "Please Don't Flush the Toilet. It's Raining." *The New York Times*, 2 Mar 2018, www.nytimes.com/2018/03/02/nyregion/new-york-reduce-water-use-in-rainstorms-flush.html

Kadinsky, Sergey. Hidden Waters Blog, 4 Oct 2019, hiddenwatersblog.wordpress. com/

McFadden, Robert. "Survey Finds High Cancer Rate In 2 Neighborhoods in Brooklyn." *The New York Times*, 23 May 1992, www.nytimes.com/1992/05/23/nyregion/survey-finds-high-cancer-rate-in-2-neighborhoods-in-brooklyn.html

Navarro, Mireya. "A Problem Rises to the Surface in Greenpoint." *The New York Times*, 8 Dec 2008, www.nytimes.com/2008/12/08/nyregion/08greenpoint.html

Newtown Creek Alliance, Riverkeeper. "Newtown Creek Vision Plan." Riverkeeper and Newtown Creek Alliance, 2018, www.newtowncreekalliance.org/newtown-creek-vision-plan/

"History of Newtown Creek." Newtown Creek Alliance, www.newtowncreekalliance. org/history-of-newtown-creek/

Newtown Creek Alliance. "Meeker Ave Plumes." 2008, www.newtowncreek alliance.org/meeker-ave-plumes/

Old Timer, The. "The Dirty Yet Important History of the Newtown Creek: Our Neighborhood, The Way It Was." QNS.com, 31 Mar 2018, qns.com/story/2018/03/31/dirty-yet-important-history-newtown-creek-neighborhood-way/

Prud'homme, Alex. "An Oil Spill Grows in Brooklyn." *The New York Times*, 15 May 2010, www.nytimes.com/2010/05/16/opinion/16Prudhomme.html

Racic, Monica. "Up the Creek." *The New Yorker*, 19 June 2017, www.newyorker.com/books/page-turner/up-the-creek

Smith, Peter Andrey. "The Toxins Lurking in Newtown Creek," *New York Magazine*, 6 Dec 2013, http://nymag.com/news/intelligencer/newtown-creek-2013-12/

Stern, Steven. "Your Guide to a Tour of Decay." *The New York Times*, 16 June 2012, www.nytimes.com/2012/06/17/nyregion/mitch-waxman-tour-guide-to-decay. html

Yardley, Jim. "Garbage In . . . and In . . . and In; Greenpoint Residents Unite to Fight Influx of Trash." *The New York Times*, 18 Apr 1998, www.nytimes.com/1998/04/18/nyregion/garbage-in-and-in-and-in-greenpoint-residents-unite-to-fight-influx-of-trash.html

Associated Press reporter. "NYC's Newtown Creek Awaits Long-Overdue Cleanup." *USA Today*, Gannett Satellite Information Network, 2 Mar 2013, www.usatoday. com/story/news/nation/2013/03/02/nyc-newtown-creek-cleanup/1958605/

author unknown. "Greenpoint Oil Spill." Atlas Obscura, 12 Sept 2010, www. atlasobscura.com/places/the-greenpoint-oil-spill-brooklyn-new-york

author unknown. "Parcel / Building Outlines Map of New York City, NY." Parcel / Building Outlines Map of New York City, NY | PropertyShark.com, 2019, www.propertyshark.com/mason/ny/New-York-City/Maps?fbclid=IwAR1VY1xZ n2xT50RPs-9_oAAYmNCnEoUdw-K5M_vONftk701mXyALov18gKo

author unknown. "Greenpoint Oil Spill on Newtown Creek." Riverkeeper (date not listed), www.riverkeeper.org/campaigns/stop-polluters/newtown/

author unknown. "The Brooklyn Oil Spill: A Timeline." *Mother Jones*, 27 June 2017, www.motherjones.com/environment/2007/09/brooklyn-oil-spill-timeline/

author unknown. ExxonMobil press release. "Our Greenpoint Commitment | Our Greenpoint Commitment." Our Greenpoint Commitment | Our Greenpoint Commitment, (date unknown) www.ourgreenpointcommitment.com/

author unknown. "Broadway Stages Receives $1.5 Million Grant for 1.4 Acre Green Roof." press release. Broadway Stages, 28 Jan 2019, www.broadway-stages.com/news/2019/1/28/bws-blog-broadway-stages-receives-15-million-grant-for-14-acre-green-roof

author unknown. "Queens Residents Lawyers Cheer Anti-ExxonMobil Stance Comments," 17 May 2006, *Queens Gazette*. www.qgazette.com/articles/ residents-lawyers-cheer-anti-exxonmobil-stance/

author unknown. "Lots of Conflicts of Interest Keeping Boathouse Plan Afloat." 17 Feb 2014, Crapper, Queens. Queens Crap, 17 Feb 2014. *I found a lot of articles from this blog to be useful in my research queenscrap.blogspot.com/2014/02/ lots-of-conflicts-of-interests-keeping.html

ONLINE APPENDIX DOCUMENTS

"AUDITOR: Let the Audit Speak for Itself." Gary Jones, Press Release, 2018.

"Greenpoint 197-A Plan." Community Board 1, Borough of Brooklyn, 2002.

Jakosky, J.J., et al. "Geophysical Investigations in Tri-State Zinc and Lead Mining District." *State Geological Survey of Kansas*, vol. 44, Dec 1942, doi:10.1306/3d93358e-16b1-11d7-8645000102c1865d.

Tim, Kent. "Quapaw Tribe Remedial Efforts at the Tar Creek Superfund Site." Environmental Justice Forum, 12 June 2018, Dallas, Texas.

Lawrence, Eugene. "Hunter's Point and Its Victims." *Harper's Weekly*, 20 Aug 1881, p. 566.

Luza, Kenneth V., and W. Ed Keheley. *Inventory of Mine Shafts and Collapse Features Associated with Abandoned Underground Mines in the Picher Field Northeastern Oklahoma*. Oklahoma Geological Survey, 2006.

Manders, Gina C., and James S. Aber. "Tri-State Mining District Legacy in Northeastern Oklahoma." *Emporia State Research Studies*, vol. 49, no. 2, 2014, pp. 20 21.

Oliver, Mildred, et al. *A Preliminary Report on Living, Working, and Health Conditions in the Tri-State Mining Area (Missouri, Oklahoma and Kansas).* Tri-State Survey Committee, Inc., 1939.

Office of the Secretary of the Environment. "Governor Frank Keating's Tar Creek Superfund Task Force Final Report." State of Oklahoma, 2000.

Petition for Declaratory and Injunctive Relief for Violation of the Oklahoma Open Records Act. *Campaign for Accountability vs. Mike Hunter Attorney General State of Oklahoma.* Freedom of Information Act request, 27 Nov 2017.

Schwarz, Katherine, et al. *Right to Breathe/Right to Know: Industrial Air Pollution in Greenpoint-Williamsburg.* 1992.

United States, Congress, Cong. Senate, House of Representatives, and James Oberstar. "Water Resources Development Act of 2007." House of Representatives, 2007. 110th Congress, 1st session, resolution 280.

United States, Congress, House - Transportation and Infrastructure; Energy and Commerce, and Carson, Brad. "Tar Creek Restoration Act." Congress.gov, 2003, p. 1. 108th Congress, 1st session, resolution H.R. 2116.

United States, Congress, "U.S. Environmental Protection Agency Abandoned Mine Lands Team Reference Notebook." EPA, 2004.

Wilson, Gary D., "Superfund Evaluation: The Families of Tar Creek" (2012). *Theses and Dissertations.* 455. scholarworks.uark.edu/etd/455

United States, Congress, The Picher Planning Commission, et al. "Picher: the Comprehensive Plan." City of Picher, 1964.

United States, Congress, Allen, Lloyd K., et al. "Preliminary Report Economic and Population Data Picher and Ottawa County." 1963.

United States, Congress, "Regulations Governing the Leasing for Lead and Zinc Mining Operations and Purposes of Restricted Indian Lands in the Quapaw Agency, Oklahoma: under Section 26 of the Act of Congress Approved March 3, 1921." U.S. Dept. of the Interior, Office of Indian Affairs, 1922.

United States, Congress, Office of the Secretary of the Environment, et al. "Report Governor Keating's Tar Creek Superfund Task Force by the Subsidence Subcommittee." 2001.

United States, Congress, Office of the Secretary of the Environment, et al. "Mine Shaft Subcommittee Final Report to Governor Frank Keating's Tar Creek Superfund Task Force." 2000.

United States, Oklahoma State Auditor & Inspector, and Gary A. Jones. "Investigative Audit: Lead Impacted Communities Relocation Assistance Trust." 2018.

If you want to help at Tar Creek please give to:
LEAD Agency, Inc.
223 A Street, SE
Miami, Oklahoma 74354
(918) 542-9399
www.leadagency.org

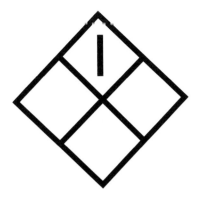

INDEX

**Earth A.D.: The Poisoning of the American Landscape
and the Communities that Fought Back**

Edited by Christina Ward

Process Media
1240 W Sims Way #124
Port Townsend WA 98368

www.processmediainc.com

Cover design by Jacob Covey
Interior and back cover design by John Hubbard

ISBN: 9781934170786
Printed in the United States of America
10 9 8 7 6 5 4 3 2 1